My Beloved Zebulon

Courtesy of the State Department of
Archives and History, Raleigh, N.C.

Harriett Newell Espy Vance, at about the age of twenty-six

Courtesy of the State Department of Archives and History, Raleigh, N.C.

Zebulon Baird Vance, at the age of twenty-eight

My Beloved Zebulon

THE CORRESPONDENCE OF ZEBULON BAIRD VANCE
AND HARRIETT NEWELL ESPY

edited by
Elizabeth Roberts Cannon

with an introduction by
Frances Gray Patton

The University of North Carolina Press
Chapel Hill

Copyright © 1971 by The University of North Carolina Press
All rights reserved
Manufactured in the United States of America
Printed by the Seeman Printery, Durham, N.C.
ISBN 0-8078-1157-2
Library of Congress Catalog Card Number 72-132258

To Mary Hendren Vance

Contents

Preface ix

Introduction xi

Part I. March 15, 1851, to March 16, 1852   1

Part II. March 30, 1852, to October 23, 1852   69

Part III. November 2, 1852, to March 14, 1853   141

Part IV. March 23, 1853, to July 26, 1853   197

Appendix A. Record of the Marriage of Harriett Newell Espy and Zebulon Baird Vance in Their Family Bible   265

Appendix B. Letter from Captain Charles McDowell to Zebulon Baird Vance   267

Index   269

Preface

———•———

Twelve years ago there came to light a letter book in which is tipped the correspondence of Zebulon Baird Vance and his first wife, Harriett Espy Vance. The contents of the book—580 items in all—fall easily into four parts. There are 121 love letters exchanged by Vance and Harriett Espy from March, 1851, to the eve of their marriage in August, 1853; 68 letters from Harriett Vance to her husband and 6 from him to her, written between 1854 and 1878; letters to both of them from family and friends; and, finally, messages of condolence to Governor Vance after Harriett's death on November 3, 1878. The present volume comprises only the letters of their courtship—75 from Zebulon and 46 from Harriett.

In preparing these letters for publication, care has been taken to reproduce faithfully the spelling, punctuation and paragraphing used by their authors. The reader can note that Zebulon's letters, carefully written at first, become more and more casual as he becomes surer of Harriett. Dates that were penciled on the original letters in Vance's handwriting appear here in brackets.

Thanks to my husband, Edward L. Cannon, the letter book escaped destruction, for it was he who preserved the battered old trunk in which it was found. That trunk belonged to my aunt, Mary Hendren Vance, widow of Major Zebulon Baird Vance, Jr., a son of the governor. After Mrs. Vance's death the letter book was given to the North Carolina Department of Archives and History by Mrs. R. G. (Harriett Espy Vance) Cobb of Mobile, Alabama, and Mrs. W. J. (Ruth Vance) Pillow of Metairie, Louisiana, only grandchildren of Zebulon Baird Vance, and by me as executrix of

Mrs. Vance's estate. In my project I have had the blessing of Mrs. Cobb, now deceased, Mrs. Pillow, and Mrs. Pillow's daughter, Mrs. Richard S. Ordway of Metairie, Louisiana.

Both the late Dr. C. C. Crittenden, director of the State Department of Archives and History, and his successor, Dr. H. G. Jones, have helped me in numerous ways, among others, in furnishing me typescripts of the letters. These were made with remarkable accuracy by Mrs. Violet C. Kidd. Members of the staff of the Department of Archives and History as well as the staff of the North Carolina State Library have been untiring and gracious in assisting me.

I am indebted to Professor Frontis W. Johnston for use of materials in his book, *The Papers of Zebulon Baird Vance*, and for permission to quote directly therefrom. His footnotes have been invaluable not only in identifying individuals but in suggesting sources for further exploration.

Dr. Edward W. Phifer and the Honorable Sam J. Ervin, Jr. have been generous with their time and knowledge, answering many questions in conversations and in letters. I have drawn heavily upon Dr. Phifer's articles on antebellum Burke County which have appeared in the *North Carolina Historical Review* and upon Senator Ervin's manuscript, "The Tates of Burke County, N.C."

My sincere appreciation is extended to Miss Myra Champion, librarian, North Carolina Collection, Pack Memorial Library, Asheville, North Carolina, for her knowledgeable help in my research.

Old friends have rallied round, making contacts, setting up interviews, and getting information for me. I refer particularly to Helen and Paul Story, Nellie and Edward Loftin, Frances and Kenneth Lee, and Kingsland Van Winkle.

I gratefully acknowledge also the contributions of the following: Mr. Albert S. McLean; Miss Edith Holmes; Miss Virginia Sevier; Mrs. B. Bryant Northcutt; Mrs. Walter White; Mr. Samuel McDowell Tate; Miss Ruth Greenlee; Mrs. John Keetch; and Miss Della Shore, cataloguer, Library of Davidson College, Davidson, North Carolina.

Without the advice and encouragement of Frances and Lewis Patton my manuscript would never have been completed.

Elizabeth Roberts Cannon

Introduction

In 1851, the year he attained his majority, Zebulon Baird Vance made two resolutions that were to have a profound effect upon his personal history and upon the history of his native state. He decided to do his utmost to win the heart and hand of Harriett Newell Espy, a pretty, pious, well-connected, redheaded girl, and, while engaged in that tender effort, to enroll in the University of North Carolina where he hoped to prepare himself for the practice of law and for public life. For the previous seven years, ever since the death of his father and its consequent financial difficulties had cut short his schooling, his life had lacked direction. He had been, as he himself said later, "a wild mountain boy." But from 1851 onward he pursued, without serious deviation, a course which was to take him at the age of thirty-two, and at a time when his state was in mortal peril, to the governorship of North Carolina.

Whether his attachment to Harriett—his desire to become worthy of her—sent him to Chapel Hill, or whether the same appetite for self-advancement which inspired him toward learning drew his fancy toward a lady of Harriett's refinement, is a matter for conjecture. Probably the duality of his purpose (in which he was successful) resulted chiefly from his time of life—that green season in which dreams of glory and dreams of connubial bliss are apt to be equally in the ascendant. In any case, this union of passion and ambition revealed in the young Vance a precocious knowledge of his own nature and its needs.

As a political animal—and by blood, environment, and inclination Zeb Vance was that, indeed—he was to derive great benefit from the climate of university life. At Chapel Hill his mental faculties, congenitally strong, were disciplined and sharpened. His vision was broadened. Training in the classics and in the rules of rhetoric put the polish of oratory on his already agile vocabulary. (Though here, for truth's sake, it must be admitted that Vance never lost his love for the vernacular and that his verbal "polish" was to become more famous in the breach than in the observance.) Above all, his genius for understanding the minds of his countrymen gained sensitivity from the enduring friendships he formed with persons of humane and cultivated tastes. Such teachers as William Horn Battle, Samuel Phillips, and Elisha Mitchell opened new windows for his mind, and David L. Swain, president of the University, did even more for him. Swain, an ardent Whig who had been governor of North Carolina before assuming his post at Chapel Hill, was an old friend of the Vance family. He was a perceptive and sympathetic man who liked to discover talent in the young, and there must have been much about Zeb that reminded him of his own youth as a poor mountain boy rustling for an education. Both as a student and later as a statesman Zeb found Swain's advice and encouragement to be of incalculable value. "I had the honor," said Vance in his memorial oration on Swain in 1877, ". . . to be on terms of confidential intimacy with him from my first entrance into the University until his death. . . . So affectionately was his interest in my welfare always manifested that many people supposed we were relatives. . . ."[1]

As a man of volatile temperament with an imagination as expansive as the landscape of the upcountry that bred him—a man of quick generosity and quick resentment; of compassion, patriotism, and self interest; wit, conviviality, and irrepressible humor; and of dark though fleeting moods of introspection—Vance needed more than most men a homing-place for the complexities of his nature. He found that place in his devotion to Harriett Espy and in her devotion to him. From the time he began to woo her, until her death twenty-seven years later Harriett's firmness of character—what he often called her "nobility"—was to be his steadying influence.

The courtship of Zebulon and his Harriett was conducted almost entirely by letter (during its course of two and a half years the couple met in the flesh—the fully-clothed flesh, of course—only nine times, always briefly and usually in company) and by a

1. Zebulon B. Vance, *Life and Character of Hon. David L. Swain* . . . (Durham, N.C.: Wot Stockwell & Co's Steam Presses, 1878).

fortunate chance almost the entire correspondence, bound in an album, has recently come to light. To say it was found "in an old trunk" has the ring of cliché. Nevertheless it is true.

Zebulon Vance and Harriett Espy shared the same kind of ancestral stock—chiefly Scotch-Irish—but they shared it with a difference. Vance, the orator, claimed proudly that he came from stock which "has given most color and tone to our society and ... furnishes the key to our public character ... a happy mixture of miser and spendthrift, of cool prudence and headlong rashness, of usquebaugh and poteen whisky ... the best middle class in the world."[2] Harriett made no public speeches about her family background or anything else, but if she had she would never have pointed to rashness or whisky as ornaments of her scutcheon. And it is doubtful that she ever thought of either herself or her ancestors as belonging to the "middle" class.

Although they both grew up in western North Carolina, the circumstances of their childhood and early youth were not alike. Harriett lived in an atmosphere of gentility and sheltered ease. Zebulon experienced no luxury, even while his father was alive to provide for him, and from the time he was fourteen he knew the privations, the uncertainties, and the necessity to fend for himself that came from real poverty.

Zebulon Baird Vance, "a fine hearty child,"[3] was born on May 13, 1830, to David and Mira Margaret Baird Vance at the Reems Creek homestead about twelve miles from Asheville. The homestead had been established by his pioneer grandfather, David Vance I, who was the first of his Scotch-Irish family to be born in America. David I had met and married Priscilla Brank, daughter of a German settler, during a sojourn on the Catawba in Burke County just before the Revolution. Zeb's maternal grandfather was Zebulon Baird, a Scotch trader who moved from New Jersey in 1793, arriving in the first four-wheeled wagon ever seen west of the Blue Ridge. Baird became a respected merchant and a state legislator. His wife was Hannah Erwin, daughter of Alexander Erwin of Irish descent, a prominent politician and the first clerk of court in Burke County. The Erwin connection was to be valuable to Vance, both socially and politically; through it he could

2. Zebulon B. Vance, *Sketches of North Carolina* (Norfolk, Va.: The Norfolk Landmark, 1875), pp. 23-31 passim.
3. Mira Margaret Baird Vance to Margaret Davidson, September 14, 1830, Z. B. Vance Papers, State Department of Archives and History, Raleigh, N.C.

claim kin by blood or marriage to almost every family of distinction in Burke County.

Grandfather David, who died long before Zebulon was born, had been the kind of man with whom any boy would like to identify. The Vances were a "talking family," so it is easy to imagine that before the fire on long winter evenings little Zeb heard much of his grandfather's exploits. How he had volunteered in the Continental army and had served under the great Washington at Brandywine, Germantown, and Monmouth, and had endured with him the cold and hunger of Valley Forge. How he had led a company at the Battle of King's Mountain. How, after the war, he had made the long journey to New Bern to represent his county in the state's first legislature, and had been appointed one of three commissioners to go into the wilds and survey a boundary line between North Carolina and Tennessee. In the legislature he had voted for the loan of $10,000 which made possible the first buildings at the University of North Carolina. He had also sponsored the bill that created the county of Buncombe from part of Burke and had been elected first clerk of court of the new county. This honor, which had come to his grandfather because he was an educated man—a former teacher and surveyor—was less impressive to the young Zeb than were the heroic honors of war. It may, however, have given him an early inkling that excellence of the mind was not necessarily incompatible with derring-do.

There was still more lore that must have persuaded the lad that he belonged to no commonplace family. His great-aunt Rebecca Brank had been scalped by Indians and yet had lived to honored old age with only a small bald spot on the top of her head to show for it. And his uncle, Robert Vance (his father's elder brother), had fought a pistol duel with Samuel Carson, who had defeated him for re-election to Congress; Uncle Robert had been killed but only, Zeb was bitterly certain, because Mr. Carson's shooting coach had been Davy Crockett.

Upon the death of his brother Robert in 1827 David Vance II had come into full possession of the 638-acre Reems Creek farm—beautiful valley land—and a number of slaves. However, when his son Zeb was six, he moved his family and slaves to Lapland on the French Broad River, where the town of Marshall now sits. There he built a "stock stand" huddled between mountain shoulders and the Buncombe Turnpike. That was the enterprising thing to do in 1836.

The turnpike, completed nine years earlier, stretched from

Saluda Gap to the Tennessee line and joined, at either end, a Greenville road—one to Greeneville, Tennessee, and one to Greenville, South Carolina. Thus it became the "great connecting link between Kentucky, Tennessee, South Carolina and Georgia,"[4] and brought unprecedented prosperity to the region between the village of Asheville and the summer resort at Warm Springs. All kinds of vehicles passed over the road. There were elegant carriages of South Carolina gentry seeking relief at Warm Springs from heat and mosquitoes; there were lumbering six-horse wagons of merchants making the thirty-day trip to Charleston or Augusta. But the most profitable traffic came on the hoof. That traffic consisted of livestock, mainly hogs. Each fall, at a speed of eight miles a day, thousands upon thousands of those creatures—squealing, bellowing, and stinking—were prodded along by their drivers from mountain pastures to southern markets.

To provide accommodations for men and beasts, stock stands sprang up on the turnpike, much as motels and hamburger joints spring up nowadays on heavily traveled throughways. The proprietors of such establishments were combination hotelkeepers and merchants, and often farmers as well. As a farmer David Vance must have sighed for the gentle slopes of his forsaken Reems Creek valley. A traveler who exclaimed in astonishment at the sight of corn growing on the steep mountainside was told by David's brother-in-law that "they shot it in with a shotgun."[5]

Here Zeb Vance spent his formative years and acquired the primary education of his heart and mind. Here amid wild, grand scenery he came to love his mountain country with an intensity which later included his whole state. Here in his father's public house he was thrown with a variety of people and began that "proper study of mankind" at which he became such a proficient scholar. If, as reported, he had an evening's conversation with John C. Calhoun, he must have had hundreds with cursing, uncouth hog drovers. With his older brother Robert, Zeb attended various "old field schools." He seems to have been a vigorous, merry little schoolboy, truthful and manly and given to profanity, whose pugnacity and daring often got him into trouble with his elders and with the law of gravity. Once he fell from a tree and broke his thigh. According to the practice of the time, the Asheville doctor

4. J. M. Ray, "Reminiscences of Forty Years Ago," *The Lyceum* 1, no. 7 (1890): 16.
5. Clement Dowd, *Life of Zebulon B. Vance* (Charlotte, N.C.: Observer Printing and Publishing House, 1897), p. 6.

who came up to attend him placed his leg in a box in order to immobilize it while its bone knitted; consequently that leg was always shorter than the other and gave Vance the rolling gait which made him look bowlegged from a distance. When he was fourteen he set out on horseback for Jonesboro, Tennessee, to enter Washington College, but he did not stay there long. Before a year was out his father died and he returned home to help his mother with the stock stand.

Although David Vance had come fairly early into a considerable inheritance, he died leaving little more than enough to pay his debts. A contributing cause for this sad state of affairs was his well-known charity: time after time he had redeemed the goods and chattels of neighboring families "where the sale had been forced under the hammer."[6] While David Vance's life was less glamorous than that of his father, it was by no means undistinguished. He had volunteered for service in the War of 1812 and only the declaration of peace had prevented his fighting in it. He was a sober and upright man, a Christian who really believed in the Second Great Commandment. If he left his children few worldly goods, he left them an honorable name and an example of probity and compassion. He also left them a remarkable mother.

Widowed at the age of forty-two, Mira Vance had nothing but dower in an embarrassed estate with which to provide for her seven young children. Yet by her energetic efforts and business acumen "she reared respectably and educated tolerably all of them, not only without debt but actually increasing her property."[7] She was a woman of devout religious faith, which no doubt sustained her in her hard life, but she was not able to convey that faith to her son Zebulon. Devoted as he was to his mother, he had "no feeling which might be strictly termed religious"[8] and he refused to pretend to what he did not feel. By far the most valuable gifts that Mira gave her son were a strong sense of humor—this by inheritance and example—and a love for reading. "Not withstanding her own imperfect education, she was extremely literary in her tastes"[9] and, by rare good fortune, she had a good library. Her husband had inherited from his father and older brother more than

6. Ibid., p. 7.
7. Zebulon B. Vance to Cornelia Phillips Spencer, October 21, 1878, Cornelia Phillips Spencer Papers, State Department of Archives and History, Raleigh, N.C.
8. Zebulon B. Vance to Harriett N. Espy, October 2, 1851.
9. Zebulon B. Vance to Cornelia Phillips Spencer, October 21, 1878, Cornelia Phillips Spencer Papers.

five hundred volumes, among which were the best works of English literature, the histories of Greece and Rome, and the Bible. From them, pausing now and then to puff on her clay pipe, Mira Vance used to read aloud to her family. This she did with such verve and delight that young Zeb took to books as naturally as he took to hills and people.

Many years later Kemp P. Battle wrote of meeting Zeb, his contemporary, in Asheville in 1848: "I thought I knew something of Shakespeare, but his familiarity with the characters and words of the Titan poet put me to shame. I claimed to be in a measure intimate with the personages of the romances of my favorite, Scott, but he had evidently lived with them as with home-folks. I had been from childhood, not always a willing, but certainly a regular attendant on Sunday school and church services. I thought I had at least an amateur familiarity with the Bible but his mind seemed to be stored with Scriptural texts as fully as a theological student preparing for an examination. Candor compels me to admit, however that his application of these texts conduced oftener to risibility than to the conversion of souls."[10]

But neither literature nor maternal solicitude had charms to tame the spirits of the boy. Ebullient, fond of rough company, scrappy (though not malicious) Zeb was constantly getting into trouble. Years later he described an incident of his early youth: "I headed a procession on mule back . . . marched 16 miles to the election precinct through the mountains of Madison Co., filled with patriotism, zeal for the Whig cause, and hard cider. Fifteen separate and distinct fights were then and there had, in part of which I participated and for all of which I might be set down as the proximate cause."[11]

By the time he was twenty years old he was living in Asheville where his mother had moved in order to find better schools for her younger children. For a short time he attended Newton Academy, and it is highly probable that the whole fresh scene of Asheville caused him to take serious and practical thought for his future. Small as Asheville was (population 420) it seemed metropolitan in comparison to the primitive isolation of Lapland. It was the seat of Buncombe County, where court met, where affairs of the world were discussed, where political careers were made or lost;

10. Kemp P. Battle, "As Student at University," in Dowd, *Life of Vance*, pp. 16-17.
11. Quoted by Hugh Talmage Lefler and Albert Ray Newsome in *North Carolina: The History of a Southern State* (Chapel Hill, N.C.: The University of North Carolina Press, 1954), p. 339.

and since it had begun to attract visitors from Georgia and South Carolina it had become a modest center of urbanity. ("Our village . . . excells any near us in the fashionable amusement of dancing," boasted the Asheville *Messenger* of June 19, 1850.) The town's two hotels, the Buck and the Eagle, were often filled with ladies and gentlemen whose air of command and *savoir-faire* must have made Zeb discontented with his own raw condition.

On December 5, 1850, Zebulon Vance, with one other young man, began to read law under John W. Woodfin, an able attorney, and the threads of his destiny began to gather. His fellow student was Augustus Summerfield Merrimon, who was to be his lifelong political rival. His preceptor, Mr. Woodfin, had a cousin named Harriett Espy.

Early in 1851 Zeb wrote to David L. Swain requesting that the University of North Carolina grant him a scholarship loan of $300. Later, Kemp Battle recalled that when Governor Swain smilingly recommended Zeb to the faculty as the son of an old sweetheart, the loan was approved.

In the middle of March, presumably made confident by good news from Chapel Hill, Zeb wrote to Harriett, about whom he was evidently beginning to have some deep thoughts.

Harriett Newell Espy, named for a famous Presbyterian missionary, was born in Salisbury, North Carolina, on July 11, 1832. Her parents were Thomas Espy, a Presbyterian minister from Cumberland County, Pennsylvania, and Mary Louisa Tate Espy of Hickory Grove Plantation in Burke County, North Carolina.

Thomas Espy had been educated at Washington College in Pennsylvania and at Princeton Theological Seminary. In 1828, after several years in Virginia, he came to preach in Burke County, sponsored by the Young Men's Missionary Society, and shortly thereafter was called to a pastorate in Salisbury. He went about the Lord's work with dedicated enthusiasm, and it was said that his success, which was notable, was due as much to his example of fervent, uncompromising piety as to his magnetism in the pulpit. But his body was frailer than his spirit. He died at the age of thirty-three, survived by his wife and his only child, Harriett, who was then less than a year old. To Harriett, the father she never knew became a living legend—almost a holy martyr—and exerted the most important single influence upon her personality and character. She felt that, spiritually at least, she wore his mantle.

Three years later, when her mother died, little Harriett was taken into the home of her guardian, Captain Charles Mc-

Dowell of Quaker Meadows. There she was brought up as a member of the family.

Captain Charles, overshadowed in history books by his more illustrious kin—leaders of the Revolution in western North Carolina—had been a soldier in the less glorious War of 1812.[12] He was a prosperous farmer, a respected member of his community, and an ardent Whig who had represented Burke County in the General Assemblies of 1809, '10, and '11. He was Harriett's half-great-uncle as well as her cousin. His mother and Harriett's great-grandmother had been the brave and beautiful Grace Greenlee Bowman, a heroine of the Revolution. Hearing that her husband, John Bowman, had been desperately wounded and was lying in a house near the battlefield at Ramsour's Mill, she had "mounted a fleet horse and taking her 15-months-old child [Harriett's grandmother] in her arms, rode like the wind [40 miles] to the bedside of her husband, who expired a short time after her arrival."[13] Two years later, Grace married General Charles McDowell, went with him and her daughter Mary Bowman to Quaker Meadows, and, in due time, became the mother of Charles, later known as Captain Charles, and to Harriett as "Uncle." Captain Charles's wife, née McDowell, was also Harriett's cousin. In this involved fashion Harriett Espy was related to many of the first families of Burke County. This was a fortunate situation for a female orphan.

In a county famous for its fine plantations there was none more beautiful than Quaker Meadows. The two thousand acres of rich bottom land inherited by Captain Charles have been described as a "magnificent and lordly estate."[14] They spread out below the house, situated on a low hill near the western boundary of the property, to the Catawba River a mile to the east. The house itself, a sturdy brick structure, was two miles from the courthouse in Morganton. Just across the river, and in full view of the house, was the property settled by Zebulon Vance's great-grandfather Robert Brank. There were slaves to work the fields at Quaker Meadows and to cook in the kitchen. For the McDowell household living was easy.

Harriett was as happy in her family life as in her surroundings. The McDowells had six children of their own, four daugh-

12. His father, General Charles McDowell; his uncle Colonel Joseph McDowell; and his cousin Colonel Joseph McDowell of Pleasant Gardens, who was also his father-in-law.
13. W. C. Carson, "Grace Greenlee," *North Carolina Booklet* 15 (1915): 17, 18.
14. Alphonso C. Avery, "Historic Homes of North Carolina: Pleasant Gardens and Quaker Meadows in Burke County," *North Carolina Booklet* 4 (1904): 9.

ters and two sons, and though Harriett called the older girls "cousin" in deference to their age, she called the three younger children "brother" and "sister." When Harriett was nine, the benevolent McDowells took into their fold another orphaned grand-niece. She was Sarah Butler—the "Sallie" of the letters to Vance—who was Harriett's first cousin and who became her close friend.

The McDowells reared their children, own and foster, with equal kindness, though Captain Charles was particularly indulgent to Harriett because of her delicate health. She had inherited a comfortable estate from her mother and he often said, "Let the child have everything she wants; it does not matter how much she spends, for she will never live to come into her property."[15] But of course she did live and, responsive to the warmth of her treatment, grew up to be affectionate and loyal. At fourteen she was described as "not a beauty, but possessed of her father's magnetism, erect and graceful in figure, with much vivacity and sweetness of manner, a musically modulated voice, and an unusual strength and quickness of mind . . . captivating."[16] However, though her appearance was fragile and her manner demure, she had, to her sorrow, the quick temper that goes traditionally with red hair. Though the McDowells were Methodists, Harriett, at the age of sixteen, joined the Presbyterian Church in Morganton. She embraced all its tenets with her father's own zeal. Among her contemporaries she was known as one who "preached righteousness."[17]

Righteousness did not interfere, however, with Harriett's enjoyment of social life in Burke County, which was very pleasant. There was much visiting among the well-to-do county families as well as among the prosperous citizens of Morganton, many of whom were sons and daughters of the planters. There were picnics and masquerade parties and a Reading Society. In July and August entertainment was especially lavish, for then three justices of the state's Supreme Court came to preside over the summer sessions of the court at Morganton; and among the lawyers and litigants attendant upon those sessions were enough eligible bachelors to brighten the eyes of the Burke County girls. As Vance himself was to write later, "The valley region became . . . the seat of culture and refinement of western North Carolina. . . . No portion of

---

15. *In Memory of Mrs. Margarett M. Vance and Mrs. Harriette Espy Vance* (Raleigh, N.C.: Edwards, Broughton & Co., 1878), p. 30. This is a collection of news clippings and periodicals.
16. Ibid.
17. Ibid., p. 31.

our state better illustrated that southern country life which so much resembles that of the British."[18]

By 1850 the handsome McDowell girls had married well. Two of them had married the Woodfin brothers, John and Nicholas, of Asheville, and the hospitality of their new domiciles enlarged the social sphere of their little Espy cousin. It was in a Woodfin house surely that Harriett made the acquaintance of Zeb Vance. Poor, half-educated, with a name for wildness, he was hardly the catch her friends hoped she would make; but she must have recognized in him, as he in her, some quality as compelling as it was alien. And through the veil of her well-bred reserve, he must have guessed that she recognized it, for on March 15, 1851, he made bold to write her the first of his many letters. "Miss Espy," he wrote, "The object of this intrusive epistle is to beg to be allowed the favor of your correspondence." Within the fortnight "Mr. Vance" was granted that favor.

There are 121 letters in the prenuptial correspondence of Mr. Vance and Miss Espy, or—quite early in the game—of "My dearest Harriett" and "My beloved Zebulon." Primarily they are love letters, couched in the elaborate style of their time, and have as such a romantic charm for sentimental antiquarians. But because they were written by candid young people who sought to achieve intimacy by telling each other all about themselves—their hopes and ideals, their fears and faults, the milieux in which they moved—they have a more substantial charm than that. They reveal, as nothing else could, the salient traits of two high-minded beings—one of whom was to play a major role in the drama of human events. Furthermore they afford fascinating glimpses into the society of antebellum North Carolina—particularly that of Chapel Hill and of the western counties which were emerging into consequence.

Zeb's letters generally begin with long passages of regard, which, though passionate, is expressed in terms of the utmost correctitude. (That correctitude is noteworthy when one reflects upon his lifelong flair for pungent phrases and "fuliginous yarns.")[19] His language gives offense to his lady only when it trespasses upon divine territory. Once he calls himself her "idolatrer" (Harriett shivers in her boots for his immortal soul!) and adds that "my love for you absorbs and transcends every other feeling within my boozum."

18. Vance, *Sketches*, p. 79.
19. Kemp P. Battle's words. Dowd, *Life of Vance*, p. 29.

Not that Harriett lacks a certain delicate ardor. "In the sweet stillness of the night," she begins one letter, "when all in the house have retired to rest (save me) I with the greatest imaginable pleasure devote a short time to communing with my Dear absent One . . . I know that I shall sleep all the better . . . for visions of my beloved one will hover round my pillow." But she remains alert to moral danger: "We should beware lest we allow the Creature to usurp the place in our hearts that the Creator alone should possess."

Aside from love, Harriett's letters tell of her daily concerns at Quaker Meadows. Visits. Parties. Neighborhood weddings. The departure of relatives and friends for the gold fields of California. Reading matter. (Zeb sends her *Harper's Magazine* upon which she comments with a polite restraint of enthusiasm; she recommends to him a new novel called *The Wide, Wide World*.) Church services. Illnesses. Deaths. Harriett dwells hard on death, for that of course is the best known literary vehicle for warning against error and for persuasion to faith. Once, transparently hoping to be contradicted (which she *is* in Zeb's next), she calls her letters "prosey"—and she speaks truer than she knows.

Implicit in Zeb's letters are two innate characteristics which he kept to the end of his life. One is a strong, headlong determination to get what he wants—in this case, Harriett. The other is a refusal to play the hypocrite. Thus, while his protestations of affection are so voluble and exuberant as to constitute almost an assault upon her mind, and while the slightest doubt of *her* affection puts him in a frenzy, he never gives her any hope of realizing her dearest wish, which is to bring him to "the throne of Grace." "I make no pretentions to religion," he states simply. He even goes so far as to twit Harriett about her excessive piety, though under a guise of solemnity that he is confident she will not pierce. When she suggests that he forsake politics, he replies that there are some things about him that cannot be changed. And yet he realizes, as he was to do in his political campaigns, that candor has its limits of usefulness. When he writes to Harriett from Asheville, where he set up a law practice after his year at the university, he stresses the town's elegant society and ignores the brawling, bawdy crowd around its grog shops. When he describes Chapel Hill, he sketches an idyllic village, given to things of the mind, and tells of his association with learned professors and their cultivated families; he does not speak of the rough behavior of his fellow students whose chief diversion was that of "deviling," and actually stoning, the faculty—a sport in which he did not engage but of which he was well aware. He is apparently quite open about certain young ladies he visits. He speaks of Miss Sue Battle, of "noble" Miss May Wheat, and of "the exquisite pleasure of meeting Miss Ann Williams of Charlotte." But he makes no mention—and the omission *must* be calculated—of his acquaintance with Miss Cornelia Phillips (later Mrs. Spencer) for whom his admiration knew no bounds. ("She is the smartest woman in the State, yes, and the smartest *man* too,"[20] he was to declare much later.) Evidently he was shrewd enough to surmise that though Harriett would not stoop to ordinary jealousy, an intellectual intimacy between her beloved and a woman of sharper wits than hers might awaken uncharitable feelings in her Christian breast.

Seldom was there a less assorted pair of lovers. She was cautious, complacent, almost entirely humorless, and religious in a way that would seem fanatical today and must even then have seemed obsessive. He was impetuous, earthy, profane of speech, and untroubled by the least shadow of mystical faith. In common they had only warmth and character. Those are not mean rations to share, of course—many a union has survived on less—but it was probably from their dissimilarities that each was to gain most. Zeb had enough wit and humor for an army and some to spare. What he needed in a wife was a "limpid fountain of purity," which was his image of Harriett. As for Harriett, her evangelical fervor would have been wasted on a saint—she needed a brilliant sinner to save.

During the course of their married life, Zebulon and Harriett Vance wrote regularly to each other. They were separated much of the time—by Harriett's poor health and frequent pregnancies which kept her at home when her husband went off to the General Assembly at Raleigh and to Congress in Washington, and by war—so that their habit, formed early, of communicating through the written word stood them in good stead. But that correspondence was of a different order. Though always affectionate, it dealt with the real and often cruel exigencies and anxieties of human existence in parlous times. The letters of this present collection reflect a time when the lark was on the wing and almost anything—even perpetual felicity—seemed possible, and the last of these marks the

20. Phillips Russell, *The Woman Who Rang the Bell: The Story of Cornelia Phillips Spencer* (Chapel Hill, N.C.: The University of North Carolina Press, 1949), p. 20.

end of a chapter. That letter was written by Harriett on July 26, 1853, exactly a week before her marriage. It is sweet and a trifle choppy. (Naturally, the girl was somewhat rattled by preparations for the great occasion.) She reminds Zeb to write to the minister who is to marry them and warns him that if he spends the Sabbath at Quaker Meadows he will have to go to church. She hopes he is "happy in the contemplation of that future which appears so bright."

They were married in the Presbyterian Church at Morganton on the evening of August 2, 1853. (Earlier in the summer Zeb had referred, with an apology for his pun, to the coming "august event.") It is significant that the wedding date was set for a political reason. It enabled the groom to be back in Asheville on the fourth of August, which was an election day.

So Zebulon Baird Vance got what he wanted—a loyal wife, a good mother for his children, and freedom to follow his natural bent. Harriett was not immediately so fortunate. It was only after she had departed this life that Zebulon took the step toward salvation that she had constantly urged upon him. She had been right about death—its persuasive power was very great.

Suffering from a double bereavement (he had lost his mother only two months before he lost Harriett) and awed by the recollection of his sick wife's patient submission to the divine will, Vance felt welling up in him "a trust in God—her God—"[21] and illustrated his trust by publicly professing his allegiance to the whole doctrine of Presbyterianism.

On December 10, 1878, he wrote to Mrs. Cornelia Phillips Spencer, addressing her as "My dear Friend," who had congratulated him upon his godly move. He wrote of "the wife of my youth—my inseparable companion, counsellor, helper and *friend* for more than a quarter of a century—who loved and trusted me with her all when a wild and obscure young man . . . God have mercy on me, how am I to face the world and make good my new and solemn profession without her!"[22] A few days before, he continued, he had visited, for the first time since her death, the home they had shared in Charlotte. There, "One white Japonica alone was in bloom, pure and white as the angel-raiment she now wears. Instinctively, my first thought was to cut it and take it to Hattie . . .

21. Zebulon Baird Vance to Cornelia Phillips Spencer, November 10, 1878, Cornelia Phillips Spencer Papers.
22. Cornelia Phillips Spencer Papers.

I then sought for her letters and spent most of the day in reading . . . weeping over her words of love and my replies to them from those of the time of our sweethearting down to the last poor scrawl she wrote me. . . ."

Frances Gray Patton

Part I

March 15, 1851, to March 16, 1852

Asheville. March 15th 1851

Miss Espy,

The object of this intrusive epistle is to beg to be allowed the favour of your correspondence, or at least the privilege of addressing a more full and expressive letter to you than this one—It is asking a considerable favour I, am aware, probably more than you would feel justified in granting, under existing circumstances, but let me say by way of apology for my presumption, that justice to my own feelings demanded that I should run the risk of incurring your displeasure by making the solicitation—I have been led to hope from the candour of your disposition that you deal with me promptly and justly, and therefore trusting that I shall receive an answer at your earliest convenience, and *earnestly* hoping that it will be a favourable one, I take the liberty of subscribing myself with all the
      Sentiments of due Respect
                Yours &c.
                Zeb. B. Vance

Miss H. N. Espy
Morganton
N Ca

The first four letters of Harriett Newell Espy are missing.

Asheville April 2d '51

Miss Espy,

Suffer me to tender you my sincerest thanks for the pleasure I experianced on the reception of yours this morning, finding as I did that the privilege of writing to you was granted me in compliance with my request—I duly appreciate your goodness, and with a feeling of varied and strange emotion, I hasten to avail myself of it—It has been said by a celebrated French writer [La Rochefoucauld], that "Silence is the best course for any man to adopt who distrusts himself", and yet though I tremble to attempt the task of expressing myself fully to you Miss Espy, yet the above maxim would be at fault if applied to myself; believing therefore that silence is not always best, tho' perhaps it is sometimes, I shall endeavor to explain to you the object for which I solicited your permission to write—The cant of false and unfeeling hypocrites I despise, and unwilling to cultivate hopes, which if too long and too fondly cherished without sufficient reason, might, if blasted, reduce me to the verge of distraction and despair. I deem it preferable for my own peace to say directly and frankly, Miss Espy, that you have inspired me with a sentiment of love deep and lasting, and of the most sanguine and even enthusiastic character—I make this declaration with a deep impression of my presumption, of my entire unworthiness—If this poor offering, this sincere tribute of the unworthy to the good, should meet with the scorn which probably it may deserve from the presumption of the giver, I can but pray your forgiveness, and my hopes for your pardon are grounded upon the fact that I have heard you declare that you believed in the existence of *such* a *passion*, and if so, you would not act in consistency with such belief if you refused to extend your forgiveness to one of *its* sincerest, but perhaps erring votaries.

Having thus stated my feelings in full it is now my object to know if, in the plenitude of your goodness, you will allow me to retain, of that hope, which has hitherto been to me as something too ideal and blissful to be of earthly origin, one ray in reality—which would be sufficient to support me in the greatest task that could be imposed on me; the struggle to render myself worthy of the slightest thought which could pass through your mind—Take not alltogether from me that life preserving and soul-sustaining principle, hope:

> "Cease every joy to glimmer on my mind,
> But leave—O! leave the light of *hope* behind.
> Yet still may Hope her talisman employ
> To snatch from Heaven anticipated Joy."[1]

The time which shall intervene between the reception of this letter, and the reception of the answer to it, will be passed more unpleasantly than any mind can conceive, which has never endured the torture of suspense in its most horrible forms, but I forbear urging haste relying upon the promise contained in your letter that "I will endeavor to be more punctual in answering your future epistle", for which I thank you. Tossed upon a sea of doubts and fears, amidst the conflicting struggles of hope and despair, like the over-wearied pilot who resigns helm and calmly awaits for the tide to waft to the shore, or dash him headlong to destruction, I shall

---

1. Thomas Campbell, "Pleasures of Hope."

await your reply, and having full confidence in your justice and generosity, I shall be prepared to bow to the sentence which you may pronounce upon me whether for weal or wo, for it would be virtually impeaching the justice of Heaven itself to impeach of injustice one of its noblest and most perfect beings—

What more can I say? Or rather what more need I say? My happiness is at your disposal—Deal with it as you please—I could extend this letter several sheets more, but I deem needless, for alas! I know not the reception this much will meet with from you—Earnestly, soliciting, therefore, your pardon if I should incur your displeasure in anything this contains

With due Respect I remain &c

Zeb B Vance

Asheville, May 20th '51

Miss Espy,

For near one month I turned from my empty box at the post office, sickened with disappointment and despair. I came to the conclusion that I was not only rejected but despised, and that you had determined to deny me the mournful favour of seeing your opinion of myself expressed on paper, and would leave me to infer from your silence your intention toward me—At length I heard you had been very ill, which caused me to excuse your delay immediately, and I reproached myself for my uncharitable suspicions—Your answer came. I took it from the box, but trembled to open it. O what a moment of suspense is that which precedes the opening of a letter! What a world of joy or sorrow is contained within the four corners of that little inanimate paper, so lifeless within itself yet rendered by the ingenuity of man, so eloquently expressive of weal or wo!—I tore it open and read —— ——

Probably Miss Espy, your sympathising soul can imagine something of the pang which I suffered then. How void, how useless this existence seemed to me—My spirit was crushed, bitterly crushed, and my heart sank within me—Active and enthusiastic Hope had before conjured up the brightest most blissful visions of the future, so brilliant that the eye of imagination turned dazled and overpowered, as does the naked eye from the contemplation of the Tropical sun, now my gaze rested upon nought but the shadowy forms of black despair, grim and horrible as hell—What a terrible transition for the mind to experiance! O why is not my reason destroyed that I might bury those recolections in insanity, in blessed madness:

Your reply Miss Espy, was the more cruel to me from the very effort you made to soften the blow, by clothing it in the most polite and gentle language and by the assurances of your esteem and sincere friendship—I thank you, again and again I thank you for it, and duly appreciate your motives in making them but they served not the purpose for which you probably designed them—Had you been less kind, had you scorned or despised, pride would have come to my relief and I could have repaid your scorn with equal haughtiness; but no; your nature was too high and noble for that, and I am compelled to see that you are faultless, and that I must expect nothing more than your *friendship*—The friendship of one so worthy as yourself, would confer an honour on any individual in the land Miss Espy and much more on so unworthy and obscure an individual as myself and I feel grateful to you for it, but truly friendship is,

"A shade that follows wealth & fame
And leaves the wretch to weep"[2]

and at best requites O, how coldly a love so deep and undying as mine. But you have willed it so, and I have nothing to do but to submit. I have nothing to complain of at your hands; your sex is the Arbiter of ours in that respect at least, and as a subject having sworn fealty to the blind God, it behooves me to yield ready obedience to his will, as expressed by his ministers—

I expect to start to Chapel Hill on the 1st of July. I shall stop a day or two in M—— [Morganton] to see some of my relations. Shall I be denied the pleasure of calling upon you in the capacity of a friend?—I suppose of course that you wish this correspondence to close, which if such is your will shall be done, but might I request an answer to this? Why I ask it, I know not, but yet I will take it as a favour of you to reply to this. I will also be much obliged to you if you will enclose my letters and return them as soon as convenient and I will return yours if you wish. And now Miss Espy suffer me to say in conclusion that though time and change may enable me to master a hopless passion, yet oblivious self will be unable to lessen the esteem and respect which will ever be entertained for you by

                          Your sincere friend
                          Zeb B. Vance

2. Oliver Goldsmith, "The Hermit."

On the second day of his six-day stagecoach journey to Chapel Hill, Zebulon Vance stopped over in Morganton to see Harriett Espy.

Chapel Hill, July. 18, '51[3]

Miss Espy,

With feelings, which none but those who have been in my situation, can describe, I once more begin that correspondence with you, I once deemed broken off forever. Your goodness, in partially recalling that cruel judgement which was suspended over me, and suffering me to indulge in the pleasing, tho' destructive sweets of hope, again forms another ingredient, to increase if possible, the strength & holiness of my passion. "Thanks, thanks, ever the exchequer of the poor",[4] is all my bounding heart can utter.

I arrived here on last Tuesday, met with a cordial and patronising reception from Gov. Swain,[5] and having with difficulty procured a room[6] (as there is an unusual number of students in attendance [251]) I seat myself tonight to address you before entering upon the arduous duties of tomorrow.

How much I regretted that I was unable to remain longer in Morganton! How I wish that I could have protracted that short and interrupted conversation which I held with you, into hours, instead of moments! But few as were the words which fell from your lips, they were heavenly music to *my* ears. My heart bounds wildly, and my temples throb allmost to madness when I recall

3. The first session began six weeks after commencement. *Catalogue of the Trustees, Faculty and Students of the University of North Carolina, 1851-52*, p. 32.

4. William Shakespeare, *King Richard II*, act 2, sc. 3, line 65.

5. Even after he became president of the University of North Carolina, David Lowry Swain (1801-68) was usually called "Governor." A native of Buncombe County, Swain was a close friend of the Vance family. He had been a classmate of Mira Vance in Asheville when they attended the school run by the Reverend George Newton. After studying law, he rose quickly in politics. A Whig, he became, at thirty-one, the youngest governor North Carolina has ever had. After serving three successive terms, 1832-35, he was elected president of the University of North Carolina, an office he held until his death. Frontis W. Johnston, ed., *The Papers of Zebulon Baird Vance, 1843-62* (Raleigh, N.C.: State Department of Archives and History, 1963), 1: 9, n. 45.

6. No. 5, West Building. *Catalogue of U.N.C., 1851-52*, p. 17.

the words which you spoke to me. And have *indeed* your feelings changed toward me? Have you at length become convinced of the sincerity and endurance of my protestations and consented that I might indulge the hope of one day becoming worthy of a warmer sentiment at your hands than *esteem*? If such is the case, then I have indeed an object to obtain, worthy of toil and labour, then indeed have I an inducement to struggle for the honours of the world; that I might lay them at your feet, that I might devote my life to her, whose smile of approbation would be a sufficient reward, and is all I ask!

Miss Hariet, I hope, that in the prosecution of this correspondence, in which I at least am so much interested, you will show toward me the utmost candour in all which you may say—I expressed that desire when with you, and you promptly replied that you would do so. In that respect I shall place entire confidence in you. If then you think that your feelings have so far changed, as to justify me in cherishing, yet and forever the passionate sentiment which I entertain for you, please, I beseech you, tell me so. You said to me, when speaking of this subject, that you *"had been thinking of it"*, and thought upon reflection, that you would give me some encouragement. That was quite correct, I wish you to reflect upon it. I wish you to consider the strength and reality of my love, and that no man could make the woman unhappy, whom he really loved, the despair and misery you would inflict upon me, by rejecting me, and the misery which would attend us both, if through a mistaken feeling you should say "yes" to my suit and your heart was not responsive. But as I have said, I rely upon you. I know that you will act in this matter as becomes the high opinion which I entertain of the nobleness and goodness of your character.

Will you write to me early and at length? If you knew what extacy the smallest note from your hand occasioned me, you would excuse me for pressing you to write to me punctually and lengthily. How impatiently I shall count the weary hours untill I receive an answer to this, and how bitter the disappointment if your answer be long in reaching me! Let me hope you will be more merciful to me. It may not be improper to say that my prospects at this place, for improvement and advantage, are exceedingly flattering, and I sincerely hope that I shall be able to fulfill the expectations of my friends, in not abusing the golden opportunities here presented me.

My respects to Miss Butler,[7] whom I presume is aware of this correspondence, and believe me to be

>Yours sincerely and devotedly
>Zeb B. Vance

>University of N. C.
>Chapel Hill Aug 27, '51

Miss Espy,

I rec'd your note by Mr. McDowell's[8] letter dated Aug. 5th and have been waiting anxiously and impatiently for the "long letter" which you promised to write me. I need not say that it has not come, although the time is past when it was to have reached me. Neither need I say that it has caused me the bitterest disappointment. It is useless to dwell upon the pang, which I suffered, as each day I returned empty-handed from the Post Office—I leave you to imagine the pain of suffering so sudden a transition from glowing hope to bitter despair. Beside this, it is quite natural, that, in meeting with so many disappointments, a shade of suspicion should involuntarily creep into the mind in regard to the fidelity of those who are the authors of them. Despair is indeed ever near, and taking advantage of the slightest circumstance or cause of discontent, will pour his dark suspicions into the ear, and drown the more pleasing voice of hope. That such is the case, to some extent with myself, it would be untruthful to deny. If subsequent events should establish the truth of my fears, I need offer no excuse for them, but should they on the contrary prove to have been too hastily formed, and unjustly indulged in, I can offer you no better apology, than to refer you to the circumstances in which I am placed. I am not exacting or unreasonable, at least I think I am

---

7. Sarah Louisa Butler, an orphan, lived at Quaker Meadows. She stood in the same relationship to Captain and Mrs. Charles McDowell as Harriett Espy. Her father was William Claiborne Butler, a farmer who had been sheriff of Burke County in 1831 and 1832. Her mother was Margaret Tate Butler, HNE's aunt. The unpublished manuscript from which this information was obtained, "The Tates of Burke County, N.C.," by Sam J. Ervin, was kindly supplied by Samuel McDowell Tate of Morganton, N.C. *Census* of Burke County, 1850.

8. James C. S. McDowell, HNE's "Brother James," was the younger son of Captain Charles McDowell of Quaker Meadows. He had attended Davidson College in 1848. At this time he was foot-loose though studying law intermittently under his brother-in-law, John W. Woodfin, in Asheville. Louise Manly, comp., *The Manly Family* (Greenville, S.C.: n.p., 1930), p. 53; *Alumni Catalogue of Davidson College*, 1924, p. 62.

not; on the contrary, I can rest satisfied and in confidence, if I have any positive or reasonable grounds on which to rest my hopes. Now Miss Harriet, have I such grounds? Have I sufficient grounds to say to myself that all is right? Has my warm, enthusiastic, devotional love met with such a reception at your hands as should banish every fear and doubt from my breast? Your candour will give a correct answer to these questions.

Considering these things, let me beg you to excuse my importunity and my uneasiness. I thought I would defer writing to you again, untill I received your letter, but my feelings would not suffer me to remain silent, with such an incubus upon my mind—and therefore with the distant and faint hope of affecting something, at least a letter from you, have I taken up my pen to address you again. At any rate, it is somewhat a relief to my feelings to communicate with you even in this distant and formal manner, and in so unsatisfactory a way as writing upon paper. Would to God it were so that I could be allowed to approach you in a way and style more in accordance with the warmth of my feelings! Then indeed it would not only be a relief, but extacy, to address you—'Miss Espy, what can I say that would please you? What can I do that would cause you to take an interest, the slightest interest, in my humble fate? How can I act, how can I live, to render myself worthy of your esteem and confidence? What can I urge upon your consideration that would wield any influence in my behalf, but the sincere and ever living love of this heart? O! could you but hear its appeals and its pleadings, its petitions and its prayers, that arise upon the mention of your name, in the glare of the day or the dead hours of the night, I could not fear for the result!'

Will you please forgive my impetuosity; I can not speak upon a subject of such importance to my future destiny, in the calm, cold-blooded and deliberate style of most folks—I am not constituted like some persons. I may say like very few persons I am neither a wild enthusiast reared in the School of Romance, nor am I one of those narrow hearted Philosophers who view the feelings and affections of the heart as something ideal and imaginary, which form the capital of the novelist and the poet, but too frivolous and effeminate to engage the attention of the man of sense and reality—But I regard the subject of marriage as involving one of the most important events in the history of a man's life; and I confess, that I look forward to the peaceful and holy scenes of love and happiness in connection with female society as the *Chief* of the few sources of pleasure, which makes life worth enduring or at all supportable.

Indeed if I thought that the sun of life was yet to set upon me, in the way in which it frequently does upon others, I know of no other consideration which would prevent me from closing my miserable existence at once, without burdening the world with my support—Ambition is the great support and prompter of the young, but when not properly restrained and directed it is more frequently a source of wretchedness and misery than of happiness—A boundless and insatiate ambition is indeed the greatest curse that ever was inflicted upon a young man, when not tempered with the nobler and milder virtues which alone produce contentment and adorn the *man*, in the true sense of the term, as God created him. Knowing that I have ambition enough, more than enough, I strive to cultivate alone those virtues, which my own common sense and the experience of all the world tells me will lead to happiness or usefulness. You will think perhaps that I have wandered from the subject and perhaps I have, but my brain, while talking to you becomes so full of the bright images of the future in which your name predominates, that it is scarely possible for me to refrain from touching upon a subject to which I justly attach so much importance—

Again I beg you Miss Harriet to forgive me if I have done you injustice—I do not write this letter in a spirit of complaint, but merely as expressive of the thoughts and fears, which at this distance from you, pervade my breast—You can remove my heavy thoughts and dissipate my fears at a single breath, and forever—Will you do it? Will you write me a letter which shall be able to give me full and complete satisfaction? I shall await the result with a patience sufficient to astonish a stoic himself under such circumstances, for it is the patience, still and death-like which precedes despair—

I have nothing in the way of ordinary news to give you, as all my news comes from Buncombe and I suppose you are well posted from that quarter, by your correspondents there. I have been quite unwell for a few days past, but attend recitations again. I hope you had a pleasant time at D[avidson] College commencement.

Yours truly, and devotedly,
Zeb. B. Vance

University of N. C.
Chapel Hill Sep. 9.

My Dearest Harriet,

I received yours on the day before yesterday, and avail myself of the first leisure moment to comply with your request, and also, the urgent dictates of my bounding heart—

The joy, the rapture and gratitude, that pervaded my breast on reading your kind and affectionate letter, can not be described— But my transports were somewhat lessened by self reproach when I reflected upon the last letter I wrote you, and which I presume you had not received when you wrote. In that letter, I indulged in some ungenerous and ungrateful complaints in consequence of your long delay, which I find that I had no grounds for making, and in which I did you injustice, the grossest injustice—O how my conscience smote me, and how bitterly I repented when I had your letter, so full of kindness and affection. *Forgive me, forgive me!* You say that "you can no longer doubt the affection that I profess for you," you have confidence in me—I am not behind in placing my confidence in you; nay, my confidence was placed in you before you probably ever thought of beholding me in the character of your devoted lover, from the first time that I became acquainted with you, you took possession of my entire confidence; and let me add, that as high as is my estimate of your character, *I never fear of being deceived.* My love can admit of no increase, I believe that it is as great as falls to the share of man to bear toward a fellow creature; if it could be increased, or if it had not been complete, your letter would have been sufficient to complete it. You said that *you loved me!* What more do you suppose is requisite to fill up the measure of my happiness? What more can I ask of you? Thanks, my dearest Harriet, thanks—Your goodness in thinking of me, as you said, during every moment since I bid you farewell, and your kindness in advising me I am sincerely obliged to you for— You say you will be glad to hear of both my health and happiness. It is in my power to assure you of both. My health is and has been good, and since the reception of your letter my *happiness is complete* and if you desire my happiness continued in future life you have but to order it so, and it will be so—You say also, that you had several things to ask my opinion about, if you had had the time when I was in M—— [Morganton] You will greatly oblige me if you will ask me about them yet—I long to answer anything which you may wish my opinion concerning. I too regret exceedingly that I could make no longer stay in Morganton as I came on through there. But I had made my arrangements with the view of coming directly on before I left home. I could have spent my time for a week very pleasantly in Morganton under any circumstances with my friends and relatives, but to have been with you would have been my chief happiness.

I am much pleased with this place—it is exactly the place for a student. There are but few attractions of any kind to draw him from his study. The circle of society is quite limited, being composed allmost entirely of the families of the Professors. I have made the acquaintance of but two or three Ladies here, and attended but one party—I have been introduced to Miss May Wheat,[9] the young lady with whom my friend Jas. McDowell was so deeply enamoured. For his sake I have been persuading her that it is her duty to go to the mountains to live. Did you see Miss May, and Miss Battle[10] while they were up in our country?

With my present situation I am content, but the future, the bright misterious future, do you ever think about that? O, with what an intense interest I gaze forward to future years! That future looks only bright and promising to me. I gaze upon it without trembling or dread; I look upon it, and resolve, that as far as it is in the power of man to control his own destiny, will I control mine by making all the efforts so to do, which are consistent with sacred honour and rectitude. My situation for improvement here, is extremely favourable. I have friends who are profuse in their assurances of assistance to me hereafter, as well as for the present, and I have health and a hearty good will to enter bravely into the arduous duties before me—With the sky so clear before and around me, and such a prize before me, I have set myself down withe determination to succeed or perish in the attempt. I am in-

9. Mary Wheat was the daughter of Dr. John Thomas Wheat, an Episcopal minister, who came to the University of North Carolina as professor of rhetoric and logic in 1850. That same year Mary entered St. Mary's School. Mary Wheat Shober, "Reminiscences of My School Days," *St. Mary's Muse* (November, 1910): 93.

10. Susan Catherine Battle was the only daughter of Judge William Horn and Lucy Plummer Battle. Judge Battle, on the Superior Court bench at this time, was professor of law and head of the Department of Law at the University of North Carolina. His sons, Kemp, a tutor in math at the university, and Richard, a student, became Vance's devoted friends. Kemp was throughout Vance's life his confidant and adviser. Richard was his personal secretary during two years of his war governorship and the one who made the memorial address in 1900 at the dedication of the Vance monument in Raleigh. *Census of Orange County, 1850; Catalogue of U.N.C., 1851-52*, p. 31; Clement Dowd, *Life of Zebulon B. Vance* (Charlotte, N.C.: Observer Printing and Publishing House, 1897), p. 17; Johnston, *Papers of ZBV*, 1; xxiv, 8, n. 42.

deed labouring, labouring with all the strength I possess; I am interested more: there is *one* who watches my struggles and takes an interest in my success, and I feel the strength of a giant at the thought. From 5 O'clock in the morning, until 10 O'clk at night, I am at my duties. I saw Mr. McKesson[11] and James McD. as they passed through this place on their route North. They halted but for a few moments. You ask if you can see me in December—Alas, I am sorry to say, I expect not. The Supreme Court sits in Raleigh about the midst of the vacation,[12] and I am preparing to apply[13] then. I do not expect to see you untill next June—Will you continue to think of me untill then? Will you be unaffected by my absence? O, I hope and trust in you—This letter is getting too long. Please write again and at an early day, it would be pleasant to exchange sentiments upon the future with you often. I remain yours & yours only

       Sincerely & devotedly,
       Zeb. B. Vance

11. William F. McKesson, a native of Pennsylvania, was a son of James and Maria McKesson. Having been successful earlier in Burke County gold mining, he was at this time a wealthy merchant in Morganton. His wife, Margaret, nee McDowell, was a daughter of Captain Charles McDowell of Quaker Meadows. HNE usually referred to him as "Brother William." A Whig, he was sent to the General Assembly by Burke County in 1846 and 1854. During the latter session, John Gray Bynum, another of Captain Charles's sons-in-law (married to his daughter Mary), and ZBV were also serving in the lower house. Margaret McKesson and Mary Bynum were with their husbands in Raleigh, but Harriett, being pregnant, stayed at home. On January 20, 1855, she wrote Zebulon, "How is Sister Mag? My love to she and cousin Mary—poor things. I reckon their husbands are just going the whole figure. I understand Mr. McKesson is quite popular on account of his *shampain* dinners and sister suffers." *Census* of Burke County, 1850; Alphonso C. Avery, *History of the Presbyterian Churches at Quaker Meadows and Morganton from the Year 1780 to 1913* (Raleigh, N.C.: Edwards and Broughton Printing Co., 1913), p. 26; Colonel Thomas George Walton, *Sketches of the Pioneers in Burke County History* (n.p., n.d.), p. 37; R. D. W. Connor, comp., *A Manual of North Carolina Issued by the North Carolina Historical Commission for the Use of the Members of the General Assembly Session 1913* (Raleigh, N.C.: E. M. Uzzell and Co., State Printers, 1913), pp. 522, 523; Zebulon Baird Vance, Harriet Espy Vance letters, from Z. B. Vance Papers, State Department of Archives and History, Raleigh, N.C.

12. The vacation between sessions lasted six weeks, from December 5, 1851, to January 16, 1852. *Catalogue of U.N.C., 1851-52*, p. 32.

13. ZBV was planning to apply for county court license. At this time two examinations were required, one for county court license and one for superior court license. A year had to elapse between the granting of the two. Oral examinations were given by not less than two of the three justices of the supreme court during the first seven days of each term of court. Fannie Memory Farmer, "The Bar Examination and Beginning Years of Legal Practice in North Carolina, 1820-1860," *North Carolina Historical Review* 29 (April, 1952), 160, 161.

I send you a plain ring, which I wish you to accept to assist you in remembering me. I must apologise for the engraving. I sent it to Raleigh to have the letters engraved upon it and it was done so wretched bad, that I gave out sending it to you, but I can get no other one in this place. Please confer an additional favour on me by accepting it, for my sake.

            Zeb

          Quaker Meadows[14] Sep 20th 1851

My dearest Mr Vance;—

 I received your highly valued letter day before yesterday & you can well imagine the pleasure it gave me to hear that my last communication had been the means of making you so happy— A few days after I had written I received a letter from you, reproaching me for my unkindly negligence. I must confess that I deserved reproach, although I could offer the best of apologies— but still it was my duty to have answered your epistle at an earlyer period—I hope that in future you will have no cause to complain of me about letter writing—for I think now that I shall write very often, in order that I may hear from you more frequently—it would afford me great pleasure to receive a letter from you every week, but I feel that it would be asking too much of you & it might perhaps, cause you to neglect your other duties. I was delighted to learn that you were getting on so well with your studies & hope that you will be rewarded for your diligence—I trust that you will not only labour to obtain the honours of the world but to obtain the reward of a *higher power*. You say that you are so "interested now that there is one who watches your struggles & takes an interest in your success"—this certainly is the case and be assured that I not only feel deeply interested in your Temporal welfare, but also in your Spiritual—Many are the prayers that your unworthy Harriett offers at a throne of Grace for you—and My Dearest *One* there is another who sends up many petitions to a Heavenly Father for your Success—it is your most estimable Mother.[15]

 14. The land claimed by Captain Charles McDowell's grandfather, Joseph McDowell, was called Quaker Meadows long before white settlers came to Burke County. Cleared by the Indians, the fertile bottoms had become grassy meadows. According to tradition, a Quaker had camped there and traded for furs with the Indians, hence the name. Alphonso C. Avery, "Historic Homes of North Carolina: Pleasant Gardens and Quaker Meadows in Burke County," *North Carolina Booklet* 4, no. 3 (1904): 7.

 15. Mira Margaret Baird Vance was a daughter of Zebulon Baird of Bun-

You say that if I desire your happiness in future life that I have but to order it so & it will be so—but I fear you are expecting too much of one so unworthy as I know myself to be—I will with the greatest of pleasure imaginable, do all in my power to contribute to the happiness of one that I love so tenderly—but the happiness of no one is complete without the love of God in their hearts—You, I fear, are allowing your imagination to picture out the future, too bright—& you have also formed too high an opinion of the Character of your devoted Harriett—When you come to know me well you will find that I (like the rest of the fallen race) am a frail creature of earth and possess many imperfections—I am well aware that a very quick temper, is one of my numerous falts & that it is a very glaring one—I allude to these things, Mr Vance, in order that you may not be deceived in my character.

You ask me if I ever think about the future? O yes! with intense interest,—do I look forward to future years—but— (My One) not as you say you do—I know that it is not the lot of frail mortality to pass undisturbed, through this world of trials—nor should it be—I have many bright anticipations of enjoyment with you My Dearest Mr V——but we should be careful to guard against trusting too much to our own selves for happiness in this life. I am fully persuaded that your affection for me is very great—& I can assure you of my sincere attachment—& as I have said before we should beware lest we should allow the Creature to usurp the place in our hearts that the Creator alone should possess—I trust that a Heavenly guide will prevent idolatry from creeping into our hearts.

I regret exceedingly that I cannot have the pleasure of seeing you in December—but for your sake I willingly submit to such a disappointment. I hope you do not think me so treacherous as to forget you before next June—No My Dearest, though absent, you will not be forgotten by her who thinks of you daily—Allow me

---

combe County and Hannah Erwin Baird, who came from Burke. In 1825 Mira Margaret Baird married David Vance II and by him had eight children. A son, David Leonidas, died in childhood. Her seven remaining children lived in Asheville at this time. The two oldest, Laura Henrietta (Mrs. Morgan Lines Neilson) and Robert Brank, were married and had homes of their own. In Mira Vance's household were an invalid son, James Noel, eighteen, and three daughters: Ann Edgeworth, fifteen; Sarah Priscilla, thirteen; and Hannah Moore, eleven. *In Memory of Mrs. Margarett M. Vance and Mrs. Harriette Espy Vance* (Raleigh, N.C.: Edwards, Broughton & Co., 1878), pp. 3-6, a collection of news clippings and periodicals; Dowd, *Life of Vance*, p. 7; Samuel A. Ashe, Stephen B. Weeks, and Charles L. Van Noppen, eds., *Biographical History of North Carolina From Colonial Times to the Present*, 8 vols. (Greensboro, N.C.: Charles L. Van Noppen, 1905-17), 6: 469.

to thank you many times for the beautiful ring that I received with your letter—I return you one of mine, but am not so unkind as to think that you need any such thing to remind you of me—I hope though that you will ware it, for my sake.

I was pleased to hear that you had made the acquaintance of Miss May Wheat—I did not see either she or Miss Battle when they were in the mountains & regretted it very much indeed—I understand Miss May is quite intelligent, besides being beautiful; she was very much admired by both ladies & gentlemen in Morganton—& from all I can learn she must have made quite an impression upon some of the gentlemen—I dont know that Brother James was particularly smitten, though he spoke in the highest praise of her.

I suppose you have ere this received the sad intelligence of the death of Mrs Henson[16] (Cousin Kame's Mother—poor Kame,[17] he has lost his greatest earthly treasure—but I trust his loss has been her gain. Now that my sheet is almost filled I must close my letter—I hope to hear from you *very soon*—I will defer (until I see you) asking your opinion about those things that I told you I wished to know your views on—And now My Dear Mr Vance May God bless you—May joys immortal be yours—May your life glide smoothly & sweetly along the stream of time & when you reach the ocean of eternity, May the evening shades gather around you in all the softness of twilight. Hoping to hear from you soon I am

Your own sincere & devoted
Harriett

University of N. C.
Oct. 2, 1851

My dearest Harriett,
You can probably imagine something of the pleasure with

16. Sara Myra Erwin Henson (Mrs. Freeland) was a half sister of ZBV's grandmother, Hannah Erwin Baird. For the Erwin family genealogy, see John McHugh McDowell, *The McDowells, Erwins, Irwins and Connections* (Memphis, Tenn.: C. B. Johnson & Co., 1918), pp. 193-95.

17. John McKamie Wilson Henson had been a student at the University of North Carolina from 1847 to 1849. He studied medicine prior to 1853 and returned to Burke County at that time to practice. He was related to HNE by the marriage of a Tate to an Erwin. *Census* of Burke County, 1850; D. L. Grant, *Alumni History of the University of North Carolina* (Durham, N. C.: The General Alumni Association of U.N.C., 1924), p. 276; Edward W. Phifer, "Certain Aspects of Medical Practice in Ante-Bellum Burke County, N.C.," *North Carolina Historical Review* 36 (January, 1959): 46.

which I throw aside my text-books for to night, & take up my writing materials to enter upon the truly delightful & willing task of answering your last affectionate and welcome letter—I was charmed with your promptness in writing so soon; and knowing that you did it to give me pleasure, the gratitude of my heart knew no bounds, as I devoured its contents. But above all do I thank you for the frank, confiding and affectionate manner in which it was penned, so free from anything cold or formal! Let those of less feeling, less kindness, or more of the cold, stoic, calculation of hypocrisy speak in terms less warm and truthful! but O, my *beloved Harriett* do you ever speak to me as you did in your last, let me never hear anything ceremonious or formal from a heart whose nobleness it becomes so ill!

You could form a better idea of the pleasure I enjoy in writing to you, probably, if you knew my state of mind, my situation here, H——Would you believe it if I were to tell you, *that I consider you a terrible pest?* Such is the fact really—Like an ungrateful scamp, I have to struggle all day-long, to drive you away from my mind—I am obliged to fight against your lovely image all the time, tho' it pretty nigh breaks my heart to try to banish even *a thought* of you from my breast—All the way I can get to study any at all, is to promise myself that at a certain hour I will lay down my book and spend a certain time in thinking about you—Why don't you let me get my lessons? If I am reading a proposition of any kind, and it is asserted that A. B. is equal to C. D., I arrive at the immediate conclusion that my sweet Harriett is not only equal, but vastly superior to all the terms in the whole proposition put together, and tho' the author of the book may not think so, *yet I do*, and that's enough—But my dear Harriett excuse this momentary strain of levity, and I will speak of something else. You say that you do really feel deeply interested in my efforts, and pray both for my temporal and spiritual welfare—Thank you, God bless you for your goodness in praying for me so unworthy as I am. I am, as you probably know my dear Harriett, a sinful, wicked, nay extremely wicked young man—I have as yet been callow and indifferent to religious matters, let them be presented to me in what manner soever, tho' my better sense, united with the "still small voice" of conscience, tells me that there is a time when the follies of youth should cease and be forsaken. *Common Policy*, in the world's language, tells me that it is getting high time to put on the garb of seriousness and discretion, and my small experiance in life, irrespective of any religious considerations, has allready taught me that there is a peace and beauty in the ways of virtue and duty which far surpasses all the fluctuating and stormy enjoyments of the fashionable, foolish world. Having considered these facts in their proper light, I may say here, without any desire of boasting upon my firmness and resolution, that I am a reformed man, in a great many respects; at least when compared with myself twelve months ago. I have gained some important victories over my bad habits since I came to this place, and which I am exceedingly proud of, as I think they auger well for the future—I have allready received my reward for my efforts in well doing, as well from the members of the Faculty as from my fellow students. As to any feeling, which might be strictly termed, religious, I am frank enough to acknowledge, that I feel none whatever; but let me say, my Dearest Harriett, that if any impression can ever be made upon me in that way, the fact that Heaven is petitioned in my behalf by one so pure and so good as you, will certainly sink deep into my heart, and burn bright in my memory day by day, & night by night. Tho' my conduct hitherto, would seem to indicate the contrary, I scorn not the serious advice of any one, and those gentle and tender admonitions which come to me from you will be armed with a double authority; besides the desire I feel to do anything to please you, they bear upon them the unmistakable impress of eternal truth. You say you wish me not to suffer idolatry to enter my heart and to love you with an affection so entire as to exclude the homage due to my Creator—I confess I am unable to draw the distinction so as to set bounds to my love—If it runs into idolatry I cant help it, *for it knows no bounds*—You say again, that you expect that I have been forming to high an opinion of your character, of my *devoted* Harriett. Excuse me if I still say that I discover new beauties in your character every day and that my estimate is formed upon judgement and not a distempered imagination—You were so anxious to undeceive me as to accuse yourself of faults which I do not think you possess—But granting you possessed of the faults which you attribute to yourself, and even if you possessed a thousand more, it matters not to me, your heart, the great regulator and moving spring of human happiness or misery, your heart is right—It is pure, generous, forgiving and affectionate, and would leap for joy in having gained a victory over its hasty or thoughtless promptings—A heart that would repent an injury committed or a pang inflicted, and forgive one suffered, is far nobler than one whose self-denying powers have never been tested successfully either one way or the other. My own faults are so numerous and so glaring that I need not mention them. You are probably allready aware of enough to condemn me as unworthy of your love if your goodness did not plead for me. It will be our duty to bear with each other and to cultivate an affectionate love so strong that it can not be disturbed or interrupted by any of the many frailties of our nature, but like a stout bark may bear us safely and joyously thro' the waves of life. I look to it for my hope in future years, which is to bless and cheer us in prosperity, and be our stay and solace in the dark and trying hour of adversity, as the Poet beautifully expresses it,

> "The evening beam that smiles the clouds away
> And tints the morrow with prophetic ray."[18]

In the strength and purity of *that love*, do I found my hopes of future happiness in your society, nor do I fear the result, let our mutual faults be what they may—To know our faults, is to guard against them, and to guard against them is to conquer them—

The question is constantly occurring to me, since you have given me your heart, when shall I be enabled to claim your hand? Who can give an answer to this? Can you? I confess, that with all my eager impatience I am as yet unable to answer it myself—It seems to me that a century will intervene before I get through my studies, and become prepared for the *consumation of my happiness* —and then I will have much to do after I get Superior Court License, before prudence would approve of our taking any *final steps* in the affair—What are your thoughts on this important point? What shall be done, to make the heavy hours fly with lighter wing, I know not—But let me strive to the utmost to improve them as they pass, lest the time should approach and find me still unprepared— Please speak to me on this subject in your next—It is important that we should interchange opinions on matters of this kind—But my dearest love, I fear I am wearying you with this long letter—I was extremely sorry to hear of the death of Aunt Sally Henson, and can sympathize with Cousin Kame, for the loss of an only parent. I have still excellent health, and of late also good spirits—I have been attending some very pleasant parties in the village during last week, and made the acquaintance of some very pleasant ladies— Accept my thanks for the ring which I received in your letter and be assured, I will wear it for your sake, though not as you said to help me think of you—it could not do that—You say you would

---

18. Lord Byron, "The Bride of Abydos." Canto II, St. 20.

like to hear from me once a week if possible, but fear it would interfere with my duties—It will *not* interfere with my other duties and you shall receive letters from me as often as once a week if such is your wish, for I assure you it gives me as much pleasure to write them as it does you to receive them. That which gives you pleasure is law to me—I shall close with the hope of hearing from you soon again as you so generously promised in your last. May the guardian Angel of the good watch over you and keep you in health and happiness. Your sincere and devoted lover—

Zebulon

Quaker Meadows Oct—13 (51)

Mr. Vance;

Little did I think when I wrote you last that my next letter would be of such a nature as this one is compelled to be—I have been informed by disinterested persons that you were, when you addressed me, engaged to a young lady[19] near the Warm Springs[20]— & that you have since you addressed me treated her very ungentlemanly—I also understand that she has received a letter that you had written to me, & directed to her, in which you spoke very disrespectfully of her—Now Mr Vance it is against my principles to allow any young gentleman to speak unkindly of a lady to me & if you have written such a letter, I feel that you have done me a great injury—I can scarcely believe that such is the case—but if it

---

19. Sara L. Garrett, daughter of James R. Garrett, a native of South Carolina, and Jane Neilson Garrett. James R. Garrett was a son of Stephen Garrett, probably the "Captain Garret of South Carolina" mentioned in the *Asheville Messenger* in 1850 as having purchased the Warm Springs about 1817. Jane Neilson Garrett had inherited considerable acreage in Madison County (then Buncombe) from her father, William Neilson, the original owner of the Warm Springs property. ZBV may have met Sara Garrett the summer he clerked at the hotel at Warm Springs. She was a first cousin of his brother-in-law, Dr. Morgan Lines Neilson. Information furnished by Miss Virginia Servier of Asheville, N.C., from family records. Foster Alexander Sondley, *A History of Buncombe Co., North Carolina*, 2 vols. (Asheville, N.C.: The Advocate Printing Co., 1930), 2: 588; Will of William Neilson, Buncombe County Wills, Buncombe County Courthouse, Asheville, N.C., Book A, p. 9; *Census of Buncombe County, 1850*.

20. John Patton owned and operated a gay and fashionable summer hotel and health resort at Warm Springs (now Hot Springs in Madison County). It was thirty-six miles below Asheville on the French Broad River near the Tennessee line. A description of the imposing building appeared in the *Asheville Messenger* in 1850 and is quoted in Sondley, *History of Buncombe Co.*, 2: 588.

should be so—I can no longer trust one that has proven so false to another—

  I have placed the greatest degree of confidence in you—& will be grieved to know that you have acted in such a manner as this—I call upon you Mr Vance, for an explination of the whole affair in order that I may know how to act—I hope you will think that I have done right—I am candid enough to acknowledge that when I first heard it I was very much incensed at you & thought that I would sit immediately down & write you a letter of positive rejection—but upon reflection, I concluded to hear your version of the matter first—Do answer this letter soon—I trust to you for a correct statement of this affair—it will be very unkind in you if you deceive me, but I dont feel afraid of it—I cant believe that one so dear as I thought you, will prove so false to me—I received your very kind & affectionate letter a few days ago—& how much more pleasure it would give me to answer *it*, than be compelled to write such a one as this—Do excuse haste—May the choicest blessings of a Heavenly Father abide with you is my sincere prayer—

           H. Espy

           Chapel Hill, Oct. 17th

Miss Espy,

  With the intensest astonishment & agitation, I rec'd and read yours this morning, and I sit down to answer it before the return mail—Of my feeling and agitation I presume you can form some idea, so I shall immediately proceed to the object of this letter—Now Miss Espy, I have some confessions to make and some falsehoods to deny, and as you generously say that you fear not my deceiving you—I will assure you that your confidence is not misplaced—But to the facts, and to the charges—First you say that you have been informed by some *"disinterested person"* that when I addressed you, I was engaged to a young lady near the Warm Springs, and whom I afterward treated *ungentlemanly*. Now this I positively deny. I was addressing the young Lady in question when you first came to Asheville, but was never engaged to her. My correspondence with her was closed at the request of the Lady herself as I have letters in my possession to establish. And again I never made any, the least, advance to you while I was corresponding with the Lady referred to—I was entirely free from any connexion with her when I first wrote to you, as the date of my first letter to you, and the last from the Lady to me which I have with me will show. Now I come to the point which excited my indignation to the highest pitch—I will give your own words; "I also understand that she has received a letter that you had written to me, and directed to her, in which you spoke very disrespectfully of her". Now this I pronounce a falsehood of the deepest dye. The interruption between me and the Lady did occur from the misdirection of a letter, which I had written to Mr. R. P. Deaver of Columbia, S. C., and not you, for at that time I had not mentioned the subject of a correspondence to you—In that letter I said things of a character not considered unusual between intimate young men, which offended her, and yet *she did not* accuse me of speaking disrespectfully of her, as a letter in my possession will show, but objected to something alltogether different which the letter contained. Neither did she accuse me of acting "ungentlemanly", since she met me since and we parted on the most friendly and agreeable terms, since which time (last June) I have not seen her, but have heard from frequently. And in particular would I never have attempted to abuse a young Lady to you, or to make any advances to you whilst "engaged" to another.

These are the simple facts of the case, and I leave them for your consideration without further comment. You said, "you called upon me for an explanation of the whole affair". You have a right to make such a call, and I answer you—Now Miss Espy, I know not as to the motive which led to the fabrication of these infamous lies against me, but I *do know your author*. At least I know who it came from indirectly, if not directly, and may the God of Heaven have mercy upon him, if without proof of his innocence, he falls into the hands of a deeply injured man—I scorn him as I do a truckling fiend of perdition, and if things were disclosed which have occured between him and myself, the tongue of the lowest would cry out against his meanness—But I forbear saying more upon that head. I thank you for not condemning me unheard, as you are frank enough to acknowledge your first impulse led you. In stating these facts, and which you have promised to receive upon my honour, as facts, you will I trust excuse me if I have done so in an apparently cold business like manner. Because under the circumstances, I can not feel myself authorised to speak to you in the same tone of my former letters—You acknowledge that you thought of writing me a positive rejection; you seem to speak as if you credited the charge which fastened upon me an act of baseness; how can I do more than simply make my defense? The feelings which fill my breast when I sit down to write to you, rise tumultuously struggling for utterance, but I restrain them. My heart thrills and struggles to utter its warm and devotional appeals to your nobleness and generosity, but I will not suffer it. I will not endeavor to prevent you from exorcising your judgement in all its calmness and candor. It is a point which involves too much happiness or misery to be decided by passion—My pride has been too much mortified and my feelings too much wounded, to permit me to urge for anything but justice. I leave my case in your hands again Miss Espy, as I did once before, earnestly hoping that you will be enabled to act wisely and for the happiness of us both. I hope Miss Espy, if you should retain any *pity* for me, that you will answer this letter soon, & let me know what you say—I hope you can know how to act from what I say in this letter—

With sentiments of the deepest respect will I *ever* remain

Yours Sincerely
Zeb. B. Vance

Morganton Oct—30—[1851]

Mr Vance;

I received your letter a few days ago, & I leave you to imagine the pleasure it afforded me to learn from its contents that the report of your being engaged to another, while you were addressing me, was false—It appears that you think I was disposed to believe this falsehood—here you are mistaken entirely—for when I first heard it I was very much incensed & denied it positively—althoug my authority was good—You seem to be very confident that you know my auther but allow me to assure you that you do not. I fear that you have censured a perfectly innocent person—I am disposed to believe that you think it was Cousin Augustus[21]—it

21. Augustus Merrimon had sought to "address" Harriett and had been rebuffed. In a letter to HNE dated March 29, 1851, Merrimon reveals his romantic attachment. His letter to her of September 7, 1851, shows that he is accepting his "disappointment." [Both of these letters are in the possession of the editor.] Augustus Summerfield Merrimon of Asheville was a great-nephew of Captain Charles McDowell. His grandmother was Sarah Grace McDowell Paxton, a sister of Captain Charles. His father was a Methodist minister, at this time connected with the Holston Conference and living in Buncombe County. From December 5, 1850, until about March 15, 1851, when ZBV dropped the course, he and Vance had read law together under John W.

certainly was not him for he never has spoken to me, of you, in any other way, than in the kindest manner—of course he would not—I dont think that my informer had any unkind feelings towards you & indeed I know that they have not—for since the occurance I have heard them speak in very high terms of you—I will tell you all about how it came to me when I have the pleasure of seeing you—but not before—Do excuse my delay in answering your letter—I know you have spent many unhappy moments since you received my last—but I hope in future never to be the cause of making you unhappy—for I am determined never to credit any charge of the kind against you—I would write much more but have not time this evening—& the mail leaves very soon—I am anxious to hear from you & hope to enjoy that pleasure very soon—Do excuse great haste —Sisters little Anna[22] is quite ill, I am in the village with her & have very little time to write in—May the choicests blessings of heaven rest upon you is the prayer of Your Sincere

Harriett

University, Nov 11th '51

My dearest Harriett,

To use your own words, "I have indeed felt many unhappy moments," since I received that *cruel letter*. I have indeed experianced all the agony of wretchedness and distraction within the last few weeks, but I am unhappy *no longer*—You can well imagine that I was rendered supremely happy on perusing your long ex-

---

Woodfin of Asheville. Merrimon was to have a distinguished career as lawyer, state legislator, solicitor, judge of the superior court, United States senator, associate justice, and finally chief justice of the Supreme Court of North Carolina. He actively promoted the candidacy of Vance for governor in 1862, and their relations remained cordial until 1872 when Merrimon defeated Vance for the United States Senate. Thereafter relations were strained. Johnston, *Papers of ZBV*, 1: 13, n. 65; Augustus Summerfield Merrimon's Diary, vol. 2, December 5, 1850, to August 5, 1851, an original manuscript in the Augustus Summerfield Merrimon Collection, Southern Historical Collection. The University of North Carolina at Chapel Hill, Chapel Hill, N.C. A. R. Newsome, ed., "The A. S. Merrimon Journal, 1853-1854," *North Carolina Historical Review* 8 (July, 1931): 300, n.1.

22. Anna Maria McKesson was the infant daughter of William F. and Margaret McDowell McKesson, the latter being the youngest daughter of Captain Charles McDowell and a real beauty. HNE called her "Sister." Avery, *Presbyterian Churches*, p. 36; Kemp Plummer Battle, *Memories of An Old-Time Tar Heel*, ed. William James Battle (Chapel Hill, N.C.: The University of North Carolina Press, 1945), pp. 88, 89.

pected note. It was doubly gratifying to me, in that you expressed yourself completely reconciled to me, and added that you were determined to be the cause of my unhappiness no more, that in future you would credit no such reports against me. My pen is incapable of expressing my thanks for that kindly assurance.

You can form no idea of the distracting thoughts that pervaded my bosom while awaiting for your reply. Measuring the extent of your affections, by my own, I could not conceive it possible that you were going to forsake me—Then by reading over your letter again I would conclude from its contents that I was allready condemned, prejudged, and that a defense would avail nothing. Pride would whisper in my ear to attempt no defense, that you loved me not or you would not forsake me in that way. But thank Heaven, I had confidence in your character as I have often told you. I believed you were actuated by the purest motives. I justified you before I knew your answer and I threw myself and my happiness upon that nobleness which forms the object of my unceasing admiration, and I was not disappointed—As to the circumstances of the case, I frankly own to you as I did in my last, that when I first became acquainted with you in Asheville, I was engaged in a rather boyish correspondence with a young Lady—Thoughtless young men are addicted to such things, unjustifiable though it be. They seem to enter into such a correspondence without motive or design, other than merely to be doing something, and I *have been* no better, I blush to own, than others—But as I have said I made not the slightest advances to you untill I was entirely free—That was one reason why I did not speak to you on *the subject* before you left A——In regard to the person whom I suspected of trying to injure me with you, if I have done Mr. M—— [Merrimon] wrong or injustice in my suspicions, I am heartily sorry for it. I had my reasons for thinking it was him, and I must acknowledge that it would have been extremely unfortunate if he and I had met in my then state of mind, as I would have been perfectly indifferent to the consequences of wreaking vengeance upon him in any manner—You know of the unpleasant circumstances under which we parted. You know that I had the misfortune to incur, in consequence of that silly transaction in regard to Mr. M—— also the displeasure of Mr. J. W. Woodfin[23] whom I regarded as one of the

23. John W. Woodfin was the prosperous and respected Asheville lawyer under whom Vance and Merrimon had read law. His wife was the former Mira McDowell of Quaker Meadows. HNE called him "Cousin John." *Census* of Buncombe County, 1850; Johnston, *Papers of ZBV*, 1: 51, n. 185.

strongest friends I possessed, and who had universally treated me with such kindness as to secure my sincere friendship—I told Mr. M—— & Mr W—— both however, that I felt no consciousness of having merited their displeasure, and that I deemed appology uncalled for and I was unwilling to offer any—I feel so yet, & I think Mr. M—— especially acted hastily and unworthy of himself in regard to the matter. Taking all things into consideration you can easily suppose that I could guess where your information came from— But as you say that I am mistaken I am sorry for my uncharitable and unjust suspicions, and I can assure you I am loath to do any person whomsoever an injury—You say you will relate all the facts to me when we next meet—Thank you—

But the glorious promise contained in your last has put me in a peaceful state of mind with all the world. I would not harm anything now, if it were in my power—My bright visions and youthful hopes are restored once more, and I may again give myself up to the enjoyment of indulging in my unbounded love for you my dearest *One*—I may again address you as my own and call upon your name in transports of love and warm affection—My imagination has again commenced its work in picturing out the glorious and happy future, which, by the smiles of a merciful Providence, will crown a pure and devoted affection—I can again apply my utmost energies to the duties before me, with a heart, supported and lifted above all obstacles and difficulties by *love and hope*. Let these words, *love and hope*, be my motto, and I need not fear the final result—I do not fear it. Will you forgive me for saying to *you*, that I am making rapid progress in my studies here. I have been studying Law[24] extremely hard and beside that I am carrying on the studies of the Senior Class[25] and it affords me pleasure to state that I take a "first honor"[26] in that Class. Two names have

24. The law course covered *Blackstone's Commentaries, Kent's Commentaries, Stephen on Pleading, Greenleaf on Evidence, Chitty on Contracts, Cruise's Digest of Real Property, Williams on Executors*, and lectures on the municipal laws of the state as modified by the acts of the legislature and decisions of the state courts. Completion of the course required two and a half years by members of the College Class (students like ZBV who were also irregular members of college). They recited only once a week. *Catalogue of U.N.C., 1851-52*, p. 31.

25. Vance took a partial senior course: under President Swain, constitutional law, political economy, and intellectual philosophy; under Dr. Elisha Mitchell, chemistry, geology, and mineralogy; and under Dr. Wheat, rhetoric and logic. Dowd, *Life of Vance*, p. 18.

26. Since Vance was not a regular member of the senior class, there were no reports on his class standing kept at the university. Therefore, this statement is the only known record of the fact that he took a "first honor." Kemp P. Battle, "As Student at University," in Dowd, *Life of Vance*, p. 18.

been instrumental in confering that distinction upon me, yours and my beloved Mothers—Her affectionate letters, full of pious injunctions and maternal prayers for my health and success, exert a most wonderful effect upon all my actions. A pious Mother is certainly the peculiar boon of Heaven to an erring young man, and I sincerely hope I may have the prudence to obey her instructions fully—I enjoy also the respect of my fellow students and the confidence of the Faculty—Please forgive me for mentioning these things. I mention them with no other design than to show you the influence you exert over my actions and that I am struggling to make myself worthy of your love and confidence—The time appears to be an age, that will have to pass by before I can get to see you, but constantly and actively employed as I shall be, I hope it will not hang heavily upon my hands—In the meantime let me hope my dear Harriett, that you will write to me as often as you can possibly—I do not wish you to consider me exacting, but I must insist on you writing frequently and at length—By the way; you have not answered some things I asked you about in my last letter but one—Look at it and write to me your views upon the matter if you please—The greatest pleasure I can have at this place will be to write and receive letters from you—It will besides, be a mutual benefit to exchange views upon the different objects of life with eachother—There is so much to be talked of concerning both the present and the future that I feel as if I could spend all my time in writing to you—My friend James McDowell passed through this place without stopping to see me, or even Miss May. I regretted it much—I suppose he will return by way of Charleston, so I'll not get to see him—

It is past 12 O'clock, and I will close my letter by expressing again my desire to receive a long letter from you soon, and by assuring you of my unchanging and unaltered devotion—I earnestly hope that you will never again have occasion to write me such a letter as the one I received from you some time since.

Please accept some verses I enclose—The stern realities with which I am engaged, forbid such attempts in general, but I stole an hour last night, to devote to thinking of you—

Your sincere & devoted Lover

Zeb. Vance

Letter of Harriett Espy missing.

University. Novr 28th '51

My own dear Harriett,

    I lack words sufficient to express the happiness and the delight I experianced on reading your affectionate letter which I received yesterday—I sit down this evening thus early to answer it, as next week is examination week when I will be so much pressed with my studies that I would have to postpone my reply untill the week after—This I could not do, as you say you take great pleasure in reading my letters, although they may contain nothing but my reiterated assurances of devoted and undying affection; it would give me pain to put off even for a few days, doing anything that would give you pleasure—However I must own, that I am not alltogether so free from selfishness in regard to writing to you as you may probably suppose—Self-love is more or less perceivable in all the actions we perform, and I assure you that the pleasure it gives me to sit down and hold sweet communion with you in this manner is very great, and is equal at least to that which you feel in reading my letters—

    I am as happy now, my dear Harriett, as it is possible for me to be on this earth, when you are absent—I have the fullest confidence in the affection you profess for me, and the dreadful agony which filled my soul and disturbed my peace some weeks since has entirely disappeared. I feel now nothing but love; *hopeful, faithful, impatient love.* What a strange feeling has pervaded my breast since first you consented that I should not love in vain! A new era seems to have dawned upon me, a new morning sun to have broken in upon my existence—The thought of being beloved by one so good and so pure is allmost too much for my reason to concede, and during my paroxisms of happy insanity, I ask myself doubtingly if it all is not a dream or fiction of an overwrought imagination! It colors my every action and is mingled with my every thought— With a proud heart, and a firm step, I march onward to the discharge of the duties before, and when an evil spirit would tempt me into the performance of a dishonorable or unworthy action, the good angel which ever keeps watch over erring, sinful man's career, whispers in my ear, that there is *one* who is pure that loves me and confides in me for happiness and protections, and I resolutely cast the temptation from me, blessing the lovely image which the thought recalled.

You need entertain no apprehension of my entertaining unkind feelings toward Mr. M—— [Merrimon] for I assure you I am not inclined to bear malice toward any one. I acknowledge that on the reception of your letter informing me of the report you had heard concerning me, I felt deeply enraged against him when my suspicions alighted there, but I feared at the time I wrote to you that I had been too hasty, and I was deeply grieved at having done injustice to him. As I told you myself in Morganton, I have none but the kindest feelings toward him and had done all that my sense of honor would suffer me to do to reconcile him, but had been unsuccessful in all my attempts—

You awakened a flood of tender recollections in my bosom when you mentioned the name of Mrs J Woodfin[27]—If ever there existed a *Lady* in this world, she is one—I believe my dear Harriett, she has won my entire regard and unlimited esteem, considering that I stood in no other relation to her than a mere acquaintance, more completely than any other Lady that I have ever met with. I am truly rejoiced to learn, that the opinion which I am vain enough to hope she once entertained respecting me has not been changed, by the trivial circumstance which was sufficient to change the opinions of others who made louder and warmer professions than she ever did—I earnestly hope that I may be able to retain her favour in future life and whether I do or not, I shall ever respect, (my feelings prompt me to use the more expressive term 'love') her for the many kindnesses she has shown me, and more expecially to my *Mother*—My Mothers friends are my friends and her enemies are my enemies—A kindness shown to my Mother will never be forgotten by me while treading this earth—

You ask me to give you my views respecting the dreadful affair[28] which has just been transacted in Morganton—Alas, I ex-

27. Mrs. John W. Woodfin of Asheville was HNE's "Cousin Mira," third daughter of Captain Charles McDowell of Quaker Meadows. She attended Salem Female Academy as did her sisters Eliza and Mary. *Census* of Buncombe County, 1850; Alumnae Records in the library of Salem College, Winston-Salem, N.C.

28. William Waightstill Avery, son of Isaac T. and Harriet Eloise Erwin Avery, was at thirty-five a brilliant lawyer and prominent Democratic politician in Burke County. On October 21, 1851, he appeared in court in Marion on behalf of HNE's "Uncle" Ephriam M. Greenlee of Marion versus one Samuel Fleming of Yancey County. When court adjourned, Fleming, who was armed, attacked Avery. Having disabled Avery by a blow with a stone, Fleming publicly cowhided him. On November 11, while acting as counsel in a case in Morganton, Avery saw Fleming enter the courtroom. He immediately

pect I feel concerning it, about the same as I infer that you do and that all others do who consider the tendency of Mr Avery's acquittal upon the community—All who reflect upon the subject, I think must be convinced that the stern majesty of the laws of our country have been violated in the most fearful respect of their jurisdiction, and violated with *impunity*—Stern and unbending laws and a rigid and Roman execution of them, constitute the pillars and the only hope of society. The good and the great, the low and the mighty must be amenable to them. That Mr. Avery is one of the most estimable gentleman in our state is not denied by any, and all are rejoiced that his life is spared to his friends and family, but many, very many shrink from the danger of establishing such a precedent as his triumphant acquittal—I speak these things solely for your ear, my dear Harriett.

  I come next to speak of what you wrote me in relation to the time when it would be practicable for us to unite our fates and fortunes as I trust our hearts have been allready—You say that you could not think of being married for two years yet, as it was your Mother's dying request, that you should not marry untill you were twenty one years of age—After that time you say you leave it entirely with me—I suppose of course that I will be compelled to acquiesce in that proposition—My judgement pronounces it proper and reasonable. In truth my situation at present would not admit of an earlier completion of my wishes in regard to the matter— But when did love ever listen to the voice of reason and judgement? When was ever the impatient lover willing to defer his happiness untill circumstances should be in his favour? In spite of all the common sense and philosophy that I can bring to bear upon the subject, *two years*, sound allmost as fearfully long as two centuries—I am confident however, that it is not unfortunate for us that there is an obstacle in our way—I will have full time to complete my studies, and be ready to undertake the duties of the profession which I have adopted—I hope also to be able to pass off

---

rose, shot, and killed him. Avery was tried for manslaughter three days later by Judge William Horn Battle, who had witnessed the tragedy. The solicitor being a kinsman of Avery, John W. Woodfin was appointed to prosecute. Nicholas W. Woodfin and John Gray Bynum defended Avery. The defense was temporary insanity. The jury required only ten minutes to arrive at a verdict of "not guilty." Avery's reputation was not impaired by the incident, and he held several elective offices thereafter. In a special election held in 1858, Vance ran for Congress against Avery and defeated him. A full account of the murder and its aftermath is given by Edward W. Phifer in his "Saga of a Burke County Family (The Sons)," *North Carolina Historical Review* 39 (Summer, 1962): 307-13.

the time, without regret or unwise impatience. Time hangs heavily on the hands of the idle only, as is sufficiently proven by the prominent fact that we see none but those who have nothing to do or, who will do nothing, inventing schemes to 'kill time' as it is termed—Time flies with meteor swiftness to those who can appreciate its value and appropriate it proffitably—Aged men who have grown grey in the pursuit of knowledge or in some useful and honorable occupation, ever regret that life is so short as only to suffer them to approach the threshold of science and usefulness—I will bury myself in my books, and in enriching my mind, will endeavor to think of those two years as little as may be, reflecting that for the great purposes which we have to accomplish on earth, time is flying fast, alas too fast—This is all philosophy however, which I am so bold and stoic as to write; how I will so *heroically* put it into practice is quite a different thing. Mankind is very patient under talked-of pain, and brave as regards remote dangers. Experiance is the test of all human virtues—

Our session is out next week, my room mate[29] is going home as are allmost all others here, and being too busy preparing to stand for License, I shall not visit any of the villagers, so I shall be quite lonely, my only pleasure will be in getting letters—Will you please write me a *long, long* letter soon?—It will break in upon my solitude like a bright sunbeam first gilding the dark summits of our own lovely mountains—O, how fondly I gaze toward the west as the sun sinks to rest in golden glory, to see if I can perceive any trace of the loved mountains which hold in their boosom all that is dear and sacred to me! I can only see them and you by the glowing of an ardent and warm imagination, so I turn from the scene and sooth my feelings with *hope, hope, hope.*

I feel the truth of a saying of a great writer [La Rochefoucauld], that, "absence diminishes moderate passions and incenses great ones, as the wind extinguishes tapers, but adds fury to fire". I do indeed feel as if your absence added increased fury [to] the fire of my love for you my dear, adored Harriet. I hope to see James McD. as he passes by this place and also I hope to meet Mr Merrimon here and go to Raleigh with him on amicable terms—Will Samuel McD.[30] come down for Superior Co. License this win-

29. ZBV roomed with Robert Bruce Johnson, son of William Johnson, a wealthy farmer and merchant of Haywood County. Johnston, *Papers of ZBV*, 1: 5, n. 24, n. 25.

30. Samuel Moffett McDowell, HNE's "Brother Samuel," was the elder son of Captain Charles McDowell of Quaker Meadows. At this time he was solicitor of the Buncombe County Court. He lived in Asheville with his brother-

ter too? I hope to see several of my mountain friends in Raleigh—I go down on the 1st Jan. Its very late and I will retire to rest. May Heaven shield you from harm and watch over your path my beloved One, is the heartfelt prayer of your unchanging and devoted lover

Zeb. Vance

[1851—Dec]

Although I am scarcely able to sit up, I cant allow another day pass without informing My Dear Zebulon, of my illness—I have been quite sick for several days & still feel very unwell—I would have postponed writing to you until I had entirely recovered but fearing several mails might pass before that time I [thought] that you might be uneasy & have concluded to write you a few lines to day—I have been suffering very much with sore throat & a most violent caugh—but hope to be entirely relieved very soon—I am much better this afternoon & was able this morning to go down stairs to see Cousin Kame Henson & Junious Tate,[31] who called to see me—I was also invited out to dine to day—& much did I regret having to decline the invitation—particularly so as it was given to the Reading Society and I am honored with so high an office as being President of the Society—The dining is given at Mr W.W. Avery's. I received your very dear communication the evening of the day that I was taken sick & Oh! how much pleasure it afforded me. I always read your letters with great pleasure—but that one was doubly more welcome than any one I have received from you during our correspondence—Why it was so, I leave you to infer—How much I wish I could write you a long letter in reply to it—but I am too much indisposed—and you will have to be content with only a short one this time—Brother Samuel is going down to Raleigh week after next—I hope to be entirely well by that time—& will write to you

---

in-law, Nicholas W. Woodfin, and was continuing his law studies with Nicholas W. and John W. Woodfin. *Census* of Buncombe County, 1950; Minutes of the Court of Pleas and Quarter Sessions, Buncombe County, Minute Docket, December, 1850, State Department of Archives and History, Raleigh, N.C., Book C, p. 591; Johnston, *Papers of ZBV*, 1: 6, n. 29.

31. Junius Constantine Tate, HNE's first cousin, had inherited a considerable fortune, including the family plantation, Hickory Grove, from his father, Samuel C. Tate. An orphan, he and his only sister, Mary Joe, made their home with his mother's brother, Dr. William C. Tate of Morganton. *Census* of Burke County, 1850; Ervin, "Tates" MS.

by him even if I do not receive an answer to this note. I know you will be very much engaged & if you do not write immediately I will know the cause—but if you possibly can, do write—& dont be uneasy about me, for I do assure you that I am better, & hope through a Merciful Providence to be well very soon—May God bless you My Own dear Zebulon is the prayer of Your truly devoted

Harriett

University. Decr. 20th '51

My dear Harriett,

You can probably imagine the concern with which I received and read your last letter informing me of your illness. I was truly pained to hear of it, but was much gratified at your informing me of it, while you were scarcely able to sit up. It shows me that you are not unmindful of me under any circumstances. I am hoping to hear by Mr. McDowell of your complete restoration—I was so busily engaged preparing for my examination, that I thought I would not answer your letter untill I got back from Raleigh, but I have myself been laid up in my room for three days past with a most violent attack of cold, which perfectly prostrated me, but feeling some better this morning, I thought I would write a short letter to you. I am still too unwell to study and my head aches so violent that I can scarcely write, but I am so lonely here by myself that I can not bear the solitude of my situation without doing something. I hope by tomorrow morning to be able to go to study again, as every moment of time is invaluable to me now. My fellow-law students have very generously suspended their recitations untill I get able to proceed with them. I think the class is pretty well prepared and I do not entertain any serious fears as to the examination.

My dearest One, you can not imagine with what impatience and anxiety I look forward to next June, the time when I shall again be in your presence, to enjoy the pleasure of your society. I spend all my leisure hours in picturing out to myself the joys I will experiance when I shall next meet you. My excited imagination dwells upon it continually—There is no mental pleasure greater than that of bringing by the magic of the imagination the ones we love near to us, gazing upon them with the minds eye and allmost realizing the pleasures of the reality by the intenseness of our conception. Especially is this a pleasure when our faith is strong and abiding in the sincerity and devotion of those whom we love and trust. Castle-building is in general I am aware, injurious, as it leads the mind to expect impossibilities, and has a tendency to make one dissatisfied with sober reality, and I have long been endeavoring and with some success to break myself of the habit in most respects, but in regard to my love and the object of it, I will not, can not refrain from indulging in the glories of an enthusiastic imagination. It is my greatest bliss by day and by night, in sickness and in health.

I could, if I had not been so pressed with business, have enjoyed my vacation very much, as the society here though small is quite select and intelligent. The Ladies of this place are very superior indeed, intelligent and sociable in the extreme. Through the kind partiality of Governor Swain I was introduced among them directly after my arrival here, but I have been too much engaged to mature my acquaintance with all of them, though with some, in whose company I have been more frequently thrown, I have become intimately acquainted. The Faculty are allways partial to the students who visit the ladies, and say that they are most orderly young men and industrious students in College. With such inducements before me, it is not surprising that I should be fond of their society—

For the first time my dear Harriett since I have been corresponding with you I feel the want of something with which to fill up a letter—But I am so unwell this morning that it is allmost impossible for me to gather anything from my aching brain worthy of inditing to you, indeed I scarcely know how I have written this much. I shall expect to hear from you by Mr. McDowell and sincerely hope to hear of your complete recovery from sickness and of your happiness—When I return from Raleigh I will write you a long letter and try to make amends for this poor and disconnected attempt.

I remain my dear One

Devotedly and sincerely yours
Zeb. B. Vance

Quaker Meadows Dec—22nd 1851

My Dear Mr Vance;

When I wrote you last, it was my intention to have written to you again by Brother S—— [Samuel] but when he left this morning he was undetermined about going by Chapel Hill & upon reflection I concluded that it would be best to write by mail at any rate—for you will receive it at an earlyer period—than you would have, if I had written by him—Greatly would I prefer engaging with you in oral converce, this morning, than to communicate to you, through the silent language of letters—but being debarred that greatest of pleasures, I must resort to those means which the God of benevolence has placed in my power. I hope My Dearest Mr Vance that my last letter to you, has'ent caused you any uneasiness—I am happy to inform you that I have almost entirely recovered from my indisposition—I presume that it was not of a very serious nature, although I feared at the time, that it was.

I suppose you are very much engaged making preparations for License; Cousin Augustus & Brother Samuel left this morning in high glee to apply for theirs—Success to all of you but particularly [to] My Dear Zebulon—If you should be rejected— (though I havent the most remote idea that you will be) be assured that I will love you none the less—Cousin Augustus I believe intends remaining at the College a day or two on his return—I should be very glad indeed for you & he to be friends—but My Much loved One I want you to grant me one request—it is—that you will make no more advances to him & do avoid getting into any diffaculty with him—he was very polite to me during his sojourn with us & I also was to him—I am disposed to like Cousin Augustus—but he has *many* traits in his character that I do not admire—

How delighted I should be to have you come to the Mountains with Brother particularly so, as Sallie Butler is to be married soon after his return—I will of course not insist upon your coming— knowing that it would be very inconvenient for you to do so—I presume you know her intended[32]—I am very busy making preparations for the wedding—& it will be impossible for me to write to you again for several weeks—this is why I write to you before receiving an answer to my last. I guess you are looking forward to the Christmas holidays with all your powers of fore enjoyment—I am, I do assure you,—but the thought of your absence lessens my bright anticipations in a great degree—I say that I am looking forward & with much pleasure to the holidays—but how & where am I to spend them?—around the cheerful fireside of My Dear home; where I always enjoy myself so much—When I think of giving up

32. Sallie Butler was engaged to one of her and HNE's cousins, Ephraim E. Greenlee, of Morganton. He was a druggist and a young man of independent means. *Census* of Burke County, 1850.

My dear Sallie, with whom I have enjoyed these pleasures so long it causes many tears—which Byron says is the "test of Affection"—& I am half inclined to believe him—These reflections together with the thought of My Dearest Ones absence makes me quite sad this morning & besides all this—how melancholy to think of another year being almost past—Let us ask ourselves the question, if the past year has been spent as profitably as it should have been? My answer is in the negative—& my sincere desire is that we may both enter upon the "New Year" with new resolutions, not trusting to ourselves alone to keep them but to the Alwise God—Wont you write to me often during your vacation? Do dont wait for answers to your letters—but write when ever you have time—If you only knew how much pleasure it afforded me to hear from you I think you would write at least every fortnight if not every week—there is nothing that I enjoy so much My Dear Zebulon as the perusal of your epistles—do, do write as often as possible—In my last letter but one I wrote you Brother James would return through Chapel Hill—but as Brother S. & Junious are going to California[33] he will go with them to Charleston—I am quite in the notion of California myself—What do you think of it? Write me in your next—And now as my sheet is filled, I must close and besides it is so cold that I can scarcely guide my pen—We have had very severe weather indeed—it is milder now than it has been—Do write soon—May heaven bless you & may your future life be a happy one, is the sincere prayer of

        Your own devoted
        Harriett

        Chapel Hill, New Years Day, 1852

My Dear Harriett,

  I take up my writing implements to address you to night with even more pleasure than it ordinarily gives me to commune with you. I feel in excellent spirits to night, both as to the present and the developements of the mysterious future—I feel that the duties and struggles of manhood and its attendant cares are beginning to press upon me with mountain weight, and I also feel that I am taking some essential steps in preparing to meet them in a manner which is calculated to render them tolerable at least if not

---

33. They were going to prospect for gold. The rush, which had started after gold was discovered at Sutter's Mill January 24, 1848, was at its height.

pleasant—I have just returned from Raleigh where I obtained license without any difficulty. Indeed I had been studying severely, and was conscious that I need not fear the result. From the manner in which the examination was conducted, I could not but infer a compliment to my preparation and that of several others, as the judges appeared satisfied with asking me but two or three questions—Mr. Merrimon stood a very fair examination, as also I understood from others did Mr. McDowell—They came to this place on last Friday for dinner, and staid with me untill Sunday morning—I went to Raleigh on Monday last and got back last night—As to the particulars of my trip I don't suppose they could interest you on paper so I will refer you to Mr. McD—— or Mr. M—— The latter gentleman was very friendly toward me, and as I am not disposed to bear malice toward any of my fellow creatures, of course I showed all the politeness within my power—It was politeness merely however and nothing more, as I can assure you that the request you made of me in your last, that I should not make any advances toward him found a ready compliance with my feelings—It was only because he is a relative of yours my dearest Harriet that I felt bound to treat him politely—He will never succeed in making friends in life unless he alters his carriage and deportment in my opinion—I regard him as a young man of sufficient native talent to gain him distinction, but it is under a most wretched system of cultivation undoubtedly—You can not but be aware that like other young men he is possessed of an infinite amount of self-importance and unfortunately makes it known to everybody present—But please forgive me for remarking upon the faults of others when I possess myself others equally glaring if the vail of self did not hide them from my view—I spent some very pleasant hours indeed with Mr. McD—discussing the news from the mountains—we went to see Govr Swain but did not find him at home, then called on Miss Sue Battle and spent some time with her—Miss May Wheat was not at home—He breakfasted with me on Sunday morning and was pleased with my talkative Landlady. I am somewhat a favourite of hers, and when I introduced him & Mr. M—— to her as my friends from Buncombe, she commenced praising me and telling that I visited the ladies a great deal, and finally closed the subject by telling Sam, that if I had been addressing any young Lady in the mountains to tell her that I would never leave her unmarried! He and M——both looked at me so knowingly that I could do nothing else but blush—She had me badly plagued, if she had but known it—

  I received yours on the day that the young gentlemen got

here and experianced the greatest of pleasures in reading it. You said that if I should be rejected that you would love me none the less—I thank you my dearest One, I thank you again and again. You can not conceive of the happiness such words cause me to feel, but I needed not any such assurances to make me confide in your sincerity—My soul is full of confidence in your truth and constancy, and so long as I pursue an honorable course through this life I feel that I shall have your sympathy and affection to aid and cheer me—You ask me what I say to California? At present I can say nothing—What notion the future may inspire me with I can not tell, but now I can think definitely of nothing but my immediate and engrossing duties—When I shall once be prepared to enter upon the struggles of active life, I care not where my lot be cast upon the broad expanse of this continent, whether upon the shores of the Pacific or in mountains of N Carolina, in the forest wild, or the populated city, so you my Love shall stand by my side and bless me with your devotion—The things that I pray for are health & your love—Grant me these and the fickleness of fortune shall be conquered by the iron hand of toil and ceaseless industry—There is such a thing as controlling ones fate at least to a great extent. The miseries which prey upon us we either bring directly upon us, or invite by our negligence and carelessness—

As to what you said in relation to my coming home with Sam and Mr. M—— you can not imagine the pleasure it would give me to do so. I am nearly destracted to see you, but in my present circumstances it would be allmost impossible for me to leave here untill next June. I will leave here finally then, and as soon after as the nature of things will admit I hope to be so united to you as never more to know any seperation—I wish Miss Butler and Mr. G—— all the happiness that I myself hope to enjoy on a similar occasion. I should like very much to be present at the wedding. If you should be lonely after Miss Sallie leaves you, I hope you will spend a part of your time at least in writing to me, and recolect that I too am lonely, though surrounded with company—

"The heart, the heart, is lonely still"—

Whilst in Raleigh, I was looking around for something to send you, and after spending some time in visiting the different shops and stores, I concluded that I could not send you a more appropriate present than Harpers New-Monthly-Magazine. I forwith ordered it sent to you at Morganton—The popular Ladies Magazines of the day with the exception of the fine engravings I regard as worthless, not at all instructive and scarcely entertaining—The last years numbers of Harper's work I think stood as high as anything of the kind in America and I am [in] hopes the ensuing numbers for 1852 will be equally as good and that you will be pleased with it—Indeed I know you will like it, as it generally contains a great deal of matter from the first intellects of the Union of a solid and learned nature and a sufficient quantity of spicy and elegant light literature to make the variety most agreeable and pleasant. I am in hopes each number will act as a remembrancer of him who needs no remembrancer to recall your image to his mind.

I hope you enjoyed yourself during the days of Christmas pleasures, among your friends and acquaintances. As for myself, I read law all day on Christmas, with the exception of attending morning service in the Episcopal Church.[34] I scarcely knew that it was the anniversary of our Saviour at all. I never spent a Christmas so quietly, and I think I may add so profitably in my life. I believe it much the best way to observe that day, in tranquility and peace instead of boisterous mirth and dissipated revelling to which young men are too much given—I hope I may live to spend many more in such a way, or at least in a manner no worse. This day, Newyear, I have spent in calling upon some of my friends in the village, and in writing letters—I expect to be engaged for the next two or three days in writing letters, as I have not replyed to any during the vacation and they have been accumulating on during that time—I have now two weeks untill the next session begins, which time I shall employ mostly in writing, as I feel that I need some relaxation from study very much—It is necessary for the health of my body, but as to my mind I feel like going right ahead without a moments intermission—I suppose I shall not be able to get another letter from you untill some time after the festivities of the "14th" are all past and over with. I regret that very much for it constitutes my greatest happiness to hear from you frequently, but I can not insist on you giving your time to me under such circumstances. I hope however that you will write to me as soon afterwards as possible—I will write to you again about the 12th inst. as I am allways happy to give you pleasure, and you flatter me by saying that my letters are so interesting as to bear a second reading—I do not stop at the second reading of yours, for I believe I read them all over from first to last at least once a week.

34. The Chapel of the Cross.

It is getting very late and I have nothing more to write which could interest you in the least, so I will close by assuring you that I am

Sincerely and devotedly yours

Zeb. B. Vance

C. Hill. Jan. 18th 1852

My dear Harriett—

In my last I promised to write to you again about the 12th inst. and should have done so but I thought you would be so much engaged with the ceremonies of the wedding that you would willingly defer hearing from me untill you should again enjoy quiet and leisure—Supposing you to be in possession of that now, I have laid aside the book which was engaging my attention to night, and betaken myself to the more pleasing task of holding communication with her I love—

The session commenced yesterday morning, and I recited my first lesson this evening—Nearly all who were in attendance last session have returned, and some twenty others I believe besides, so you see the attendance will be very large especially for the winter term. Since my last I have been endeavoring to obtain some recreation, and with the exception of some general reading, have not looked at books at all. I mostly employed myself in hunting, and visiting the ladies here, with the most of whom I have the honor to be on very good terms—They are all intelligently accomplished, and most of the[m] classically educated, so that owing to the literary atmosphere which they breathe around this place their society can not but be both agreeable and proffitable to gentleman of much greater capacities than my humble self—It is especially more pleasant to me, since owing principally to the kindness of Gov Swain, whose good opinion I am so fortunate as to possess, I meet with the kindest treatment from all the families of the village in which I visit—Indeed my intercourse with the citizens of this place has been so pleasant that I am allready as much attached to it as it is possible for one to be who can see nothing beautiful or charming in any place but the spot where dwells the idol of his soul. I shall doubtless leave here with regret, nothwithstanding the *inducements* which would hurry me back to "my mountain home," as it is allways more or less unpleasant to leave friends—Tomorrow I resume the regular duties of the session and also my law books to prepare for my Superior Court license—I expect to study even harder than I did last session, always keeping those noble incentives in my view of which I have spoken to you so often—To my law studies I expect to devote my most particular attention, as I have the best of instructors[35] and I can stay no longer here than June. After getting Superior Court License there is yet another *license* to be obtained in obtaining which *you* will be my Judge instead of Ruffin Pearson & Nash,[36] and I sincerely hope that I may be so well prepared that you will not find any room for rejecting me. If I should [be] found deficient, yet I hope by casting myself humbly upon the mercy of the court that I may be able to *pass muster.*

But how did you enjoy yourself during the nuptial festivities of Mr. and Mrs [Ephraim] Greenlee? and how much longer will it be untill I shall have the pleasure of hearing from you? I have been waiting very patiently for you to find leisure to write to him who can allways and under all circumstances devote his time and thoughts to you— Now that I consider myself again at liberty to urge you to write, I beg you to write me at an early date. It is beyond your imagination to picture the pleasure it gives me to receive your affectionate letters when engaged in the studies and duties which press upon me here, and for a moment while reading them lose sight of everything but my bright visions of you, and love, and hope. You doubtless have time sufficient, and will you not then spend a large portion of it in making your devoted lover happy, and in making his exile from your presence as tolerable as it is possible to be? I do not in the least, my dear Harriet, complain, for I have been gratified extremely in your punctuality heretofore, but I am as greedy of your letters as the miserable miser is of the glittering gold, and would fain receive as many from you as possible—Write me about the departure of Sam McDowell for California and those who went with him— Have you received the first number of Harper's Magazine yet, and how do you like it? The first number of the "University Magazine"[37] will be issued by the first of February, edited by the Senior Class. I will send you a copy probably as it will contain an article

---

35. Judge William Horn Battle and Samuel F. Phillips.

36. The three justices of the North Carolina Supreme Court, Thomas Ruffin, chief justice, of Hillsborough; Richmond M. Pearson of Rowan County; and Frederick Nash of Hillsborough.

37. The *University of North Carolina Magazine* was established in March, 1844, and suspended later that year. When it was resumed in 1852, it became the state's first permanent literary magazine. Hugh T. Lefler and Albert Ray Newsome, *North Carolina: The History of a Southern State* (Chapel Hill, N.C.: The University of North Carolina Press, 1954), p. 387.

from my humble pen, and I have the vanity to think you would feel an interest in seeing a production of mine in print. Am I mistaken or not? I will see if you will be able to guess which piece is mine and therefore I shall not tell you at present—For the second number I shall have a piece of poetry (this is prose) which I am certain you will have no difficulty in recognizing—All the moments I can snatch from other things, I delight to employ in composition of some sort, but as my hours of leisure are few and interrupted when not stolen from that time which is due to repose and my health, my compositions are disconnected, incoherent and scarcely ever completed and touched off so that I would be willing to trust them to the public gaze—I beg you therefore to look upon those of mine which you may see in the magazine, with clemency and a proper consideration of all the circumstances. I write them for improvement, not with the boyish expectation of hearing others praise that which my own common sense says is quite undeserving of laudation.

It is probable that I may be with you before the session is out, as the studies of the Senior Class will close on the 1st of May and as I am an irregular student I will have no duties to perform at commencement and unless I stay for the purpose of reading law, I shall have nothing to detain me here after Senior vacation.[38] But I can not speak positively on that point as yet—
My health is still good and I feel in excellent spirits for study. My room-mate [Robert Bruce] Johnson of Waynesville has not yet returned and I am anxiously looking for him, in expectation of his bringing me a bundle of news from home and my friends in the mountains—

It is past 12 O'clk so hoping to hear from you very soon, I shall close by subscribing myself in truth and sincerity
Your devoted lover
Zeb. B. Vance

Quaker Meadows Jan 22nd 1852—
My beloved Zebulon;

This is the first leisure time I have had for the last two weeks, & I gladly devote it to writing you a short letter. I was quite disap-

[38]. President Swain initiated the custom of giving seniors a month's holiday just prior to commencement. Kemp Plummer Battle, *History of the University of North Carolina*, 2 vols. (Raleigh, N.C.: Edwards & Broughton, 1907), 1: 555.

pointed last mail evening, when Brother William returned from the Office without a letter for me from you—I certainly expected to hear from you though as you wrote me in your last that you would write again about the 12th of the month—You are generally so punctual, that if I dont receive a letter tonight I shall really be uneasy—you are surely not waiting to hear from me? If you only knew my anxiety to hear of your well being & the pleasure it affords me to peruse your epistles, I think you would have written, but perhaps you have written & I should not be writing to you in such a manner —I hope, dearest, you have & as I go to the Village in the morning I shall be quite disappointed if I do not receive a letter.

I must now tell you something about the weddings, as I have had the pleasure of attending two, since I last wrote—the first one, My dear Sallies took place on Tuesday the 13th the second the Tuesday following, which was Mr P. W. Robberts & Miss Corpening[39]—both weddings I enjoyed exceedingly but my happiness was greatly marred by your absence—Your image, My beloved, was constantly before me—I could do nothing without thinking of you—I could converse about nothing that would drive the thought of you away—but to return to the subject—Sallies & E.s attendents were Isaac Avery[40] & myself—Mary Jo Tate[41] & brother Sam—Miss Dorcas Happoldt[42] Cousin June Tate—Tene Avery[43] & Brother James—the other parties had none, as they only concluded to have a wedding the week before they were married—how very embarrassing it must have been—though Mr R. told me that he was not the least agitated—they were married by the Episcopal Ceremony

---

39. Philetus W. Roberts, son of Buncombe attorney Joshua Roberts, was an able young lawyer of Asheville. His bride was Salena M. Corpening of Morganton. John Preston Arthur, *Western North Carolina: A History (From 1730 to 1913)* (Asheville, N.C.: The Edward Buncombe Chapter of the Daughters of the American Revolution of Asheville, N.C., 1914), pp. 391, 392; William S. Stoney, *Historical Sketch of Grace Church, Morganton, N.C.* (n.p., 1935), p. 21; *Census* of Buncombe County, 1850

40. Isaac Erwin Avery was a son of Isaac Thomas Avery and Harriet Eloise Erwin Avery of Swan Ponds plantation in Burke County. Phifer, "Saga (Sons)," 39: 326.

41. Mary Joe Tate, daughter of Samuel C. Tate and his wife Elizabeth Ann, nee Tate (first cousins). Orphaned at an early age, Mary Joe and her brother Junius were reared by their mother's brother, Dr. William C. Tate. On her father's side, Mary Joe was a first cousin of HNE, and on her mother's, a distant cousin of ZBV. *Census* of Wake County, 1850; Ervin, "Tates" MS, McDowell, *MsDowells, Erwins, Irwins*, p. 193.

42. Dorcas Happoldt was the daughter of Dr. John Michael Happoldt of Morganton. *Census* of Burke County, 1850.

43. Harriet Justina (Tene) Avery was a daughter of Isaac Thomas and Herriet Eloise Erwin Avery of Swan Ponds plantation. Phifer, "Saga (Sons)," 39: 149.

& Sallie & Epharam by Mr Rowley[44]—I admired the latter most, though my strong Presbyterian principals would not allow me to adopt either mode for myself—I find I am growing stronger in *"the faith"* every day—Dont think from this that I am becoming Sectarian in my feelings, for indeed I am not—My wish is to follow the command of God's holy word, which is to "love the bretheran."

Although we have had a gay lively time, my dearest, all of our pleasure has been mixed with sorrow—the departure of our dear friends for California[45] (the day after Sallies Nuptials) seemed to cast a gloom over the whole Village & neighborhood for a few days—it was truly a sad time to me—Brother Sam & June had both been Brothers to me & it was with great reluctance that I could give them up for such a long time—I cant express to you my grief at parting with them. It was really very affecting to see Brother take leave of his good Mother & June of his only Sister—it may be that we have only taken leave of them for years but it may be forever—it is always best though, to look on the bright side—so I hope, through a Merciful Providence, to welcome them back to the dear "old North S[t]ate" at the expiration of two years—Sallie & Ephram will leave in a few weeks—so I will be all that will be left at the dear old "homestead" with my much loved Aunt & Uncle[46]—My greatest pleasure will be in writing to & receiving letters from you, dearest Zebulon.

44. Dr. Erastus Rowley of Asheville, a Methodist clergyman and a teacher, was originally from Massachusetts. Richard N. Price, *Holston Methodism From Its Origin to the Present Time* (Nashville, Tenn.: Publishing House of the Methodist Episcopal Church, South, 1913), 4: 128; *Census* of Buncombe County, 1850.

45. A member of Junius Tate's and Samuel McDowell's party was Robert M. Dickson of Lenoir, a first cousin of the latter. Dickson's letters, March 19, 1852, to March 12, 1853 (William Dickson Papers, Southern Historical Collection, The University of North Carolina at Chapel Hill, Chapel Hill, N.C.) describe the expedition. Taking slaves, they embarked at Charleston for Havana. Thence they went to Panama, crossed the isthmus to Panama City, and boarded a sailing vessel for the thirty-five-day trip to San Francisco. They prospected in Tuolumne County, California.

46. Captain Charles McDowell, sixty-six, was Harriett's half great-uncle and guardian. Son of General Charles McDowell and Grace Greenlee McDowell, he had inherited the Quaker Meadows plantation from his father. He was a successful farmer, a Methodist, and a Whig politician, having represented Burke County in the House of Commons from 1809 to 1811. His wife Anne was a second cousin, being the only daughter of Colonel Joseph McDowell, Jr. and Mary Moffett McDowell of Pleasant Gardens in McDowell County (Burke County at the time of her birth). Ashe, *Biographical History*, 7: 304; Ralph Stebbins Greenlee and Robert Lemuel Greenlee, *Genealogy of the Greenlee Families in America, Scotland and England* (Chicago: privately printed, 1908), p. 238, seen through the courtesy of Miss Ruth Greenlee, Old Fort, N.C.; Connor, *Manual*, p. 521; *Census* of Burke County, 1850.

Accept my many thanks for the Magazine, that you were so kind in forwarding to me—I have received the first number & find it quite interesting—I saw several numbers of it during last year & was quite delighted with them—you could not have sent me any thing that I would value more highly—an interesting book is my delight—& I too often neglect other duties for it—We have some intensely interesting works in the Reading Society at this time, among the number is Mrs Ellets Women of the Revolution[47]—which I am completely charmed with—By-the-way, I had almost forgotten to tell you that the Ladies of the Reading Society give S. & E. a Fancy party tomorrow evening—What would you guess was my character? It is a conversational party—how delighted I should be to see you there—as my Noble Zebulon—I will write you more about it in my next. As it is now very late & I am suffering, as usual, with a severe cold, you must excuse me from writing more—Remember Dearest that heaven is often petitioned for you by one that will never cease to love you devotedly—Write very soon—I hope to be able to write you oftener in future—I have much to talk with you about & am becoming very impatient to see you—I must bid you goodnight. The prayer of your unworthy Hattie is that you [illegible] the night pleasantly—Remember me at a Throne of Grace & May God guard you My Own One is the prayer of your still devoted

Harriett

Chapel Hill. Feb. 3rd 1852

My dear Harriett,

    I myself began to feel uneasy before the reception of your last, as I had not heard from you since sometime in December. If you felt uneasiness about me during such a short silence, you must know that I felt some considerable anxiety in regard to you since the reception of your last—Your delicate health allways keeps me in a state of uneasiness, and I never open a letter of yours without fearing to hear of your illness—Do my own dear Harriett, take care of your precious health, avoid exposure of any sort and the thousand and one foolish things by which young ladies ruin a good constitution—Excuse me I pray you for speaking in this manner: it results from my intense anxiety for your happiness in which

---

47. Mrs. Elizabeth Fries Ellet (Lummis), *The Women of the American Revolution*, 3 vols. (New York: Baker and Scribner, 1848-50).

consists mine also. I know your health is not robust and consequently I am ever desirous of your taking especial care of it—My own is good and is quite likely so to continue whilst I continue at this place which is quite healthy and I am constitutionally very stout. Well the weddings are all over & taking your county and Buncombe I see there has been several lately—What effect did the witnessing such events have upon you? Did you cast any glance into the mysterious future and picture out any such similar era in the history of your own life? I must confess that I never take up a newspaper from home and read over the marriages, but what I imagine to myself how euphonious the names of *somebody* else would read in a similar announcement! How pleasant, nay, that word is too cold and inexpressive, how blissful and extatic must be the feelings of two mutually loved and devoted hearts when they are thus blended forever into one! But my beloved, how many, who are thus made one by a union of soul and sympathies as well as of hands and destinies, remain unsevered throughout the whole journey of their existence! How many have their bright morning prospects buried beneath the dark clouds of sorrow and domestic misery! How many are unable to withstand the force of those obstacles to happiness which the many imperfections of human nature and rude buffettings and vicissitudes of life never fail to present! Oh my own dear one, let us cultivate that philosophy of spirit and those principles of love, which will enable us to defy those elements of disaffection so fatal to happiness and peace and to disarm adversity of its bitterness if it should ever seek to envelope us in its gloomy folds—May our souls be so mingled, our hearts and affections so entwined together, that the evening of death may find the stars that gleam in the little firmament of our love still gleaming as brightly and joyously as they did on the morning of our union—May we ever truly and emphatically [be] *one*, having but one destiny, but one source of joy and but one of tears, create a little world within ourselfs and people it with house-hold Gods at whose altars our hearts can worship in sacred unison—

I look forward to those coming days with mingled hope, impatience and fear. Many who have been able to climb the highest steeps of ambition and wring from stern fate the laurels of immortality, have been incompetent to the apparently simple task of securing domestic happiness in their private relations. More can successfully command an army or direct the helm of state than act successfully their part among the many vicissitudes of domestic life. But I look at it with such intense interest and as a matter of such paramount importance that I entertain the most sanguine hopes of passing away this life in your society with as much happiness as man has ever been allowed to enjoy—It is the theme of my constant thoughts and I am bringing myself to shape my actions and habits with a particular regard to the attainment of that end—Let me ask you to meditate upon these things practically and unromantically, and let us during the time which we are yet to remain disunited strive to study each other with a view to proffit by sounding the particularities of character with we each may be endowed. I have often thought, in regard to this subject that, long engagements—though undoubtedly most disagreeable to lovers might yet be not without advantage in enabling persons to thoroughly acquaint themselvs with the dispositions, peculiarities &c of each other. It is undoubtedly a test of affection and I should feel satisfied that it was no common feeling which causes one to remain faithful thus for years. Well are you not getting tired of this somewhat protracted essay? I hope you will pardon me if I have taken up too much space in discussing this subject. The truth is, I am unusually prolix whenever I happen to touch upon it, and feel that I could spread out my remarks untill thay approximated the magnitude of a volume without feeling wearied with the task. I hope however I have not failed to excite some degree of interest in your breast, as I know the subject affects you equally with myself—

My friend Mr Roberts is also married. I have seen the lady of his love, but had no acquaintance with her. I suppose indeed that you felt much grieved in exchanging adieus with your friends who left for California. I wish them all success possible and hope as you say to welcome them back to the old North State in a few years with health and wealth. I see that the "fever" is raging also in Buncombe very high and among others my restless Brother-in-law Dr Neilson[48] is wild to get off and take his family with [him]. I have entered my solemn protest against his taking his wife whose health is quite delicate with him and am much in hopes he will either decline going or taking her with him—I heard from James & Samuel, Junius & the others as they passed through Charleston. You say that when Mr —— and Lady leave you will be the only one left at "the dear old homestead"—Then I suppose I will get the last Lady-inhabitant

48. Dr. Morgan Lines Neilson, a native of Tennessee and son of Archibald D. Neilson and Elizabeth Lines Neilson, was a practicing physician in Asheville. He had married ZBV's oldest sister, Laura, in 1844. Their five-year-old son was named Archie. Gaillard S. Tennent, "Medicine in Buncombe County Down to 1885," reprinted from the *Charlotte Medical Journal* (May, 1906), p. 12; *Census* of Buncombe County, 1850.

of the Quaker Meadows which will be somewhat romantic, won't it? But although, last, I will not agree that you are least of all the ladies who have from time to time been taken away from that place—To me at least the grand prize yet remains; the gem of greatest value is left as yet untouched, but thank kind Fortune, not unspoken for—You will I know have the inducement of solitude to spend your time in writing to me, and blessing me with the continued assurances of your affection—I hope you will so employ it, at least a great deal of it. I think you may look to see me early in May as I have decided to leave here then. Of course I will *have business which will cause me to go through Morganton* on my way home. I am getting along finely with my books again, and have so far succeeded in acquiring a studious disposition that I have not the least inclination to neglect my studies on any ordinary occasion. I hope to be able to get license next winter for Superior Court practice and then I will go to work to see what can be done in the way of establishing myself in the world. I shall expect to hear from you again before long, so bidding you adieu for this time, I am yours truly & devotedly

Zebulon

Quaker Meadows Feb—11th 1852—

My beloved Zebulon:

Now in the sweet stillness of night when all in the house have retired to rest, (save myself) I with the greatest imaginable pleasure devote a short time in communing with My Dear absent One, for I know I shall sleep all the better for a bit of conversation with you; "Not the more soundly—no—but the more sweetly," for visions of my beloved one will hover round my pillow. I received, on Sabbath, your very welcome epistle & accept my many thanks for so dear a treasure—I read it with great interest, even more than usual. After perusing your letters I often ask myself if it is possible for my prosey compositions to interest one who writes so beautifully—and I console myself by thinking that you will receive them as tokens of my unchanging affection—for this, & nothing else are they intended—I am vain enough to think that a piece of paper containing nothing but information concerning my health & happiness & assurances of my devotedness, would be welcome to you—At-any-rate you have had to content yourself very often with such communications, but enough of this. I would infer from your letter, that you considered me quite a romantic somebody, & I must confess to the truth of it—but My dear one, I hope I have not allowed my romantic disposition to lead me astray. I have, as you desire me to do, meditated practicably & unromantically upon the subject of matrimony—I have envoked my heavenly Fathers guidance in such things, & I pray that He may direct us both what our duty is towards Him & towards one another. I entreat you, My Dearest, to write me many such letters as your last, & never fear of my tireing of your *'esseys'*, no matter how protracted they may appear to you—Nothing would afford me more pleasure than to receive just such epistles from you every week until I can welcome you to my dear home—which I am delighted to learn from you, will be the first of May. I hope *the business* that calls you through Morganton will *not be so urgent* as to *detain you* from spending the greater part of your time with me. You ask me, what effect the witnessing of the weddings of last month had upon me? I must confess that it caused me to cast a glance into the future & to picture out the time when our hearts would be thus forever united. I do not allow myself to think of the future as being only bright for *we* are as liable to be enveloped in the gloomy folds of adversity as others—but true Love "though strong in prosperity is still stronger in adversity."

My dear Sallie left on Monday last—she and Mr Greenlee have taken up their abode at Uncle Logen Carsons,[49] until they leave for Tennessee which will be the latter part of next week—I will then, feel more than ever the loss of my much loved companion & friend—Since their marriage they have been boarding at Dr" Happoldts[50] where I could see them every few days, & besides they visited us often so that it did not appear that she had left me entirely, but now I have to give her up to go some distance, with her chosen companion—it is quite a trial for me to part with her, but it is her choice, & I must submit—They think of returning in May—What a joyful time for me—for besides their return, I hope to en-

---

49. Jonathan Logan Carson, son of Colonel John Carson, was a half brother of Mrs. Charles McDowell. He ran the home, Pleasant Gardens, which he had inherited from his father, as an inn and stagecoach stop. "Carson's" was twenty-eight miles from Morganton and thirty-two miles from Asheville. Avery, "Historic Homes," 4: 18, 21; Henry E. Colton, *The Scenery of the Mountains of Western North Carolina and Northwestern South Carolina* (Raleigh, N.C.: W. L. Pomeroy, 1850), p. 21 and information from map.

50. Dr. John Michael Happoldt, a practicing physician, owned and operated the Mountain House Hotel in Morganton. Phifer, "Medical Practice in Burke County," pp. 40, 46.

joy the pleasure of a visit from one whom I love above all other earthly friends; there is rumour of another wedding in our Village about that time, & I suppose there is no doubt about the certainty of it—Mr Victor Barringer[51] & my friend Miss Maria Massey are the parties—I understand I am to be one of the attendants—I hope you will be here at that time, for your presence would add greatly to my enjoyment. I have been visiting at Belvidere[52] for the last day or two, where I met a friend of yours, Mr Marcus Erwin,[53] or at least I presume he is a friend as he spoke in very high terms of you—which was of course, gratifying to me—There were several of the young Ladies there—& they were teasing me a great deal about you, & Mr E— remarked, that if it was the case (as Mr. Merrimon said) that you & I were engaged, he admired my taste. In your last letter but one, you spoke of the University Magazine being issued by the first of this month—& that you would probably send me a copy, as it contained an artical from your pen; now be assured you are not mistaken in thinking that I will feel an interest in seeing a production of yours in print; I imagine I will find no difficulty in deciding which piece is yours.

I continue to be pleased with Harpers Magazine—I spend a great part of my time in reading aloud to Aunt, & she is also delighted with it—She & Sister are speaking of going to Rutherfordton[54] the latter part of next week, & I will perhaps write to you frequently during their absences but dont be disappointed if I do not—for it is quite likely that some of the young ladies will spend most of the time with me—I thought of going to Rutherfordton myself a week or two ago—but have given it out until their return, when perhaps

51. Victor Clay Barringer, lawyer of Cabarrus County, was secretary of the American Legation in Spain and private secretary to his brother, Daniel M. Barringer, American minister to Spain (an office he held from 1849 until 1854). Perhaps he was on leave at this time. Victor Barringer's fiancée was the daughter of George Massey and Maria McKesson Massey of Burke County. Ashe, *Biographical History*, 1: 125-30.

52. Belvidere was the plantation on the Johns River in Burke County established by William Willoughby Erwin, a first cousin of ZBV's grandmother, Hannah Erwin Baird. His descendants were known as the "Belvidere Erwins." At this time Belvidere was the home of HNE's friend, Margaret Erwin McDowell, and her sister Katherine Ann (Kate) McDowell, McDowell, *McDowells, Erwins, Irwins*, pp. 188, 193.

53. Marcus Erwin was a son of Leander Erwin of Belvidere in Burke County. About 1849 Marcus moved to Asheville where he practiced law. A Democrat, he represented Buncombe County in the House of Commons in 1850 and 1856. He had assisted John W. Woodfin in tutoring ZBV and A. S. Merrimon in law. Johnston, *Papers of ZBV*, 1: 20, n. 93; Merrimon's Diary.

54. Mrs. Charles McDowell frequently visited her daughter Mary, wife of John Gray Bynum, politician and successful lawyer of Rutherfordton.

I will make a flying visit there—It is now past midnight & I must retire—but not until my prayers go up to Heaven for you, my dear & faithful one—though we are separated—as the same sun shines upon us, so the same guardian care protects *us*; the same patient & merciful ear receives our prayers—the same final & blessed home, through His goodness, I trust awaits us—I will expect a letter from you very soon—Goodnight My dear Zebulon & believe me, as ever your devoted

Harriett.

University. Feb. 15th

My dear Hattie,

I set down again this morning to pen you a short communication, as in consequence of the illness of Dr. Mitchell[55] we have no service in the College Chapel this morning—I hope you will not consider it a violation of the Sabbath for me to write you to day, for I assure you that to me at least it seems allmost a sacred duty to commune with one I love so deeply, and on the quiet of this day, I have nothing else to do but to think of you, and I assure you that the day is spent in that manner almost entirely. Even whilst in Church, the words of the Sacred Orator fall unheeded upon my ears, but it would be a mistake to suppose that because I was not attending to the service, I was not at worship, for I was pouring out my heart to the object of my adorations as fervently as the most pious persons there. If others were equally sincere and fervent in their religion as I am in mine, the land would overflow with devout Christianity. But lest you should conceive that there was occasion to warn me again to beware of what you term idolatry I will forbear. But truly, my own dear One, I am afraid that, within the terms of your definition I am and shall allways continue to be an idolatrer, for as you are aware that I make no pretentions to religion, I must confess that my love for you absorbs and transcends every other feeling within my boosom. That is to say it is the ruling principle of my heart and all others are of less force, and operate only in an inferior capacity. If this should be wrong, and so you pronounce it to be, then I must own that I am such a

---

55. Dr. Elisha Mitchell, senior professor at the University of North Carolina, was an ordained Presbyterian minister. He preached in the chapel alternate Sundays. Johnston, *Papers of ZBV*, 1: 9, n. 46; Battle, *History of the University*, 1: 467, 537.

hardened wretch as to glory in my wrong doing. I can not help it, my dearest Harriett, and to try to moderate my passion for you, would be like tearing my heart from its dwelling place—These are not mere unmeaning words, for 'tis the genuine truth that my passion increases and gathers strength with each successive day that passes over my head. Absence seems to swell the flame the longer I stay from you, and the anticipation of meeting with you in May fills me with the wildest delight. To make a confession, I can say that I am not doing so well now as I was last session. The philosophy I boasted of to you that I possessed, which would assist me in my studies when so deeply in love, instead of impeding me, has nearly been overthrown, and I now frequently give myself up to dreaming of you, when duty forbids. But I will strive against it for a few months longer and *then* ——, but no that cant be, those odious *two years* you spoke of are still between me and happiness—Oh for patience, patience, patience. My dearest, noblest Harriett, shall I find you as warm and devoted when I meet you as your letters lead me to hope, or rather let me not doubt that, but will I find you as warm and devoted as my fancy paints you? Oh, let me hope so!

I hope your health is quite good again, although when you last wrote you said you were suffering with cold "as usual"—I am afraid you are not sufficiently careful of youself, as allmost every time you write you complain of cold. I can only repeat my earnest exhortations, as expressed in my last letter. My own health is still good, and my situation as comfortable and advantageous as I could desire in most respects. I have been so highly honoured by my fellow students as to be elected one of the Editors of the University Magazine in place of one of the former Editors who resigned in consequence of ill health. We have been delayed in getting it out this long, but it has at length made its appearance, and I will send you a copy this week. It will contain nothing very interesting for a Lady I presume, and only send it to you thinking it might interest you by reason of my connection with it (vain mortal that I am). I received a letter from Jas. McDowell last week. He is well and is undoubtedly much smitten with Miss May Wheat of this place, and I should not be much surprised at seeing him here before I leave. Allmost every letter I get from the mountains contains the intelligence of *certain strange reports* in relation to you & myself. I can not tell how it got there unless through the agency of Mr A.S.M— who seems to take a somewhat lively interest in all my affairs. Of course however, I am not in the least agitated by those reports.

I hope Mr. G—— and Lady are well. Have they left you yet? I trust you enjoyed yourself very much at the party you spoke of. Do write to me immediately and say something if you can that will control or at least calm in some degree, my burning impatience. This is my second letter since your last and I will look for a long one from you at an early day. And now my loveliest and adored Harriet, I must bid you a short farewell again, trusting that Heaven will protect and bless its own, and in such keeping may you remain is the prayer of your sincerely devoted

Zebulon

[1852]

My beloved Zebulon—

I received your letter on Sabbath afternoon & must thank you for it; it was quite an agreeable supprise to me, and as this afternoon finds me at home alone, inclination leads me to spend a few moments in replying to it—I do not think that it was a violation of the Sabbath for you to write to me, but My Dear one it certainly was a violation both of the Sabbath & the holy word of God for you to write such an idolatrus letter as I pronounce your last to be. I do not doubt your devoted love for me, but I must doubt that adoration you express—It is always a source of pleasure for me to peruse your epistles, but I must confess that some parts of your last gave me pain. & if I receive any more similar to it I fear I cannot appreciate them as I have your charming compositions heretofore—To be an object of adoration would cause me many unhappy hours, & My Dearest I know you donot desire to make me unhappy, so hoping you will consult my pleasure the next time you feel inclined to pour forth such sentiments, I will change the subject but I must ask you to pardon me for the manner in which I write—I know it to be my duty to warn you against such an error as I know you to be commiting when you say that your love for me amounts to Idolatry—I cant bare the idea of one so dear to me as you possessing such a fault—so, My beloved—Zebulon do express your self differently—it is only a fancy of yours—for I cant believe that such an unworthy person, as I, could be adored—& even if it could be, I think it would make me miserable. You ask me to write & say something that will control or at least calm in some degree your burning passion? What shall it be, that I continue to be your sincere Harriett—& that those *odious two years* (as you call them) will make no change in my devotions—unless indifference is manifested by you—which I do not fear?—So you see I am also a vain mortal—if this be vanity. You ask again, if you will find me as warm & devoted when we meet, as my letters lead you to hope?—If you do not, you will be the cause—I am, by no means, fickel—& do not make up my mind without mature reflection—I consider this a good trait in any one & if I possess none other—I am I assure you in possession of it—but I must lay aside my letter till another time

I was prevented from finishing this letter yesterday, & will have to conclude it in great haste this afternoon as Cousin Sallie McDowell[56] is with us & says I must go to the Village with her to remain a few days—so if I did not write by this mail, you would not hear from me before another week & I cant think of causing you uneasiness. My Dear Sallie [Greenlee] left last Saturday for Tennessee—I am quite lonely without her but I have some delightful Books—& the time passes very pleasantly—I visit a great deal & have a good many visitors—Aunt has not left for Rutherfordton yet, but will very soon & I will then be entirely alone unless some of the young ladies stay with me during her absence, & I imagine they will.—I understand Dr Lester[57] is in the Village, this is the second time he has been over this Winter—I presume his business is to see my fair friend Miss Ann Judson[58] I trust he will be successful— She is a great favorite of mine & she is one of my most particular friends & truly a charming girl. I heard from Asheville a few days ago—Your Brother-in-Law Dr Neilson I believe hires for California very soon—I hope he has abandoned the idea of taking Mrs Neilson along with him. We received a letter from Brother Sam—at Havana. He wrote in fine spirits & appeared as much as ever in the notion of California, though he said many that were with him were wishing themselves back home—notwithstanding all this the fever still prevails in Burke & companies are constantly leaving—& by-the way—I am quite in the notion my self, but I guess I will never

56. Sarah McDowell was the daughter of John McDowell of Rutherfordton, a brother of Mrs. Charles McDowell. John H. Wheeler, *Reminiscences and Memoirs of North Carolina and Eminent North Carolinians* (Columbus, Georgia: Columbus Printing Works, 1884), p. 85.

57. Dr. Thomas C. Lester of South Carolina moved to Asheville about 1841 and developed an extensive medical practice. He also kept a drugstore, the first of its kind in Asheville. Tennent, "Medicine in Buncombe County," p. 11; Arthur, *Western North Carolina*, p. 147.

58. Ann Judson Happoldt, daughter of Dr. John Michael Happoldt of Morganton. *Census* of Burke County, 1850.

see California. I must close my hastey epistle—I will write again very soon—I am sorry I cant write a longer letter this time, but I know you would prefer a short one, to none at all. I will expect to hear from My Beloved Z—— very soon—My health is pretty good, but I have been suffering a great deal with tooth ache for the last month— I want to have two teeth extracted tomorrow but am fearful I cant summons up courage sufficient—I must confess that I am very imprudent & do not take care of my health—but I think I have learned a lesson this winter & am determined to be more careful in future. May the choicest blessings of a Heavenly Parent rest upon My dear one—is the prayer of your still devoted *Hattie*

The following is a reply to HNE's letter of February 11, 1852.

Chapel Hill Feb. 23d, 52

Dear Harriett,

I received yours a day or two after I had written and I suppose you received mine just after you had written in the same manner. Thinking of course that you would wait until I should write you again, I sit down thus early in order to hasten your reply, and I must confess this to be the great secret of my punctuality. You profess to be much pleased with my letters at which I feel exceedingly gratified as well as flattered, but indeed I think you attach more merrit to them than they are in fact entitled to. I am not vain enough to believe that they are written "so beautifully" as you term it, but I *am* vain enough (and perhaps this is greater vanity than any other) to believe that you overate them because they come from one who loves you so fondly, and for nothing else. You say you "often wonder how such prosey compositions as mine can interest one who writes so beautifully." Now my Dearest Harriett that was allmost unkindness in you; I say *almost* for you qualified it afterwards, but still I do hope you do not think I would be disposed to critticize a letter from you admitting it to be ever so faulty. But such is by no means the case with your communications. Let the pleasure you experiance in reading mine be as great as possible yet it can not be greater than the pleasure I receive in reading yours. I can with all truth and sincerity assure you that I am almost wild with delight and love when ever I open a letter from you. The mail from the west gets in about one O'clk and if I get a letter from you by it, I invariably make a bad recitation on that evening at four O'clk. It awakens the flame which burns within my breast to such fury that all thoughts of the task before me are driven away; I can do nothing but lock my door to prevent intrusion, and read your letter over and over again until I have it perfectly fixed in my memory—Never, never, by beloved One, speak to me of "prosey compositions" again. They are not "prosey" or they would fail to create such emotion within me. They are just such letters as I want ever to get from you; well written, neat, and are so full of affection and confiding love that I prize them above all things else. The only objection that I can possibly make to them is that they are sometimes too short. But this is not a fair or equitable objection, and I do not wish you to consider me as complaining in that respect. I know that in writing so much and so frequently it is oftentimes difficult for the most fertile imaginations to collect matter on the moment sufficient to fill up a long letter, even though it be to one with whom, if present, we could never fail of something to talk about. I am in general happy then to receive letters from you that contain as you say nothing but intelligence of your health and happiness and assurances of your continuing and unchanging affection. Those are the main items and the others are put in merely for the sake of filling up the page. But still I may hope that you will write me letters as long as the most of the ones heretofore received have been.

I am glad to hear you say that you have been reflecting upon the topics proposed in my letter. You have, you say, studied it in a practicable light and not as most people under similar circumstances would do. I thank you for so doing. I need not I presume trouble myself with trying to impress upon you the vast importance of such study and consideration, as I have done before, for you seem to be aware of it equally with myself. I think with all the rashness and headlong precipitancy which my friends attribute to me, that I am disposed to view these things in a far different light from the generality of young men let them be possessed of ever so much moderation and prudence. I look forward, as I have often told you, to domestic life as one of the very greatest and surest sources of my future happiness, and consequently feel willing to make any sacrifice to obtain it. Oh how much I want to see you, face to face! I have so many things to say to you. So many topics to discuss and every one I feel like talking to you upon incessantly. I am looking forward to the time when I shall be with you at the Quaker Meadows with impatience amounting allmost to distraction. You say Mr. Erwin, you suppose, is a friend of mine, and that you had met him at Belvidere &c—He *is* a friend of mine. He has always professed the greatest friendship for me, and takes an interest in my success in my profession of which I have several proofs. I hope you may think well of him, he is so talented and noble-hearted. Like myself he is struggling to get himself up in the estimation of the world by his own exertions and I sincerely hope he may succeed. There is only one thing I know of that would be likely to prevent him, and I am in great hope that he will have firmness sufficient to keep clear of that rock upon which so much that is noble and generous has been forever wrecked and stranded. I suppose from the way you write about the young ladies teasing you and from what I hear by my Buncombe correspondants, that it is well known to the good people of the up country that you and I are engaged. Well, let them know it. Its a *fact*, and the object of any and every people ought to be to seek out *facts*. That has been the aim of philosophers of every age and country, and I suppose they are as fond of cultivating philosophy in the Mountains as other people. I am still in excellent health. I had almost forgotten to tell you that I am going to take the liberty of sending you my Daguereotype. I intended to have done it some time ago, but didn't have the opportunity of getting it taken until a day or two ago—I think it is very correct and hope it may be of some pleasure to you. But the chief object I have in sending it is to obtain yours in return. Please my own loved One dont deny me. Oh, how I would kiss even the cold image! Let me hope to receive it then at an early day. I am not aware of the least shade of impropriety in it, or of course I would not make the request—I hope you will avail yourself of the leisure you will have in the absence of Mrs McD[owell] and Mrs McK[esson] to write me a long letter. You will get the Magazine I suppose at the same time with this letter. I have ordered it to you for a year. I have a great quantity of writing to do for it now, which interferes materially with my studies, but it is of so much benefit to me that I do not regret it—And now my noble love, after invoking for you the shielding wing of the Great Protector of innocense and virtue I will bid you adieu again and subscribe myself, as ever

                               Your devoted and faithful
                               Zebulon

The following is a reply to HNE's letter dated "1852."

Chapel Hill March 6 [1852]
—Once again my dearest one I sit down to write to you and to seek your forgiveness for giving you pain in reading my last letter.[59] You say you hope I will consult your pleasure when next I shall feel inclined to pour forth *such sentiments*. I certainly shall, and not only in that respect but in all others when ever that pleasure shall be made known. You have only to intimate your slightest wish my own sweet Harriet and if within my power it will be gratified. Most sincerely do I beg your forgiveness if my passionate letter caused you pain. God knows how unwilling I would be to cause you the slightest shade of pain and I hope you will forgive me. You probably did not feel more pain in reading my "idolatrous letter" than I did in reading yours. The idea of my having offended you grieved me exceedingly; and although the rebuke was kindly given and penitently received, yet words of rebuke from my gentle & beloved Harriet sounded strange and chilling to my heart and made me for a while feel miserable indeed. I thought that you felt more than you said and nothing but your goodness saved me from more severe censure. Oh, how strange sound the first words of disapprobation from the lips of those we love! Let me so conduct myself as never to deserve them again, and my noblest love do you administer them ever when needful, but tempered with mercy. For I assure you, without any mixture of imagination or exaggeration in what I say, that my love for you is of so deep and tender a nature that it has become a portion of my existence and your displeasure would be the means of my destruction and despair—

I would say however, in extenuation of my offence, that you probably interpreted my words too literally. Those figures of speech are allowable as being expressive of more than common language can convey. Of course I did not mean to say that you were in truth and reality an *Angel* whom I worshiped as we do our Saviour. I could not have been so profane as to mean that. I only used the term in the figurative sense to express my devotion for you. If you were in really an Angel, possessed of all the qualities and perfections of those beings, then the match between you and myself

---

59. ZBV is obviously referring to his letter of February 15, which was not his "last letter."

would be so unequal that I could not think of desiring it. But if you forgive me, there is no need of trying to plead my innocense—. I trust you do—

We have got our letters wrong by some means I am a letter ahead of you and your answer is in reply to mine next the last one. I wish we had them straight again. I have not yet learned whether you got the Daguerotype in safety or not, and also the Magazine. The second number is out and I think you will find it more interesting than the other number. I would reccommend you to read the first article in the March number headed "A word to the wise is sufficient." It is rather wagish and humorous—I received a letter from James McD. the other day; he is going to come here in May and he and I will probably go up the country together after he has basked himself a while in the sun shine of Miss May's eyes— I am sorry to hear that you are so beset with the notion of California. Banish it for a time at least untill we see what can be done in the poor old North State. Peace and happiness can be acquired here by seeking rightly for it although riches may not be. I do not fear for the future if my health is spared. I have a confidence in myself that I will be successful in my profession and suffer nothing like doubting despondancy to approach me—But if our prospects should be otherwise then we may look toward the land of gold.

I shall almost count the days, hours and minutes untill I see you. It seems to me that I could never say enough to you or gaze upon you enough if I could but stand before you once again. But let me be patient. You say you can offer nothing only that you are still my "sincere and devoted Harriet" to calm my burning impatience and that if you do not meet me in all the warmth which I infer from your letters it will be my fault. I ask nothing more than that, I should expect nothing more; I must calm myself, and wait for time to effect his wonders in our behalf. Do let me hear from you soon, as your letters will form my greatest pleasure during the next two months.

Begging pardon for this short letter and invoking the protection of Heaven upon [you] I still and ever will remain your devoted and ever faithful Zebulon.

The following is a reply to ZBV's letter of February 23, 1852.

Quaker Meadows March—10th 1852—

My beloved Zebulon,

 I received your letter some days ago & with it your Daguerrotype Likeness for which I owe you many thanks. I leave you to imagine the joy of my heart, when I opened it & found that it was the image of *him that I love*. How much I prize it—it is such a treasure—I should be delighted to send you mine in return but I regret exceedingly that I havent it & do not know when I shall have an opportunity of getting it—if I should though, meet with one, before I enjoy the privilege of a visit from you, it will afford me great pleasure to have my likeness taken for you—I gaze often with delight upon yours & hailed its arrival with infinite pleasure & how much more welcome will be the arrival of the original—The time is drawing near when I hope to see you & the nearer its approach the more impatient I become—I was in the Village a day or two ago, at Mr McKessons & while there James McKesson[60] came in & says Miss Harriett Mr Vance is in town—he has just come—I was of course very much supprised & equally as much disappointed when I found that he had deceived me & I must confess that I was considerably teased. I did not, though (I think) exhibit the least disappointment—I only wish that it had been so—I am so anxious to see you—There are a thousand things that I have to converse with you about—I dont generally, desire time to fly swiftly away—but I am almost tempted to express myself so now—I will not indulge though—for it is sad for me to think of how unprofitably most of my past life has been spent—but I hope that the future will attone for the past—You say that it will afford you great pleasure to see me. Well, the time is not far distant (I hope) when you can judge practicably whether yours or my joy will be the greatest.

 I have had a number of my friends to visit me since I last wrote—Aunt has been absent & I have been housekeeper (& am vain enough to think my self a pretty good one). I have, been, very little of the time alone—or I would have perhaps, written to My Absent Lover, before this. Mollie Jo Tate has been with me all of this week—she certainly is the most artless creature of my acquaintance & truly a lovely girl—She sends you many messages—so many that I wont attempt to deliver them all—She says tell you that she is in love with you herself & thinks of cutting me out—What think you of it? Will she succeed—I flatter myself that she

---

60. James McKesson, nineteen, son of Thomas McKesson, a farmer of Burke County, and his wife, Sarah. *Census* of Burke County, 1850.

will not—she is a good friend of mine & also of yours—We are as intimate as sisters—I hope you will bestow much of your affection upon her—Now that my much loved Sallie has left me—Mollie Jo— will take her place in many particulars—though Sallie still shares largely in my affections, but my love for my own dear Zebulon far exceeds my devotion to my friends, but it is useless to say more on that theme—you are already convinced of my attachment for you, Dearest—

  I have another message for you from Sister Maggie McKesson—She is deeply interest in my wellfare & says you must obtain her consent (with regard to our engagement) now that you have mine—She would take pleasure in replying to a letter from you or at least she desired me to say to you that she would, & I know that she would—Dont write though unless you wish to; she will leave in a day or two for Rutherfordton & will not return before the latter part of next week or the first of week after. I will spend most of next week in the Village visiting as Uncle expects to be absent— I am anticipating much enjoyment but I must confess that home has greater charmes for me than any other place on earth.—besides the society of my dear Uncle & Aunt—there are many other sorces of enjoyment at the Quaker Meadows—& how much the presence of him, that is dearer to me than any other *earthly friend*, will add to all these enjoyments.

  I suppose you have learned ere this that your friend Mr [Marcus] Erwin has declared himself a candidate for the Legislature —I hope he will be elected. I received the first number of the University Magazine last evening—I think I shall like it—I havent been able to decide which of the articels is your production unless it is the poetry, do write me if I am correct. It is now after 12 o'clock & I must close. I know you will think me imprudent—but I am expecting visitors tomorrow & I disliked for this mail to leave without a letter for you—My health is very good, much better than it has been for some time—May your dreams be pleasant tonight— May our heavenly Father guard you during its defencless hours & may your dreams be sanctified to your Soul is the sincere prayer of one that feels an intense interest in both your spiritual & temporal happiness, especially the former, & one that never forgetts you in her humble petitions at a throne of Grace. I shall expect a letter from you very soon & will also write again very soon—Good night my dear one—

          Your truly Devoted
          Harriett.

The following is a reply to ZBV's letter of March 6 1852.

Quaker Meadows March 15th 1852—
My beloved Zebulon;
　　It is only a few days since I wrote you but having received a letter from you yesterday & expecting to be absent from home most of this week (as Uncle & Aunt are both away) I could not allow it to remain unanswered so long, so I must write you a short epistle this morning in great haste. I suppose you have before this received my letter acknowledging the receipt of the much prized Daguerrotype. I have also received the March number of the University Magazine & am much pleased with it, it is the only number that I have received—I was particularly pleased with the article to which you alluded—"A Word to the Wise is sufficient"—there is a piece of poetry that I think really beautiful, are you not the author of it? Your likeness (as I have said before) I am delighted with, but pardon me, when I say, that I dont think it, as handsome as the original—this is not flattery but dont allow it to make you vain of your appearance—When I love any one I most generally consider them handsome, even if they are not, & how can I avoid thinking you, that I love so devotedly—*fine looking*—I often gaze upon your likeness & wish that it could be really yourself, but this cant be & I endeavour to be content though it is rather difficult at times—I am anticipating many joyful hours with you when we meet which (I hope) will be certainly the first of May—You say that you received a letter from Brother Jimmy & that he will accompany you from the College at that time, after spending a short time their visiting Miss May—Do you really think that Miss Mays charmes have captivated him? If she is as facinating as I understand she is, I dont wonder at it but Brother is very susceptible & I accuse him of falling in love with all the pretty ladies that he meets—I believe that all the gentlemen are great admirers of Miss Wheat & I fear that Brother—will find some one of them, a very formidable rival—I wonder that you, My dear one, have resisted Miss Mays charmes. I am very anxious to make her acquaintance, particularly so, as there is a probability of her being a relation; I hope she will not treat my good Brother badly. I can recommed him, as a noble youth—

We heard from Brother Samuel & Junius at Panama they were both quite well & in fine spirits, they expected to leave there on the 20th of Feb. for San Francisco—I hope they have arrived safely by this time—I feel very anxious about them—yes they often rise in memory & ever with a strong, & sad impression of the pang which rent my heart when I bid them farewell—they have, (it many be) bid a final adieu to the sunny & endeared spots around the home of their childhood to the friends that love them so much—I trust not—they know not how oft, how tenderly they are remembered, or how strongly the affections of their friends cling to them— They both left home with the hope of improving their fortunes, but I know their minds yearn for their native land where every object is dear to them—I am satisfied to remain in the dear old North State and enjoy that peace of mind "compared with which" thrones & empires & principalites & powers are but vanity & dust. I must confess that I would like to go to California but not to acquire a fortune—as you seem to think. Oh! that my dear cousins had cared as little about wealth as I—they would have now, been enjoying with their friends, the pleasures of home—but it is not right that they should be so easily satisfied I suppose—May they be successful & may they as well as My dearest Zebulon remember that "we should first seek the Kingdom of heaven & its righteousness"—I regret, dearest that my last letter caused you an unhappy moment. I knew you were speaking figuratively when you wrote the letter that caused me to write the one that gave you pain, but I would prefer that you would not use such extravagant termes in expressing your love for me & I wrote that letter (not to censure) but to inform you, of this—I do not remember now the contents of my letter, but *if I* said anything that I ought not to have said—I ask pardon, most sincerely—I would not intentionaly wound your feelings—& hope that you will not be hurt at any thing I may chance to say in my communications that I ought not to. I feel deeply interested in you My own dear one & may some times express myself differently from the way in which I ought—As you say, our letters have gotten rong by some means & I will not write again until I hear from you & perhaps that will set them right—I hope it will not be long before I have that pleasure—I dont think though that you are a letter ahead of me now I will expect one from you very soon—I wish so much I could send you my Daguerrotype it would afford me the greatest pleasure. Although I have had many opportunities of having it taken I never would consent to it & regret it now as there is one that would prize it as much as I do his—Fare-

well for a while—May an Almighty Father keep you from all the ills of this life & May joy immortal be thine is the prayer of Your sincere & devoted
                                    Harriett.

The following is a reply to HNE's letter of March 10, 1852.

                                    University. March 16th 52
My dear Harriet,
    I was made so extremely happy by the reception of yours yesterday that I can not enjoy any peace of mind untill it is answered—therefore I set down this evening for that purpose thus early, although I thought when I last wrote that I would wait untill I received an answer from my last—so that we could get our letters straight again—as you know I keep one letter ahead of you—But it's impossible, I cant do it. I cant rest after receiving one of your sweet and affectionate letters untill I have immediately responded to it. I feel in addition to the love which pervades my breast, a lively and affecting sense of gratitude for your goodness and affection as displayed in every letter, and I am not content untill I have poured out my thanks and grateful acknowledgements before Her who is the author of my temporal happiness—You see I qualified the term *happiness* by prefixing *temporal*, lest you might think me *idolatrous* again as usual. But let me not dwell upon that subject, for I assure you it is a dangerous one for me. I can hardly mention it without being strongly tempted to break out into the same dangerous strain and attempting to justify myself in so doing. I am like Dame Margarett Billenden of "Old Mortality" who, whenever any of the Royal Family were mentioned could never even in the terror of death, refrain from recounting the time "when his Majesty James the first of blessed memory, partook of his *disjune* in her poor house." I am ever apt to run into extravagancies when the subject of idolatry is mentioned, therefore I shall hasten on for fear of again incurring your displeasure.
    I was pleased to learn that you were so much delighted with my daguereotype—I would have sent it to you long ago, but have not had the opportunity of having it taken before this. I am sorry

that I can not have yours to gaze upon in my solitude here—It would have been such a pleasure to me! But it matters not my dear One. Your image is so deeply stamped upon my heart and stands forth before my eyes so often and so faithfully that I have little need of anything else to remind me of you. You make mention in very warm terms, of my sweet Cousin Mary Jo. She is indeed a lovely girl and has my entire esteem upon her own account, irrespective of your wish upon the subject, which of course would have been complied with. I never had the happiness of her company, but for a short time when I paid a visit to Morganton some years since. I was then very much pleased with her. I did not speak with her as I came through that place last summer, although she was at Dr. Happoldt's where I stoped. I only saw her at the table and hardly knew it was she. I treated some more of my relatives badly, I am to confess, but I hold you responsible for it all. I was with you all the time, and felt too much anxiety on the subject under discussion between you and me to feel disposed to visit—Tell Cousin M—— she may blame you for not receiving a visit from me. Tell her also that I regret very much being under the painful necessity of telling her she can not succeed in cutting you out: at least I dont *think* she can, but there is no telling what can be done until the effort is made.

You told me also of another message which was of interest to me. I will most assuredly take pleasure in writing to Mrs McKesson in a few days. I feel much gratified at the manifest concern she evinces thus indirectly at least, for my welfare—I have been thinking upon this subject for some time, and am not certain but that I am to blame for not seeking the consent of others beside Mrs McKesson long ago. I feel that it was my duty in view of your Fatherless condition, to have asked the consent of Capt. McD—— at the outset. Shall I write to him immediately, or shall I wait untill I see him? Please write me your wish on this point—
None of the poetry in the Magazine is mine. In the first number my article is headed "Theorizing", in the second number "Americanisms", "Indian Legend" and in the April[61] number which will be out shortly a piece of poetry headed "For what I ask" and the Editorial Table are mine. Please do not let it be known. I am sorry to hear that Mr. Erwin has declared himself a candidate against Mr Woodfin[62] for the Senate. He should have been satisfied with a seat in the House of Commons.

61. This was actually the May issue.
62. Nicholas W. Woodfin (older brother of John W. Woodfin) of Asheville

Ask Cousin Mary Jo if she remembers Miss May Wheat. She was asking me about *"Tatey"* the name she was known by among the girls at St. Mary's, last evening. How do you like the March number of "Harper"? It is certainly a splendid thing. I am glad to hear that Dr Lester is making strides toward obtaining the hand of Miss Ann. 'Twas she, you recollect, to whom I used to string my lyre: forgive me for it, you know I was *young and foolish* then—didnt know any better. I shall expect an answer very soon: I am always exceedingly disappointed when your letters are delayed. Do write then immediately. May happiness and health be with you my dearest, noblest Love is the heartfelt prayer of your faithful

Zebulon

---

was the incumbent, having represented Buncombe County in the Senate for the past four sessions. He was considered one of the ablest lawyers in North Carolina. His wife was the former Eliza Grace McDowell, HNE's "Cousin Eliza," daughter of Captain Charles McDowell. HNE called him "Cousin Woodfin." Arthur, *Western North Carolina*, pp. 384, 385; *Census* of Buncombe County, 1850.

Part II

March 30, 1852, to October 23, 1852

There may be missing a letter from ZBV telling Harriett that he was returning to Asheville sooner than he had expected and asking permission to visit her. But it is more likely that he surprised her.

Definitely missing is a letter he wrote the day after he left Morganton.

Asheville. Mar. 30th 52

My dearest Harriett,

I promised, I believe, when I left you to give you the earliest possible information concerning my success in regard to the solicitorship, and I sit down to night, the first leisure moment, to comply. Do not think, however that this is the only object I have in writing, for amid all the hurry and bustle I have been in since my arrival, the pleasures of home and friends, I have been thinking of you and longing to break away and sit down to commune with you.

Well, I left Morganton about 9 O'clk on Thursday night and travelled all night without sleeping. I found it impossible to close my eyes in slumber. I felt extremely sad, yes both sad and joyful. I had just torn myself away from the one whom I loved more than my feeble faculties of expression can describe, and yet I was elevated with thought that she was mine. For many miles I ruminated in silence upon my probable and actual destiny, built castles and did every thing else that the buoyant mind of youth can do when wild with the warm and glowing dreams of love. Rousing up I attempted to talk with the driver, but finding no sentiment or congeniality in his uneducated, unpoetic soul, I gave up the attempt and relapsed into profound silence to think, think, dream, muse, bless, and adore my beloved and devoted Harriett! The last glance of that dear Ones form, as it stood in the piazza waving a handkerchief after her departing lover danced vividly before my eyes the whole of that long, long night. At Pleasant Gardens we took breakfast about sunrise and arrived without incident at Asheville at 4 O'clk. My good Mother was at Dr Hardy's[1] visiting; I got

1. Dr. James F. E. Hardy of Asheville, one of the leading physicians and social figures of western North Carolina. Hardy's wife was the former Delia Haywood Erwin of Belvidere in Burke County. It was Hardy who had been called to Lapland to set young Zeb's broken leg. Gaillard S. Tennent, "Medicine in Buncombe County Down to 1885," reprinted from the *Charlotte Medical Journal* (May, 1906), p. 8; Alphonso C. Avery, *History of the Presbyterian*

out of the stage and went in suddenly upon her, and of course almost overpowered her with astonishment & joy. I found all my friends well and happy at seeing me. On Saturday night I told my Mother all about our engagement which she approves in the most cordial manner. She had heard of it before but not from me. There is not much said about it here, and I imagine there would be nothing at all if it were not for the kindness of Mr M—— [Merrimon] who seems to delight in informing the whole village of it. On Monday morning early I went up to the village and announced myself a candidate and the vote coming off after dinner, I have the pleasure of informing you that I beat Mr Merrimon by a vote of 11. to 8. I laboured under many disadvantages, as he had been electioneering for three months and had obtained pledges from a great many magistrates who did not know I was coming home to offer. Beside this there were only about half of them in town so that I stood quite a slim chance and my friends thought I would be defeated. It was truly gratifying to me, my dear Hattie, to see how many warm friends I had. It seemed as if every body I met wished me to succeed; my young friends and associates of the village especially were exceedingly warm and active in my favour I believe without an exception. My strongest and only active enemy was my *old friend and admirer* Mr Sawyers.[2] The young gentlemen honored me with a beautiful serenade last night in celebration of my success—Mr. M—— took his defeat with quite a bad grace. He seems to possess very little philosophy, or even good policy. He got mad, accused some of my friends of acting badly and defeating him by unfair means. He exonerated me however, publicly, from any imputation of unfairness and said that I acted as a gentleman. I regret to say that I can not return the compliment with entire truth. He *did* do something in the election of which I believed him incapable and I caught him in it fairly, but as it all turned out to my advantage, I forbore coming to a rupture with him. Please for the same reason let no one know that I have said so. I did not rejoice in his ill success by any means. I really sympathized with him,

---

Churches at Quaker Meadows and Morganton from the Year 1780 to 1913 (Raleigh, N.C.: Edwards and Broughton Printing Co., 1913), p. 96; Clement Dowd, *Life of Zebulon B. Vance* (Charlotte, N.C.: Observer Printing and Publishing House, 1897), p. 12.

2. Isaac B. Sawyer, magistrate of the Buncombe County Court, was present and voting when ZBV was elected. Minutes of the Court of Common Pleas and Quarter Sessions of Buncombe County, Minute Docket, March 29, 1852, State Department of Archives and History, Raleigh, N.C., Book C, p. 635 (hereafter cited as Minutes, Buncombe County Court, March 29, 1852).

and felt in my heart as if I could willingly prefer being defeated myself to witnessing his mortification. His extreme vanity will always render him miserable under the slightest reverses. His Father to day before a large crowd refused to speak to me after I had spoken to him. From that fact it is plain to see where he obtains his unchristian-like prejudices—But enough of my own affairs: I think the road before me is bright and cheering. May God help me to walk in it correctly and honorably!

On Monday morning also I called upon Mrs J. W. Woodfin and delivered your letter. She had been gone all week to Hendersonville and only got back on Saturday evening, so I had no chance to present it sooner. You told me to present it in *propria persona* and I did so. Why did you ask me to do so? Mrs NW Woodfin received a letter from Mr Sam. McDowell on Saturday but I believe it contained nothing more than what you had heard when I was in M—— [Morganton].

Miss Mag Baird[3] spoke to me in a very friendly manner when I got home but whether she will since I have inflicted another wound upon the spirit of her lover I can not tell. The general report is that she will not. I am in hopes however, that she will be too wise to again expose herself in that manner.

I believe I told you that I would write to Capt. McDowell next week, so you might have a *chance of being out of the way* as you desired and for your sake I will try to do so, although I shall be extremely busy. I have indeed a complicated set of duties to perform; so much so that I am very much afraid I will not be prepared for license next winter. But assiduous labour will do a great deal. Have you received the letter I left with Kame [Henson] for you? I recd. yours from Chapel Hill and was delighted with it altho' you said you thought I would find it "flat." I am extremely much obliged to you for your compliments upon my personal appearance. I am afraid you stand almost alone in your opinion that I am handsome. I know of no one who would agree with you except Mother, who, good, blinded soul thinks that if I were cured of a little wildness I would be quite a charming boy—Its unkind of you however, my Dear One to try to undo the compliment by saying just after that whenever you love any one you can not help thinking them handsome let them be ever so homely. O, dear me!

3. Margaret Jane Baird of Asheville was a daughter of Israel and Mary Tate Baird. Her grandfather, Bedent Baird, and ZBV's grandfather were brothers. Frontis W. Johnston, ed., *The Papers of Zebulon Baird Vance, 1843-62* (Raleigh, N.C.: State Department of Archives and History, 1963), 1: 6, n. 26.

how could you elevate my vanity so high in one breath to hurl it down with the next? But the facts compel you to do so. How thankful am I that the truth does not thus prevent me from paying my loved One compliments. My opinion of your person, you have I presume always known. You are to me indeed beautiful and lovely in the extreme. But I never wished to dwell upon that, fearing you might think me captivated by your beauty alone, which to a lady of good sense would seem to me to be the most insipid and least acceptable of all compliments—

What shall I say of the delightful hours I spent with you at home! They flew by indeed as "golden hours on Angels wings" to me. I shall never forget them. My happiness almost made me mute. Especially when those Ladies were there, I never felt so stupid in my life. I felt conscious when they left of having made quite an inconsiderable figure. I suppose my dumbfounded expression of countenance hastened their departure. How I long for the time when I shall be with you once again! Be assured that I will let slip no pretense to cross the ridge if any occur between this and August. But my lovely Harriett its getting very late and I cant write all night even to you. Write to me soon, very soon; I am so anxious to hear from you since I left you. How did you get along at the Reading Society? I sympathized with you & deplore the vexation you must have undergone. Remember your promise about the length of letter But dont let me tax your convenience by insisting on your spending too much time with me, for I assure you I am thankful, extremely thankful for any kind of a letter from you and anything from your hand will always be revered and honored by your own devoted Zebulon.

Quaker Meadows April 8th '52

My beloved Zebulon,

I was quite pleased a few days ago to receive your letter giving the gratifying intelligence of your success in regard to the solicitorship, but not only on that account (you must be aware) was it gratifying to me. It also contained assurances of your remembrance of one that will ever think of you as the dearest object to her on earth—but remember, I do not make an idol of you—I only love you with a creature affection—this dearest is all that you ask. Althoug you are surrounded by many friends, I learn from your letter, that your own Harriett is not, nor will she be, forgotten—I have also many warm friends that I am devotedly attached to, but my affection is principally bestowed upon my absent Zebulon—the tie that binds our hearts is not to be severed—I meditate daily upon the subject of our union & feel more & more the importance of acting well my part—May the influence that I have upon you be exerted properly—May I live such an exemplary life as is becoming to one whos exampl has an influence with any one & particularly upon one who is as dear to me as you—I possess numberless imperfections, as I have said before—but your charitable disposition has assured me that you will overlook them—I know you will ask why it is that I continue my confessions of faults to you—it is for the simple reason that I dont wish you to be deceived in me—if it is disagreeable to you, do pardon me—I am anxious that you should know all my faults—I should like so much to be near enough to enjoy frequent visits from you, but I suppose it is best that I am not I might prevent you from attending to the study of your profession & perhaps would cause you to neglect other duties—I trust you have found no difficulty in resuming your habbits of study as you feared you would—I think there are many temptations to be resisted in all Villages & I do sincerely hope that you will resist those of your Village—choose not the idle nor intemperet for your associates; if you should have already formed an attachment for one who becomes inebriated at times & possesses many qualities that you admire—do endeavour to exert an influence for good—I dont feel afraid Dearest of your ever falling into such habbits—so dont think that I do from the manner in which I write—I have great confidence in you, you know—or I would not have told you that I would leave other friends & prefer you to them. You said in your letter that you had received my last to you while at Chapel Hill & that although you was delighted with it you thought it unkind in me to elevate your vanity so high in one breath merely to hurl it down with the next—You know dearest that I did not intend any unkindness—as for my own personal appearance I never thought for a moment that you were captivated by it—for if you had intended marrying a beauty I am candid in saying that you would have chosen another—if I am as you say, beautiful to you—it is I fear to you alone—You say that your good Mother agrees with me—Well, I always considered her a Lady of taste—but now I know that she is—Such a Mother as you have is indeed a blessing for which you should feel thankful—Mine has been called from me by an alwise Providence—I grieve not for her, as those that have no hope—she has taken up her abode with the Saints in heaven as has also my Father—I can think with great pleasure on their earthly cares—& my constant prayer is that our last end may be like theirs. Excuse me for alluding to the subject of my deceased Parents, it is one on which I love to dwell, although I was very young when deprived of them—Remember me very affectionately to your Mother—I was pleased to hear that she approved of our engagement. I hope she will, in future, find her noble sons, lady love, an exemplary woman.

  I received, the day after you left me, the letter that you left with Cousin Kame—he called & delivered it himself—I was quite delighted I assure you to receive it, for I was really sad at parting with you; your visit was such a short one—do come again as soon as you can conveniently do so, not until August appears a long, long time—I dont wish you to come, if at all impracticable, but you dont know how much pleasure frequent visits from you, would afford me—It is quite uncertain when I will go to Rutherfordton—I dont think I shall go until after Miss Maria's wedding which is not until the last week in May—Brother Will is going, perhaps next week & I was speaking of accompanying him, but I dont think I shall—I will write you if I do.

  I was truly sorry to hear that Cousin "Gus" took his defeat so badly & regret much more to know that he acted dishonorably—His Father, I think, acted very unbecomingly—how unlike, his conduct was, to that which a christians should have been. I fear "Gus" will never succeed in his profession while he continues to be so vain—Is it not to be regretted that a young man of such fine talent as his will continue in such error? This I guess though will not prevent him from obtaining our fair cousin Maggie—I do hope that she will not subject herself to such censure as she will justly deserve if she follows the example of her lovers Father—how absured such conduct is according to my judgement.

  I read, yesterday, your letter to Sister Mag McKesson—I was truly gratified to see it & I know she was also—I think you need have no fears about obtaining the consent of my friends—Uncle says you are a *nice* young man & he intends that little word nice to convey a great deal. You say in your letter to "Sis" that you can not but entertain hope that your petitions will be successful, from the recolection that she who was once your judge will now be your intercessor—certainly my dear One all the influence that I could have would be exerted if it were necessary—Sister will reply to your letter very soon—You ask me why it was that I requested you to deliver cousins letter yourself? I really have no particular reason & it was really foolish in me to make the request. So she received it, it did not matter by whom it was delivered—I hope to have the pleasure of welcoming she & cousin Elizia at the charming Quaker Meadows very soon—I am anticipating much pleasure during their visit—I received a letter last week from Sallie Greenlee—she & Ephram are quite pleased with Tenn—They will return to Burke the first of May & spend the summer in the gaden spot of the old North State.

Have you seen my friends Clara Patton[4] & Mary Martha Avery[5] since your arrival at Asheville: you will find them both agreeable young ladies—Mary Martha is one of the most intelligent ladies we have—How comes on, our good friend Dr Lester? Do you think Miss Anne has rejected him? I do hope not. I am afraid she has. How is your sister (Mrs Neilson) bearing the separation from the Dr?

I regret to say, that Mr William Pearson[6] who spent some time in California is now perfectly deranged, & it is thought his recovery very doubtful—he had Hemorrahage some time ago & went on to Charleston—& there, I understand the Physicians say'd he couldent possibly live three months—how very sad it is—he was engaged to Miss Caldwell[7] & they were to have been married last month—how truly sorry I am for her—her parents have opposed the mach for some years & had at last given their consent. Indeed I must close my letter I know you cant complain of its being too short—Do answer it very soon—I had almost forgotten to answer a question that you asked me in your last about my being teased—

4. Clara I. Patton was a daughter of Thomas Taylor Patton of Buncombe County and the former Louisa Walton of Burke. After the death of their mother, Clara and her younger sister Louisa were brought up by the Waltons in Morganton. Apparently the girls had at this time rejoined their father and were living at his home, Pleasant Retreat, on the Swannanoa near Asheville. Information from Dr. Edward W. Phifer, Morganton, N.C., and Miss Edith Holmes, Asheville, N.C.; *Census* of Burke County, 1850.

5. Mary Martha Avery was a daughter of Isaac Thomas Avery of Swan Ponds in Burke County. Edward W. Phifer, "Saga of a Burke County Family (The Sons)," *North Carolina Historical Review* 39 (Summer, 1962): 142.

6. William Pearson, brother of Robert C. Pearson, was clerk of the Superior Court of Burke County at the time of his death. Samuel A. Ashe, Stephen B. Weeks, and Charles L. Van Noppen, eds., *Biographical History of North Carolina from Colonial Times to the Present*, 8 vols. (Greensboro, N.C.: Charles L. Van Noppen, 1905-17), 3: 362.

7. Probably Jane Caldwell, twenty-seven, daughter of John Caldwell, a leading merchant of Morganton, and sister of Tod R. Caldwell. *Census* of Burke County, 1850; John H. Wheeler, *Reminiscences and Memoirs of North Carolina and Eminent North Carolinas* (Columbus, Ga.: Columbus Printing Works, 1884), p. 94.

I must give my friends credit—they have really dealt with me very mercifully—& have subjected me to very little vexation—I do not though, at any time get vexed with them—May the good angels guard thee Dearest is the prayer of your truly devoted

Harriett.

Letter of Zebulon Vance missing.

Quaker Meadows April 23d 52

My beloved Zebulon—

Although surrounded by many very dear friends, the dearest *one* "though absent is not forgotten." I was almost wild with delight yesterday evening, at the arrival of my dear Sallie—this morning she, Aunt, Ephram & myself together with the elder Mr McKessons family dined with Sister Mag McKesson (it being her first day in her new house) & this afternoon while we were enjoying ourselves truly our pleasure was greatly increased by the arrival of Cousin Elizia Woodfin & her interesting little children[8]—Knowing how pleasant it is for you to receive my poor productions (judging your feelings, by my own) I left them all at Sisters & came out to the Quaker Meadows, in order that my dear good old Uncle might not be allone & that the mail might not leave without a letter for my Dear Zebulon, of some discription. If you should find it too short & in possession of the many other faults that my letters usually are in possession of, I know under these circumstances you will excuse the only fault that my much loved one finds—If it was not quite late & I had not been up late, for several nights past, you would not find this letter too short, for I have much to write, that I cant to night, on this account. I was overjoyed to receive your charming epistle a few days ago. I began to think it a long, long time, coming—Dont you remember, that you promised to write me more frequently? I think you toled me that you would not wait for replys to all your letters if you did not fear my becoming negligent—now Dearest, do not fear that—for how could I neglect writing to one who never neglects his affectionate Harriett? I ought not to urge

---

8. The Nicholas W. Woodfins had three daughters: Anna, ten; Mary, eight; and Mira, four. *Census* of Buncombe County, 1850.

you to write oftener, perhaps, as it will probably cause you to neglect other duties of more importance—if such is the case—I can willingly submit to receiving letters as I have been but would greatly prefer their coming more frequently; I cant, you know write very often to you while Cousins are visiting us, but I will certainly write as *lengthly* as possible as it puts me to no inconveniance at all—it affords me great pleasure to make my beloved one happy.

You spoke of an abusive peace that Mr Edny[9] had put in his paper about you—I was glad to find that you had not gotten into any difficulty with him—do dont allow anything that comes out in his miserable paper to enrage you—he has few subscribers in our community—& those that do receive his paper I dont think are much benefited—I assure you that it can do you no injury here—I have enquired of several persons if they have read the last Messenger—& the reply of all has been in the negative—I have not seen it nor dont care to see it—I hope you will have no difficulty with him—do treat such characters as he is, with silent contempt—I will certainly acquit you (as far as is in my power) of any base motives that he has charged you with.

I was pleased to hear you speak in such high terms of my friend Clara [Patton]—I hope you will cultivate her acquaintance—she & I have ever been the best of friends—I love her very much indeed—she I suppose, will make a visit to our charming little Village soon—as I think she is to be one of my friend, Maria Massey's attendants. She is to be married the 27th of May—. I was quite sorry and some what surprised to hear that Dr Lester was rejected—you ask me if I think it advisable for him to follow your example of perseverance—really I cant give any advice on the subject, as I do not know Ann's opinion of such things. I will converse with her about it—& then write whether or not a second appeal would avail any thing—*I think it irresistable, as you very well know.*

What a very melancholy death we have had among us—last Monday I attended the burial of Mr Williams Pearson, who had been a lunitic for several weeks—if you remember I mentioned in my last letter that he was to have been married to Miss Caldwell last month,—poor girl—she has been quite *ill* ever since his

9. James M. Edney, editor of the *Asheville Messenger*. Edney was another of the magistrates of the county court who, obviously, voted against ZBV for the solicitorship. *Census* of Buncombe County, 1850; Minutes, Buncombe County Court, March 29, 1852.

death—he told his friends that he would die, a few days before his derangement—It was the will of our Heavenly Father that he should bid farewell to this poor perishing world & I trust he has taken up his abode with the saints—his friends have been called to pass throug the furnace of affliction, that furnace through which an alwise Providence often causes his children to pass for wise purposes.

  I am so much oblidged to you my own one, for the books that you send me by cousin Ephram—I am reading Dream Life[10] & am really charmed with it. I have abandoned the idea of going to Rutherfordton, until after Maria's Wedding—you say you have some notion of going there, when I do—how delighted I shall be to see you there when I go—Do come to Burke as soon as convenient & I would be so glad to see you, at any time. I am enjoying myself much at this time & when all of the family arrive, wont the Quaker Meadows be a place for enjoyment? We are expecting Brother James in about two weeks—I have no doubt that he would be pleased to meet his friend Mr Vance, here—I am so anxious for his arrival.

I received a letter from one of my cousins, at the North, a few days ago requesting me not to enter into an engagement with any one until I should make the acquaintance of a nephew of his, who he said, intended sending me his likeness soon & wished mine in return—isent that a curious way to carry on a courtship? I intend writing to this cousin that I received the letter from, very soon, telling him that I have already made choice of a noble & talented young man & one that I know is worthy of my entire love. Do write very soon, but this is a useless request, for I know that you will. I could write much more, but must close now—Have you received Sister's letter? She, I think wrote to you the first of the week— Uncle, I believe, has also answered your letter. Remember me affectionately to your Mother & do remember the request that she made of you respecting Mr Edny; May the prayers of your good Mother for you as well as those of your truly Devoted Harriett be heard an answered—Adieu My beloved One—You will hear soon again from Your Own Harriett.

  10. I. K. Marvel, pseudonym of Donald Grant Mitchell, *Dream Life: A Fable of the Seasons* (New York: Charles Scribner, 1852).

Asheville. April 27.—[1853][1]

My Dear Harriet,

I sit down with pleasure this evening to acknowledge the reception of yours of the 24 [23] inst. in which you give me another irresitible proof of your earnest and sincere attachment. You can not well imagine, my Harriet, how my boosom swells with pride and gratitude when I receive your affectionate letters, especially when I know them to be written under such circumstances as your last was. Amidst all the excitement & joy of meeting beloved friends from whom you have long been separated, I find that I, undeserving of your lightest thought, am not even then forgotten! You can break away from them to write to one who is distant indeed from you in body, but ever near in soul. You may rest assured my beloved One that I appreciate to the utmost, the delicacy and nobleness of your attention to my happiness. If anything *could* increase the violence and fervor of my devotion, your conduct toward me would surely do it; but no, that is impossible: the cup of my love is full to the overflowing, my spirit is bound up to yours with so strong a tie that no earthly power can loose or draw it tighter—O, to God your feelings may ever be thus! That you may ever be my Own noble, generous, warm-hearted, and devotedly faithful Harriet!

But let me try to answer your letter. I received Mrs McKessons not long since and was delighted not more with the gratifying sanction to our union which it gave me, than with the curtious yet kindly tone in which it was written. I replied to it last mail, in as warm terms as my grateful feelings could suggest. I have not yet received a reply from Capt. McDowell, and must own, that although I did not urge a hasty answer, yet his delay has given me a little *just a little* uneasiness—I hope however, from what you have told me, that my fears may prove nothing more than imaginary; only the frighful bugbears of an excited fancy. I trust next wednesday's mail will bring my *reprieve.*

So you are reading the books I have sent you. The[y] are very popular with the literary world and undoubtedly works of considerable merit—You will, I think, find them replete with beauty; happy conceptions arrayed in the richest garb which the English language can produce. I have marked several passages which I thought you would concur with me in thinking almost inimitable. "The Rev-

11. This letter is an 1852 reply to HNE's letter of April 23, 1852.

eries"[12] is the better of the two, perhaps. Read them all, and think of me as you read. I did not have the pleasure of calling on Mrs Greenlee while here, as it was on the Sabbath; I saw her however in Church. Mr G—— [Greenlee] called at my room and sat some time. How happy *he* must be! and miserable wretch that *I* am! But patience, patience. "For time at length sets all things even" says Byron, and I am waiting with the fortitude of a martyr at the stake for it to bring about my happiness—Please dont give yourself the least uneasiness in relation to my difficulty with Edney. I called upon him on his return home and abused him without restraint which he took without the slightest attempt at resistance. I told him to never mention my name in his vile sheet again unless compelled to do so upon the penalty of having his bones broken, and upon his faithful promise to that effect I left him—Mr Merrimon has been on nettles ever since I got back home to find out the true state of affairs between you and me, which he at length in a degree effected by going in the post office when the last mail from Morganton came and on seeing the mail opened he saw your letter to me and recognized the handwriting of the address—I can have no idea why he is so curious, but I envy not his method of acquiring information.

I was amused somewhat at the manner of begining a courtship adopted by that cousin of yours of whom you spoke and also at the prompt way in which you intend to reply to it—The ladies certainly understand how to do business when they have a mind to be frank and decisive—That prayer which I used to make for myself I will now make in behalf of others, "administer the law with mercy"—You will not go to Rutherfordton then till after the wedding. I was just going to beg you to come to Asheville with Mrs Woodfin but I suppose the wedding will also prevent you from doing that. Oh, how pleased I would be for you to come to Asheville and spend a few months this summer! I wish I could be near you all the time, but my duty forbids. I must stay at home constantly among my books and struggle to build up my fortunes by study and attention to business. During the last week I did not read a great deal. I was with the ladies most of the time. It is vacation time with the inmates of the Boarding House of the Female College[13] here and as the young Ladies are forbidden fruit to the

12. I. K. Marvel, pseudonym of Donald Grant Mitchell, *Reveries of a Bachelor: Or a Book of the Heart* (New York: Hurst, n.d.).
13. The Western Carolina Female College was taken over in 1851 by the Holston Conference of the Methodist Church, but the name was not changed to Holston Conference Female College until September, 1852. Richard N. Price,

young gentlemen during the session, it stands us in hand to "make hay while the sun shines".

However there are only a few there. Miss Remine the Teacher of French &c is quite pretty and possessed of considerable intelligence. This morning however (Monday) I sat down determined on doing a weeks *work* and I have scarcely been out of my room to day only to meals—

You remind me of my promise to write more frequently. I will do so in future. I think I will write at least once a week whether you answer or not, unless when I am from home or something else prevents me. I was not in earnest when I told you I thought you would grow negligent of me if I kept on writing to you without waiting for your reply. I am not fearful of your neglecting under any circumstances—I hope however, you will continue to write as often as possible—I should like to see my friend James McD—— very much. I want you to send him over soon after his arrival in Burke. I wonder how he is getting along with Miss May [Wheat]. I suppose he will spend at least a week with her as he comes home. How I wish I was at Chapel Hill to plead for him. Miss May and I were such good friends I think it likely I could have done him some little service. I can, at any rate, teach him the efficasy of a *second appeal*.

I have not yet delivered your regards to my Mother as she has been very sick all day and is no better tonight. She is troubled with periodical attacks of the nervous head-ache which seems to grow worse with her increasing age. She suffers exceedingly with it— I often talk with her about you—Sister Laura has been returned from Tennessee some time; her health is very feeble, and I am afraid will never be much better—She has a very interesting little boy who gives indications of great sprightliness of intellect. We have heard nothing from Dr. N. since he left Havanah—Cousin Mag' Baird has has acquitted herself toward me with more credit than one would suppose from her former conduct—She spent the evening with us not long since and fairly tendered the olive branch to me which of course as a gallant Knight I could not refuse altogether. *She is getting older*, and you know that age sometimes imparts wisdom.

Well, what have I else to say? I think I have exhausted most of the material I had on hand for a letter to night and therefore I shall begin to wind up. You must know I am something like a

---

Holston Methodism from Its Origin to the Present Time (Nashville, Tenn.: Publishing House of the Methodist Episcopal Church, South, 1913), 4: 429.

horse at full speed, or a locomotive, I cant stop all at once, but must have room to check myself—But let me mention that I was much affected by the melancholy fate of Mr P[ea]rson and the evidently deep distress of Miss Caldwell. What a mournful lot is hers! I sincerely sympathise with her, and deplore the untimely taking off of her lover—Promising to write again soon and hoping to hear early of your health and happiness I remain as ever

>Your true and constant
>Zebulon.

>May 5th 52

Dearest Harriet,

In accordance with my promise to write once a week, or at least as often as possible, I set down this morning to write you a short letter. Short it must of necessity be, for I am somewhat pushed for time this morning, and being subjected to many interruptions from the publicity of my room (which is in the Court House) I cant get my self into that *sweet* condition of mind requisite for writing long letters, as the influx of loafers keeps me continually mad.

Well in the first place, I have to inform you of the great gratification I experianced on finding a letter from Capt McDowell[14] in the postoffice when I returned from the country last evening. I read it with pleasure and found that he cheerfully gave his consent, and accompanied it with some flattering remarks concerning myself. I am extremely proud to know that my character has been so favorably represented to him as he says it has. I hope he may never have cause to regret his generosity in yielding up so great a treasure to one so humble and undeserving as myself. I shall ever strive to merit his generous consideration.

I was called to the country last week by some important business, and was gone nearly a week. Whilst down the River at the springs, I called upon my friend Miss [Sara] Garret, who received me with the utmost politeness and even friendship. She was aware of my correspondence with you and teased me about it considerably. I told her of the reports that were so current in the country in reference to my having treated her badly &c and she denied ever having given any persons ground to speak anything ill of me at all. She said she would take every opportunity to deny

14. See Appendix B.

everything of the kind accusing me of having acted ungentlemanly —She appeared to be in delicate health. Allow me to say my dear Harriet without exciting any jealousy in your generous heart, that I consider her a noble hearted and truly amiable young lady. Such she has ever shown herself to me. I had a fine time on the River, as I saw a great many of my early associates of the country. There is always to me, something charming in a country visit. The hospitality of the people is so plain and generous so free and simple, that it always makes me feel comfortable and pleasant in the extreme. There the huge and rugged mountains, just arraying their steep and rocky sides in the glorious, gorgeous garb of summer green; and the boisterous, foaming river, thundering over the jagged rocks, all conspired to make a ride down the French Broad to the Springs a unique pleasure. I got back last night and found Sister Laura Neilson down with a very dangerous attack of Neuralgia. She was very ill indeed yesterday and last night, but is some little better to day.

I have been writing letters all day, and expect to continue till late to night as I have several unanswered ones before me. I have received several letters lately from Chapel Hill. I learned yesterday that one of my fellow students there died not long since. I was not acquainted with him. In one of the letters I received, the young Lady of whom I spoke to you Miss [Mary Jane] Morrow, sent me her *love*. She said she would not send her *love* to a young gentleman but she knew Mr. Vance was engaged any how, and it did'nt make any difference with *him*! The saucy little coquette!

Our *great female College* has begun operations again, with, I think, about forty pupils. I dont think it will ever be anything extra, and I dont think it ought to, because it is a sectarian School. The only redeeming quality about it is, they have a Presbyterian Music Teacher. I intend cultivating her acquaintance, although she is somewhat up in years, ugly, and vinegar-faced. Tomorrow I want to go to hard study again as I have not read any for near a week. I hope you will excuse the shortness of this letter, under existing circumstances, and answer it as soon as possible. It seems really a long time since I have heard from you. I wish so much that you could come over with Mrs Woodfin. I hope you continue to find the books interesting. Adieu my Dearest Harriet, for a short while, and believe me as ever,

                                Your loyal and devoted
                                Zebulon

Quaker Meadows May 8th 1852

My beloved Zebulon;

  I was unusualy gratified yesterday morning at the reception of your short but sweet epistle, it being the second since I last wrote & this pleasant May morning finding me at home alone, it affords me the greatest imaginable pleasure to spend a lonely hour in communion with my absent lover; I did not think, when I received the one before the last, that I would receive a second before I would write to you again, but I have been so much engaged with my friends, that I have had very little time for any thing else—for the last two weeks I have enjoyed myself finely—we have been visiting some in our facinating Village—it has always been a great place with me but a more charming spot now than ever, as both Sister & Sallie are residing there, besides many other friends—Sallie & Ephram have gone to house keeping—our family dined with them yesterday, & be assured we spent a very pleasant day—they look quite happy & as you say *must be*. We are hoping this evening to welcome some more of our friends at the old homestead—brother James wrote he thought he would get here by this evening, & we are expecting certainly to see Cousin John & cousin Mira—you say you would like to have me return home with Cousin Mira & I should be pleased to do so, if it would contribute the least to your happiness—but it is impossible for me to visit Asheville at this time—

Marias Wedding comes off the last week in this month & I shall be oblidged to remain at home, at least ten days after it is over with —she is anxious that I should go down to Charlotte with her—I dont think of doing so though, but will certainly go to Rutherfordton at that time, & perhaps remain there until the last of July— so if I visit Asheville atall this summer my stay will be short—I hope though to see you frequently—It appears a long time to wait until August to enjoy a tête-à-tête with you & will you believe that the hope of seeing you is one great inducement for me to go down to Rutherfordton—for I certainly expect to see you there when I go. So you have seen, since you last wrote, your former lady love—how unkind it was in you to fear you would excite jealousy in my heart by saying that you considered her a noble hearted & amable lady— her character has always been represented to me in this manner— & I should be truly sorry to hear you speak in any other way of her—her conduct towards you goes to prove that she is certainly a noble woman—I hope you will ever have a very high regard for her. I am sorry to learn from your letter that you are so much annoyed with loafers & I must confess that the prevailing fault (selfishness) is one of the principal causes of my regret, for the perusal of your long & interesting letters is to me one of the greatest of pleasures. You will be deprived of the pleasure (if it be a pleasure) of receiving many of any discription from me for the next month—I would write to you again next week, but Presbytery meets in Morganton at that time commencing on a Thursday evening & after it is over I will be quite busy preparing for the nuptials of my good friend Maria—She is truly a lovely character—how much I wish you were acquainted with her—she has expressed a wish several times to make your acquaintance—if you should receive an invitation to any of the parties given her in Burke would you attend? We will have some fine ministers with us during our approaching Presbytery—I wish very much you could be in Morganton at that time for I am really gratified to know that you are a Presbyterian in principal—I do sincerely hope that you will not depart from the faith—I was very much surprised to hear that the music teacher at Asheville was a Presbyterian—I do not consider it a desirable situation, if it is a sectarian school.

You wrote in your last letter but one that your Mother was quite sick & in your last that your Sister Laura was a great sufferer—I hope to hear in your next that they are both entirely well again. We have recently had a short visit from my good friend Clara Patton—I saw her but a few moments while she was over—she is from all I can learn, a friend of yours also—have you seen her since her return? do write me if there is any thing like an engagement existing between she & Mr M. [Marcus] Erwin—by the way, how is Mr Erwin getting on electionearing? I regret so much, that he & Cousin Woodfin are opponents although Mr Erwin was never a particular favorite of mine until I found that he was a friend of yours—I think that he ought to have been satisfied with a seat in the Commons, for a while at-any-rate—I must close, hopeing to hear soon both of your health & happiness. I was quite an invalid a day or two ago—but am pretty well at this time—I will expect to hear from you very soon, but dont be uneasy if you do not receive a letter from me for several weeks—Accept dearest the adieus of Your truly devoted

Harriett.

Asheville May 16th

My dearest Harriett,

    I do hope you have not been disappointed in failing to receive a letter from me by last mail, and if you were disappointed I hope again that it is not necessary for me to entreat you not to attribute it to any neglect in me. I know you can not entertain such an idea for a moment concerning your faithful and devoted Zebulon. I was prevented by a variety of circumstances from writing by Thursdays mail, and consequently have to wait for the next one which leaves to night.

    I feel quite unwell this morning, and you must forgive, therefore, all deficiences in this letter. I went yesterday morning up into the mountains to fish for trout, with several ladies and gentlemen—We were out all day in the broiling sun, climbing mountains &c, and this morning from the violence of the exorcise, the excitement of the day and the heat of the sun, I feel quite dull and feverish. I suppose I am being repaid to day in dejection and indisposition for the enjoyment of yesterday, for I dont reccollect when I have had a day of more pleasing excitement on the whole. We left the village soon after daylight and had a splendid morning ride of twelve miles into the mountains before the sun became oppressive. The fishing was fine, and the ladies the most amiable and pleasant that the country can produce. We got home just at dusk. You ask my Sweet One, if I would attend if invited to any of the parties given to Miss [Maria] Massey in Burke? I can not. You can imagine the pleasure it would afford me to do so, but I have business in Madison County just about that time which will require a weeks attention, and I could not possibly neglect it. I will deny myself the pleasure of seeing you then, and sustain myself with the hope of getting to meet with a still greater pleasure in seeing you in Rutherfordton. There I hope to enjoy a long private talk with you, which will be far more pleasant to me than all the parties in the world.

On last friday the poor wretch Mason,[15] who has been in our jail for some time, was executed. There was a vast concourse of people from all parts of the country here, estimated about 5,000, one third

---

15. David Mason was convicted of murdering his wife in Haywood County. James T. Weaver of Reems Creek was present at the hanging and wrote a detailed and grisly account of it in a letter to M. A. Gash dated July 18, 1852. John Preston Arthur, *Western North Carolina: A History (From 1730 to 1913)* (Asheville, N.C.: The Edward Buncombe Chapter of the Daughters of the American Revolution of Asheville, N.C., 1914), pp. 376, 377; Mary Gash and Family Papers, State Department of Archives and History, Raleigh, N.C.

of which at least was *women*! I followed the crowd out to the place of execution, heard the religious exorcises usual on such occasions, and then not being of such a tender heart as most of the women there, I left and came back to keep from seeing him hung. He died denying his crime. I suppose such details are not pleasant to you by any means and I therefore forbear. I will say however, my dear Harriet, that the mournful lesson was not lost upon me. I was filled with horror of the scene, and the many and unguarded effusions of the human passions which bring men, and especially young men, into the commission of deeds of rashness, arose strong and vivid in my mind. Grant me, Oh God, the power to feel thus in the hour of temptation and I am safe from the ebulitions of passion!

It is with regret that I inform you of Sisters continued ill-health. She suffers a great deal indeed, and there seems to be little prospect of an early resoration for her. Mother is quite well and requested me to thank you for the many expressions of regard toward her which you have uttered. We heard indirectly from Dr Neilson a few days since. He was well and was not expecting to be detained at Panama but four days. I am still doing pretty well in my studies, having to some extent severed the connexion which hitherto existed between myself and the regiment of loafers which infest the place. I have been busy for a day or two preparing for our next court in looking over the cases in which I will have to prosecute for the State. I am quite anxious as you may well imagine, to make a good impression upon my first attempt. I have so much depending on my success that I shall spare no possible pains to acquit myself with credit—I almost regret that I got into business before I obtained Superior Court License, as my limited knowledge of the practical proceeding in the courts which can only be learned by experiance, will I fear, be a drawback upon me. Has Jim McD— got home yet? if so, please let him come over as soon as possible. I should like to see him so much. Have you received the May No. of our University Magazine? I believe I told you that I have nothing in that number but a piece of poetry signed "Halcro'" You would recognize it anyhow I suppose, from the great sentimentality which pervades it. How do you get on reading 'IK Marvil'? I hope you are still pleased with this noblest hearted American author. And Harper, what of it? But I suppose you have not been reading much of late in consequence of the many other things pressing upon your attention. I will beg you my dearest One to forgive the brevity of this letter for the reason of my indisposition as before stated. I want to see you *very* much. I have a great many things to talk of, and things of importance to us. But I will wait. Hoping that you will write when it is possible, I remain as ever your devoted and faithful betrothed

        Zebulon.

       Quaker Meadows May 22nd 1852

My beloved Zebulon;

  I was made so extremely happy yesterday afternoon by the reception of your dear letter, that I cant allow the mail to return without expressing my great delight to you, who I know will appreciate my feelings—I had began to think it a long time since I received your last & it was quite a disappointment to me that I did not hear from you by last mail, but I knew you must have some *good* reason for not writing, you are always so punctual. I could not think for one moment that one so much loved by me, would neglect me, No! May such an idea ever be strange to her who does love, & will ever love, you devotedly. How sorry I was to learn from your letter that you were indisposed; I hope this fine, May morning, with all nature appearing so gay, finds you entirely recovered. I was also truly grieved to hear that your sister continued in such ill-health, I hope she will soon be restored. How much you must have enjoyed yourself with that fishing party that you speak of in your letter—amiable young ladies, I think, must add greatly to the gentlemens pleasure in such excursions.

  You can well imagine how disappointed I was to find that you could not attend any of the parties to be given to my friend Maria. We intend giving a small party the Wednesday after the wedding & I was very much in hopes that I would have the pleasure of welcoming you at the Quaker Meadows at that time—though of course, my dearest, I would not have you neglect more important things to gratify me—for I do assure you that (like yourself) I would find that a long private talk with you, would be far more pleasant that meeting you at all the parties. I cant name precisely the time, now that I will go down to Rutherfordton—but will in my next— Brother James is speaking of going to Charlotte with the Wedding party & I will not perhaps go as soon as I expected—as he was to go to Rutherfordton with me—Brother has been at home two weeks— he & I have been enjoying ourselves finely—he has been reading to me that charming book—"Reveries of a Bachelor." We were both perfectly enraptured with it—but I must say that I liked "Dream Life" equally as well; you may not think this good taste, as I believe all the gentlemen prefer the "Reveries", but it is nevertheless so—The last no of the University Magazine is first rate. Do you know the Lady correspondent who has written such a severe letter in that no? We will be pleased to see letters from her very frequently—& the gentleman who is defending the ladies; I must say, deserves the many thanks of the sex. "Harpers" I find quite as interesting as ever—I am much more pleased with "Dickens" last work[16] that is coming out in it, than I was with David Copperfield. The piece of poetry of yours in the University Magazine, I must say without flattering is beautiful—I have read it again & again, with increased interest, each time Although I have not read as much of late as usual—still I rarely pass a day without reading some—I am very fond of it & sometimes neglect other things in consequence. My sheet is almost filled & I must prepare for closeing: Brother desires his kind regards & says he expects to be in Asheville very soon.

I hope my dearest one, you will ever remember that your sincere Harriett as oft sends up a petition to a Merciful Father for you, as for her self—May you resist all temptation is my constant prayer—We had a very interesting meeting of Presbytery in our Village last week, that most excellant man Mr Streetz[17] was ordained—We had some fine ministers with us.

 I hope to receive an immediate reply to this—I will write again as soon as possible—you have promised you remember not to wait for replys to all of your letters—. Adieu My dearest one, & believe me as ever Your own devoted Harriett.

            Asheville. May 24

My dear Harriet—

 I take my pen again this evening to commune with you as both my duty and my feelings urge me to do. I was not expecting to get a letter from you last mail, as under existing circumstances I knew you could not write, and yet you can scarcely imagine my disappointment in not getting one. It seemed so long since I had

16. *Bleak House.*
17. The Reverend William C. Sheetz came from a pastorate in Winchester, Virginia, to the Morganton Presbyterian Church. Avery, *Presbyterian Churches,* p. 34.

heard from you, that I thought there certainly *must be* one for me. With this idea I hurried to my box, drew it out, and found—nothing! An individual standing by could have thought from the length of my wobegone countenance that I had just got news of the loss of all my interest in the California mines or something of worse nature. With long, deep drawn sighs, I returned to my room and sat down to meditate upon the glorious light of the future whose "jeweled lamps" alone can give any light to the present gloom which shrouds me and mine. Dont think my Sweet One, that I am growing melancholly and discontented. Indeed I am not. I only feel bad and impatient when I think of the hard lot I have to endure in waiting so long for that happiness which should now be mine. Life is so short and we pass away so soon, that I wish to spend its flying moments as pleasantly as possible. And then to think that the prime of my life, which I wish to devote to your service, to labor and toil for your happiness, is gliding along imperceptibly over my books, indifferent friends and youthful follies! Oh it grieves to think of it! But this is all folly, puerile folly, and I know you will pronounce it such. I have pronounced it such myself in all the *patient* and *dignified* epistles I used to indite about the value of time, the great things I had to accomplish and all that. But dont censure me too severely, my own generous Harriet, for my ardent impatience. I strive against it, and philosophise on the subject with all my might, but it is oftentimes too hard for my fortitude. I am completely overcome at times. But let it go.———

I have been troubled somewhat of late by hearing a great deal of that old tale in regard to Miss [Sara] G—— [Garrett]. My friend Mr Erwin on his return from Burke a few days ago told me he heard a great talk about it in the Morganton circles and that the ladies entertained a very bad opinion of me over there. Of course they have heard the tale in the same distorted manner in which it first got to you and he said it was quite a common topic. I made him acquainted with the true circumstances & he promised to defend me from future attacks in his presence. I regret this exceedingly. You can not imagine the mortification I feel. People seem always so unwilling to stop talking of a bad report and are ever so eager to credit one that I shall never be able I am afraid to get the matter set right. Miss G. is also extremely mortified about it, and nothing but the delicasy of her situation as one of the parties prevents her, she said, from taking trouble to put things right. Again, what gives me the greatest pain, they have your name mixed up with it and seem inclined to reflect upon you for having anything to do with me. Do they ever talk to you about it? You told me when you first heard of it, that you knew the persons who told you did not do so to injure me with you and I was disposed to think so too, but I have found out of late that the originators of the report were instigated by deep hatred and malice against me. I have this on the best authority and there is no mistake about it. I will defer the statement of it for you when we meet. I am not fearful of being lowered in your estimation by any further agitation of the matter, but dislike exceedingly for the community to reflect upon me in this way. In the meantime, let it go.

We had news last mail from our friends in Calafornia. A hurried letter from Dr Neilson informed us of his safe arrival in San Francisco on the 10th of May, it being only 24 days from Havana to that place: a very speedy trip. He and his company were in excellent, health, and he had been lucky in getting a cheap passage from the Isthmus. He was just about stepping aboard the steam boat for Sacramento City when he wrote. He did not mention Sam McDowell or any body else but members of his own company. A short letter was received also from Dr Jo McDowell[18] dated from the same place which mentioned nothing of Sam either. Probably Dr Neilson & Company being aboard an excellent steamer, passed him and got in before him. I hope they are all at work by this time.

Sister Laura is still very dangerously ill and we have almost given up the hope of anything like a permanent recovery. Indeed she is as you said, a great sufferer. I am so anxious to hear from you! and still more so to see. How long will you stay in R—— [Rutherfordton]? I shall have to start in a week or two to the western courts and shall be gone some time. will you stay in R—— untill I get back? If you dont, I will go to Morganton as soon as I get back for I cant wait 'till August: *thats impossible*. As I have a little business to attend to in the west I should not like to fail going there. You know it behooves me to do every thing I can in the way of my business.

Jim McDowell is at home, I hear. Do send him over. I want to see him very bad. I have a great chance more which I would like to write but will have to defer it. Do, my dearest Harriet, seize the first leisure moment and write to me. I hope to hear of your health

18. Dr. Joseph Alburton McDowell practiced medicine in Asheville. He was a son of Mrs. Charles McDowell's brother James. Tennent, "Medicine in Buncombe County," p. 20; John McHugh McDowell, *The McDowells, Erwins, Irwins and Connections* (Memphis, Tenn.: C. B. Johnson & Co., 1918), p. 262.

and happiness, and that you have had an infinite degree of enjoyment during the wedding festivities. Amidst them all, think of him who is your constant, faithful and deeply devoted Zebulon.

Quaker Meadows June 4th 1852

My beloved Zebulon:

About one week ago I received your last communication saying that you had not received a letter from me for so long—I certainly wrote to you the mail before you wrote me this letter & cant imagin why it was that you had not received it, I hope it has come to hand by this time—I have been so much engaged since my good friend Marias wedding, attending her bridal parties that I have not, until now, had time to write letters—not even to you Dearest & I am now compelled to trespass upon the time that I should be enjoying sweet sleep—for I have been dissipating so much of late that I am quite willing to retire at an early hour, for a short time at-any-rate—you say, you hope I have had a great deal of enjoyment; I can assure you that I never passed a more delightful week, than last in my life—I met a great many of my friends from a distance & formed some charming acquaintances both ladies & gentlemen—the young man with whom, I waited, was certainly a noble fellow—perhaps you know him from reputation—he is a lawyer from Charlotte—Mr Hutchison[19] an old College Mate of my dear absent brother Samuel, which made him decidedly more interesting to me—but amidst all my enjoyment dearest, you were in most of my thoughts—how often I wished for you to share with me these pleasures—I expect if you had been among us you would have met with such facinating ladies, that I would often, yea very often have been forgotten—I know you will consider this unkind in me—but you must excuse it, for some of the ladies were certainly beautiful with all the other recomendations & you know such characters are irresistible. I guess you will be quite surprised to learn from this letter that I have concluded to accompany a party from Burke to Charlotte next week—Mr & Mrs [Victor] Barringer are going down & we all have received very pressing invitations from their friends to accompany them, so most of the attendants from Burke togather with others have concluded to go down

---

19. James Marion Hutchison graduated from Davidson College in 1850. Samuel M. McDowell enrolled there in 1844 but did not graduate. *Davidson Alumni Catalogue*, pp. 56, 57.

—& I cant resist so much enjoyment as I know we will all have—how delighted I would be to have you go along, we are very scarce of gentlemen—& I can assure you that the whole company but particularly your much attached Harriett would be pleased to have you make one of the company, there were ten or fifteen gentlemen up from Charlotte & I think there will only be three going down—I wish so much I could see you before I leave—We dont go until next Wednesday & the company will return to Morganton in about 9 or 10 days Brother & I will probably return by Rutherfordton & I will remain there some time with cousin [Mary, Mrs. John Gray Bynum], so if I cant see you before going down I will certainly expect to meet you there immediately after my arrival & if I should conclude to return home I will expect to see you soon, as you say in your last letter that you will certainly come to see me after your return from the western courts. Do come before August if you possible can. I will write to you if I conclude not to go to Rutherfordton. I expect now to go & will perhaps go from there over to Asheville to make a short visit—I hope you will not allow that report concearning yourself & Miss Garret to disturb you any longer, I think your friend Mr Erwin is entirely mistaken in regard to its being a general topic in the Morganton circles—I have not heard of it recently at all & I have inquired of a friend of yours if he has heard it generally talked of & he says not & I know he would know—it does not disturb me in the least—if they do cast reflections upon me —I am not governed by the opinions of others, particularly in matters of that kind—I hope you are mistaken about its being told to me, to injure you—I cant think but that the persons were friends of yours—but if they are not, I do sincerely beg you not to let it vex you with them—for they have not succeeded I can assure you. I wish I had time to write you as much more, but I have not & will have to close my very hastily written letter. Brother James desires to be remembered to you & says you will not see him at Asheville probably before July—he has been expecting a letter from you ever since his arrival at home.

I hope Mrs Neilsons health is better, I was delighted to hear that she had received such pleasing intelligence from the Dr—how much I wish we could hear of our dear friends—we are becoming quite impatient to hear of their arrival. Do write to me by the return mail—if you do not, it will be so long before I receive a letter from you—I am anticipating a great deal of enjoyment during my visit to Charlotte, but my pleasure will be greatly marred at the thought of your absence. Mollie Jo is going down with us & she wishes cousin Zeb would go—she rarely ever sees me without inquiring about you & always sends you her love & I neglect to deliver it, so you must accept it this time & write her some message in return—for she very often asks me if you never mention her—Cousin William[20] is not living in the Village & I see a great deal more of Mollie than I did—& the more I know of her the more I love her—I really will be compelled to close now, as my sheet is entirely filled—I would like so much to give you a full history of all our enjoyments, but I have not time, so I will have to defer it until we meet which I hope will be very soon—Do write to me before I leave—May God guard & guide thee dearest is the sincere prayer of your very affectionate Harriett

P. S. Please excuse great hast—

Asheville, June 23d [1852]

My dearest Hattie;

What will you think of my long silence? I am afraid indeed, that you are displeased with me; but wait untill I "define my position" which is easily done, and then you will forgive me. I assure you that I feel more concerned at having suffered you to go so long without a letter than you can feel at having not received one.

I left a few days after I last wrote to you, for Cherokee Court, intending to write to you from there, or from Macon. I had ordered my letters to be forwarded to me at Franklin—When I got to Franklin I found your last there, as I expected, in which you informed me your intention to go to Charlotte. From that place you said you were undetermined where to go: whether back home or to Rutherfordton. How then could I write, not knowing where you would be? You promised to inform me of your whereabouts, and with that expectation I have waited untill I have got out of patience. The arrival of the Rutherfordton mail last night without a letter from you determined me to write to Morganton, thinking it the more likely to find you there than at R—— I had to hurry home from the Western Courts earlier than I expected on account

20. The farm to which Dr. William C. Tate had recently moved was land originally settled by ZBV's great grandfather Robert Brank. It was only a mile from the house at Quaker Meadows. "The Vance Family of Virginia, Pennsylvania, North Carolina and Kentucky," compiled by Elizabeth Williamson Dixon, North Carolina D.A.R. genealogical records chairman, 1958, p. 230 (hereafter cited as Dixon, "Vance-Brank Families").

of Sisters health growing worse. When I got home, I found her very low indeed but the next day she took a start to improve and has been slowly improving ever since. She sat up a little to day, & seems much better. I hope it may be a permanent change, which is now giving us all so much hope.

All these things together will constitute I trust, a sufficient excuse for my delay in writing. You will reccolect I did not get your letter requesting an immediate answer untill you had started for Charlotte.

I got home on Thursday evening last. The particulars of my first trip on the circuit as an "Attorney & Councellor at Law", I do not suppose would be particularly interesting to you. At any rate I believe I will put off relating them untill I see you, which certainly will not, and certainly *shall not* be long. Suffice it to say, that as regards my success, as I did not expect much, I realized the blessing pronounced upon all such moderate spirits, for I was not disappointed. I made some Ciceronian displays, and also many acquaintances with some few *friends*, which is better—My own Court begins on the 5th of July, and after that is over, I shall be at your service for some time. That is to say, I will be with you some time, whether of service to you or not—

I have a world of things to talk about, as it has been so long since I wrote to you, but I am doubtful about this letter reaching you soon and therefore I shall defer it untill I am certain of your location.

With this slight sketch of matters and things, forming quite a poor apology for a letter, I shall for the present conclude. I must not however omit to state, how sincere my sympathy is for you in common with the numerous friends and relatives of Mr Sam McDowell, in not having as yet heard from him.

Please accept, once again, my noblest Harriet, the oft repeated assurances of the devoted and undying affection of your

Sincere Zebulon

Letter of HNE missing.

Asheville June 29 '52

My Noblest Harriet—

I recd yours by last mail and was much surprised to learn by it that you had not recd my last. I noticed however that yours was written some several days before it was mailed and think therefore you must have received mine before yours left Morganton—I certainly wrote to you by last wednesdays mail, one week ago.

Well I was truly rejoiced to hear from you again—in health and happiness. You say you enjoyed your trip to Charlotte so very much and made so many charming acquaintances that you were perfectly delighted all the time of your absence. Now you may rest assured, my dear Harriet, that I am always pleased to hear of your happiness and can only regret that I am so little able to render you always so—But as I have so often said it shall ever be the grand object of my love and exertions to promote your happiness by all the means within my power. I hope that my letter, which I presume you have recd before this, has removed all grounds of complaint against me for not writing sooner. You said you were strongly tempted to censure me for neglect on finding no letter from me awaiting your return. I hope you have forgiven and excused me before now, as you must know, my sweetest Harriet, that it is utterly and morally impossible for me to *neglect* that being whom I love even to the verge of distraction. Dont use that word to me any more; it implies too much coldness and indifferance to apply with any suitableness to a creature so warm hearted and faithful as I know myself to be.

You said during your trip to Charlotte, as everyone seemed to be aware that you were engaged it was your privelige to do as much flirting as you liked. My dear Harriet, are you fond of flirting? I hope not, at least to any great extent. Since Miss Marias wedding some of my friends have been trying, as I supposed, to make me uneasy by telling me a good many stories about you, which of course I treated as the idle winds—I have so much implicit confidence in you, and also such a perfect and thorough contempt for the gossiping stories of idle brains and the thousand little petty jealousies which affect most folks that I scorn to let such things ever trouble me in the least. I leave you to be the judge of your own conduct, not doubting but that you are fully competent to the task, and will only say here since you seemed to fear in your last letter that I might think you had erred, that if you *have* done anything wrong I readily forgive you, only hoping the like forgiveness will be extended freely to your own devoted, but frail and erring

Zebulon. I know of nothing to forgive you for—alas, it seems that it is your charity which will always be extended toward me! I seldom quote scripture, but I recollect a passage which says, "Bear ye each others burdens, and thus fulfill the law of Christ"—

You beg me to say when I can visit you. I can't go to see you untill after Yancey Court. My own court is here next week, the week after at Yancey and I have been making my arrangements to return home from Yancey through Burke. But you say you expect to visit Asheville on the first of July—If you come to Asheville then of course I will not go to Burke—If you do not come, I shall go right on from Yancey court—Do come to Asheville if you can. My visits to Morganton must always be so few and hasty that it deprives me of half the pleasure of seeing you—At any rate write soon and let me know what you will do, so that I may not miss you when I go to Burke. Now for my sweet Cousin, Mary Jo—Do express my thanks to her for the many kind messages I have got from her by you and give her all of my love that you can spare her. You know that you have all the love of my heart and I have nothing left for my friends but esteem. If you will divide with Cousin Mollie I am willing. Be generous and more careful in future in sending me her messages lest she might think me careless about them. I dont believe you send half of them. Remember me also, to James McDowell and tell him his friends over here are quite anxious to see him. We hear frequently from Dr Neilson and his company in California—They are mining in the nothern mines I believe and doing a very fair business—I wrote to him the other day at the request of Mrs Eliza Woodfin and Mira Woodfin to get him to make inquiries about Sam, which I am sure he will do with pleasure—

My dear Harriet, I am again approaching the close of a letter to you and it makes me feel almost as sorrowful as if I were leaving you in person. I do want to see you so bad! And I am getting every day so very impatient to call you mine forever, that it realy seems as if I were consuming with the fire of impatience. As usual I have filled my letter with my heartfelt expressions of love and tenderness, leaving out several items of news which might have interested you more. But forgive me and believe me when I say that I am now and ever will be what I profess to be—your own eternaly true and devout

Zebulon

It is with pleasure that I state Mrs Neilson's health is much better. Indeed I think she will soon be able to get about again. Mother's health is also good. Mr. James McKee[21] got home last evening from down the country, bringing his wife with him. I attended a party given him last night at Mr M— Pattons[22] and have just received an invitation to attend another to night at Mr J M Smiths,[23] to him also—Again on next Tuesday at the Eagle Hotel the M[illegible] (your especial friends, I believe) give a large party, to which I am invited. So you see our village is getting to be a gay place again as well as Morganton. I had forgotten to ask you if you were reading any now a days? I suppose not much however. Have you got the last number of Harpers? I will take the greatest pleasure in procuring for you any books which you may want to read. But I will close lest my P. S. be longer than my letter.

Zeb—

Quaker Meadows July 6th 1852

My beloved Zebulon—

I received your last letter a few days ago & a few days before its reception I received the one, which you say, you hope has removed all grounds of complaint against you for not writing sooner—. My dear, did I say in my letter to you, that I thought you had neglected me? No I did not, I expressly said that I considered myself the cause of your silence—I have too much confidence in you, to suppose for a moment, that you would neglect me—I only wrote, in the manner that I did, to show you what a great privation it was for me to pass a week without hearing from you—the privation of not seeing you as often as every week, is great

21. James L. McKee, son of James McKee, long-time sheriff of Haywood County who moved to Asheville before his death. According to Foster Alexander Sondley, "James S. McKee" was appointed postmaster in Asheville, February 15, 1849. *Census* of Buncombe County, 1850; Colonel A. T. Davidson, "Reminiscences of Western North Carolina," *The Lyceum*, 1, no. 8 (January, 1891): 5; Foster Alexander Sondley, *A History of Buncombe Co., North Carolina*, 2 vols. (Asheville, N.C.: The Advocate Printing Co., 1930), 2: 800.

22. Montreville Patton, successful merchant, land owner, and politician of Asheville. Sondley, *History of Buncombe Co.*, 2: 757.

23. James McConnell Smith, known as the "first white child born in North Carolina west of the Blue Ridge." Smith owned and operated the Buck Hotel in Asheville as well as a thriving mercantile establishment. Ibid., 2: 747, 748.

enough without being added to by not hearing—Never, dearest allow yourself to think that I fear being neglected by you—I am fully convinsed that such will never be the case & as for my neglecting you—it is out of the question. I intended writing to you by last mail, but about that time I expected to leave this morning for Asheville, & I thought my arrival would be an agreeable supprise to you—so I concluded not to write; & afterwards, also abandoned the idea of visiting Cousins this summer—Sister & Sallie both declined going & then I had to give up my trip as I couldent think of going over in the stage—knowing how ready the world is to censure. Brother's leaving this morning was very unexpected to me—I only knew a short time before he left th[at] he was going or I would have written by him; he expects to remain in your Village but a short time—cant you return home with him? if not, I will certainly expect you the last of next week—Saturday at fartherest— do dont break the Sabbath—I presume you are aware of my great aversion to traveling on that holy day. Besides the great happiness of meeting me when you come over— (I judge you in this case by myself) it will be pleasant, I have no doubt, for you to meet your friends the Misses Morehead who are now on a visit to Mrs Avery[24] —Mr John Morehead who I presume is also an acquaintance of yours, is now on a visit to Morganton—I flatter myself, dearest that meeting them would be the least part of your enjoyment. I am looking forward to your arrival with all my powers of fore enjoyment, for I am always happiest—when you are with me—Oh! that I could have you oftener with me, & if I could be with you always, I think I should always be happy—though I am rarely any other way, even as it is—my very great number of sins, my own dearest one is all, th[ere] is to cause me to be unhappy—you say my beloved one that you know of nothing in me that requires your forgiveness —I hope you may always be of that opinion—I have many faults that you know not of—do you think that flirting is one of them? I hope not—I think, to deceive a young man, is a great sin & I trust that I would not be guilty of sinning wilfully—I guess you are aware, that I have been considered a flirt—I will leave you to judge

24. Mrs. William Waightstill Avery, the former Mary Corinna Morehead of Greensboro, a daughter of John Motley Morehead, Whig governor of North Carolina, 1841-45. The "Misses Morehead" were her sisters, probably Marie Louise and Emma Victoria. Her brother, John Lindsay Morehead, had been at the University of North Carolina with ZBV. John Motley Morehead III, *The Morehead Family of North Carolina and Virginia* (New York: privately printed, 1921), p. 59; D. L. Grant, *Alumni History of the University of North Carolina* (Durham, N.C.: The General Alumni Association of U.N.C., 1924), p. 441.

for yourself of my character, as regards that—I have not seen Mollie Jo to deliver your messages—but hope to soon, as she thinks of visiting me this week—I will in future be more careful about delivering her messages as you appear to think I dont deliver half of them. Dr Lester was over last week & it is thought by some that he will succeed in wining my fair friend, Miss Ann—I hope so at any-rate;—have you been giving him any advice recently concearning a second appeal? I did not see the Dr at all when he was over; I think he was here only a day or two & of course he couldent leave Miss Ann any during so short a time. Mr McKee passed through our Village last week on his way home, with his wife—I did not see them, but understand he has quite an interesting, accomplished wife—do write me what you think of her—are you & Mr McKee any better friends than you were, when I saw you last? his wife has a sister & several female acquaintances with her, I believe who will, I have no doubt, captivate some more of the Asheville gentlemen—Mrs McKee, I imagine, will be quite an addition to your society; I hope you will find the young ladies who accompanied them up, very agreeable, for to meet with intelligent & interesting young ladies must contribute greatly to a young mans enjoyment, & I am anxious my dear one, that your days of single blessedness should be passed in happiness, as your after life, which I intend to do in all my power to make pleasant; but my own one let us remember that our Tem[p]oral happiness is not all that we should seek—this life passes away, but eternity is unending.

I suppose you are quite busy this week, as it is your Court—I have no doubt but that you will acquit yourself with great credit—do dont allow your time to be so much occupied as not to answer this letter next mail, if it is only to say you are well & enjoying yourself. Do you think you will be detained all the week in Yancey? I hope not—do dont make your visit to me too short—it has been so long since you were here, you ought to remain some time when you come. I know you will make your visit as long as possible.

    I was truly delighted to learn that your Sister's health was improving—I do sincerely trust that she will soon be entirely restored—I am glad she has been so fortunate as to hear so frequently from the Dr; Dear Brother Sam; it appears such a length of time since we heard of him & as for hearing from him, it really appears that we never will again—but we should not despare. I hope all fears with regard to the company are needless & that they have arrived safely; it is truly gratifying to see with what christian fortitude My dear Aunt bears the suspense. Well really I must close my epistle; I could fill several more pages with something similar to what I have written, but we have visitors & I cant occupy any more of the evening in writing. You seam to think it likely that I have not been reading much of late—I have not been reading a great deal, until the last week or two; I am now very much interested in a book by John S. Maxwell. The Czar, his Court & people: including a tour in Norway & Sweden.[25] I have received the last number of Harpers & find it as usual, quite entertaining. Do recomend something to me to read & if I can procure it I will take great pleasure in peruseing it. If you have anything that is good, bring it over when you come. I really shall have to close now. I will expect a reply to this immediately. And now My dearest one, Adieu for a while. Let me assure you again of the unchanging love of your truly devoted

Harriett

ZBV visited HNE in July, 1852.

Asheville, 21st of July—'52

My ever dear Harriet,

What shall I say to you this morning? I can not express the fulness of my feelings this morning as I wish: It is impossible! "What more can I say than to you I have said"—Oh I could say much, much more if I could find utterance: I could never cease to talk with you and of you if language did not fail me. In accordance with your request I sit down this morning, immediately after my arrival, to write you a *"long, long letter"*, but am at a loss how to do it—perhaps though as I get on a page or so, my thoughts and utterances may flow more freely and I shall find something to say which may please you—Please therefore excuse the disconnected manner in which these phrases may be thrown together, and attribute it all to the intensity of my feelings, for I assure you it is with great difficulty that I can write at all at present—

Well, well, I cam on home without any incident occurring to me of note. I met the Buncombe delegates at Carsons; staid all

---

25. John S. Maxwell, *The Czar, His Court and People, Including a Tour in Norway and Sweden* (New York: Baker and Scribner, 1848).

night with them there and resisted all their earnest entreaties to go back to M—— [Morganton] with them. I thought of what you said about my turning back on their account when you was unable to prevail on me to stay—I met Mr Woodfin next morning. He said he supposed *my* convention had met and adjourned already. I told him yes, to meet again on the first day of September or about that time. On arriving at home I found Sister so much improved as to be out on a visit. If I had known that, I certainly would have staid with you untill after the convention—We entertain sanguine hopes of her permanent recovery now—I am going to spend the next week in driving her about the country—I delivered your message to both her and Mother and they desire me to return you their sincere regards, &c. No news from Dr. N. of late. As Mrs N. W. Woodfin is in Henderson, I delivered Mrs McDowells letter to Mrs J. W—which I suppose will answer—

And now my idolized Harriet, that I am once more back at home, I would if it were possible, express to you the satisfaction I experianced during this my first real visit to you—But I can not—I can only say that it was the most delightful period of my existence. I felt and knew more joy while sitting by your side, than I thought man could ever possibly prove in this world! I have often told you that my love could not be any greater; I thought it had long ago attained the maximum point, but I found that the longer I lingered by you the deeper and stronger, and more overwhelming my love became, untill it seemed that if you were taken from me, I would cease to exist as suddenly as if my heart were torn from my breast and laid at my feet! The earth without a sun or night without a star, would not be half so dark and cheerless as my existence without you! True, how true it is! "I would not live without thee, for all this world contains". Do not think me extravagant or using the language of gallantry; you know Harriet I am above that, and especialy since you have forbidden me to use it to you. I speak only the words dictated by an almost bursting heart, so full of the one all-absorbing idea, that it scarcely contains room for any other common emotion of nature—The manner in which you received me, your generous and noble devotedness in proposing to share and lessen my humble fortunes and struggles through all the journeyings of life—your looks and smiles, all sank deep into my soul and took possession of its most secret thought—How could it be otherwise Harriet? Who could resist the many and unmistakeable evidences of a life-long devotion which you blessed me with? The generous and confiding trust, which can only spring from a pure and disinterested love, that induced you to tell me that you would believe everything I should tell you, and your faith in my love told you not to fear of my deceiving? May this tongue perish and be forever silenced, if it ever deliberately and wilfully tells you a falsehood! O! Harriet, your confiding love unnerved me when you uttered that holy sentiment! I trembled to think that I, sinfull and unworthy, was the frail pillar against which so much purity leaned for support! Oh: that I was for your sake, as firm and upright as the imperishable rocks of our own eternal granite hills! But trust me still, trust me ever Harriet. The lofty pine is bent almost to the earth by the might of the tempest, but the elasticity which nature has given its trunk enables it to gain the greater power, the stronger is the pressure; and it finally rebounds back to its former strength and pride. It may be thus with me—The more I feel the weight of the obligation which your confidence imposes upon me, the more will I exert my every faculty to stand firm under it, and if for a moment I should give way to the vast weight we will both pray to God for strength to regain the position I held when first you leaned against me for support—Yes Harriet, I labour in future only for you—My holiest ambition is now to convince you, that though you may have placed your happiness in the keeping of one who *could* not preserve it, yet that it is not with one *would* not if in his power—I know you feel assured of that now, else you would not have trusted me, but I am eager to convince by actions, so that you may *know* as well as *believe*. How I long for that time to come!

    I believe I have come to the conclusion not to go to Raleigh this winter for license. I will explain to you my reasons when I next see you and I hope you will approve them. I think I shall wait a year longer and get them in Morganton[26] in August. This will not interfere however in the least with our getting married before that time if you give your consent and as I told you before, I *think you will*. In reference to that matter however, I can say that my love outruns my discretion in wishing to get married before next July. Because, I can not deny the fact that I can not be prepared before that time. I will be badly prepared even then, but I am determined not to think of waiting till I am well prepared; that's out of the question; I might never be *well* prepared—But if I can make any arrangement which would enable me to marry before next July, I will go right after you and will take no denial—I dont think you will have the heart to refuse me. Will you? No,

---

26. The August term of the state Supreme Court was held in Morganton from 1847 to 1861. Historical marker of the Burke County Courthouse.

no, you wont—There are a great many things which I wish to talk to you about when next we meet—I did not feel like talking about them when I was with you. I have been talking with Dr Lester since I got home and it is agreed that he and I shall go over together about the 1st of September; I think things are all correct with the Dr and Miss Ann, judging from his talk. I will have to close this letter, although I have a great chance more to say; in truth my Hattie, you know I never get out of talk for you except when I am sitting with you, and then I could do nothing but exorcise my "privilige"—Do write to me as soon as you promised and believe me now as ever your still faithful and devoted

Zebulon—

Quaker Meadows July 27th 1852

My beloved Zebulon:

The letter that I received the Mail after you arrived at home, I can truly say met with a warm reception—& if I had treated you so kindly as you always do me I would have replyed to it by last Mail—but you must remember that I told you that I did not think that you would receive my epistles as frequently in future as you have during the past—I will though write you very often & expect your letters more frequently than ever. I was pleased to learn that you arrived safely & found your sister so much improved—how much I wish you had known of her improvement before you left— I would have then enjoyed the convention much more than I did, as your presence always adds greatly to my enjoyment—I was very much in hopes that the Buncombe delegates could prevail upon you to return—the ladies attended the convention & I assure you we enjoyed it—if you had only remained, you would have had the pleasure of seeing the many facinating Burke ladies—& besides, dearest your own Harriet would have been happyer.

I thought of you constantly the day you left & indeed ever since you did leave—Oh dearest what a great privation it is to me not to be more with you—these long separations are truly disagreeable— September appears a long time off—but I hope it will be spent both pleasantly & profitably by us both & if so you know it will pass *too rapidly*.—You seamed to have enjoyed your last visit so much, that I can but hope your next one will be enjoyed; you could not have spent those few days that you were with me more agreeably than I did—that is impossible—for they certainly are numbered among my happiest days. In your letter you say that you have many things to talk with me about that you did not feel like talking of when you were with me last—you really have excited my curiosity & I think you might satisfy it, by writing what these things are. I suppose Annie Happoldt & I may certainly expect you & the Dr the first of September—I am truly glad to hear that the Dr is going to succeed in wining one of the Burke jewels—I dont know how he & Ann will agree on religious matters—the Bishop[27] was in Morganton a few days ago & Ann & Dorcus were confirmed, I suppose that will not be an objection with the Dr.

Brother has just come and says he is waiting to mail my letter, so I will have to close in great haste, & with a miserable pen. We were all made extremely happy a few days ago at the reception of a letter from brother Samuel—I guess you have also heard from him as Cousins received letters—so I will write nothing more about him. Do dearest one remember & observe the advice I gave you when you were over. I wish I could write you a long letter & give you more advice, but I can not now—I will write soon again—I will certainly expect to hear from you soon. Do excuse this very short & miserably written letter—Brother keeps at me to make haste—My love to your Mother & sisters—May God bless you dearest is the sincere prayer of your own devoted

Harriett

Asheville, 30th July '52

My dearest Harriet,

I could not answer your last by the return mail as it starts back immediately, and in fact I dont expect you wished or looked for a reply that early, and therefore I am compelled to wait untill Mondays mail before I can get an answer to you. You see this is friday evening, two or three days before the mail leaves again, and I should not write this evening, but I cant help it—I cant study in peace while thinking that I have a letter to write to Hattie; had I not better do it now? Wont something happen to prevent

---

27. Levi Silliman Ives, second Episcopal bishop of the Diocese of North Carolina, 1831-53. In 1853 Ives renounced the communion of his church and became a Roman Catholic. Hugh Talmage Lefler and Albert Ray Newsome, *North Carolina: The History of a Southern State* (Chapel Hill, N.C.: The University of North Carolina Press, 1954), p. 392.

me from writing by the next mail? Such consideration induces me to sit down and write now—besides Harriet you know that I am never so happy as when I am either with you or conversing with you upon paper, and therefore I never fail to rejoice when it becomes my task to sit down, uninterrupted, to write you a long letter, full of the gushing affection of my heart—I seldom have anything but the "old theme" to write about, the same old tune, not even set to new music, my love, my love for you; but I never get tired of telling it and I must believe as well as hope, that you will not tire of listening to it—If you ever should, I must stop writing, for I cant find anything else to say to *you*.

I am somewhat more calm at present than when I wrote last. I was then not far from being crazy—my blood was considerably above fever heat—near to the boiling point. A little sober sense however soon came to my aid, and I mixed up a cold, dry solution of Selwins *Nisi Prius*, Starkis on Evidence, &c, into which I plunged head and ears—This prescription had the desired effect and I was soon in the land of stern, unromantic reality again. I went to work and take pleasure in informing you that I have studied very well for the last week. I think in future I have only one thing in the way of studying hard, and you can guess what (or rather "who") that is. When not thinking of you I can study pretty well. To night I am invited to a dance at the "Eagle";[28] I am going for the purpose of getting to see Miss Clara Patton. I have not gone to visit her since my return and am anxious to see her only because you seem to desire that I should cultivate her acquaintance. Be assured that I shall obey you in all things so pleasant as visiting Miss Clara. I am not much inclined to visit, *of late* among the ladies and to make a frank confession there are but few in this place for whom—but no I shant say, it would not be polite perhaps—I go to see Miss Towns our amiable (Presbyterian) music teacher, who grows upon my esteem every day—Miss Clara however, has had company, some relations from a distance perhaps, all week and I did not feel inclined to go to see her under those circumstances—Mrs's N. W. & J. W. Woodfin are out there to day—I have been teazed almost to death since I got back from Burke—The young and the old of all sexes, "ages and conditions" seem to take an especial pleasure in plaguing me. I set out with the determination to bear it all with good humour, but I tell you a martyr could'nt stand it much longer:

28. The Eagle Hotel was owned by one of Asheville's leading merchants and most influential citizens, James W. Patton. Sondley, *History of Buncombe Co.*, 2: 771-72.

my philosophy is fast waxing "small by degrees and beautifully less"—There is however only *one* way to put a stop to it and you and I have discussed more than once the propriety of putting that into effect—You will doubtless remember what it is, and that you are opposed to stopping these annoying reports *before next summer*—Well, Well,

"Faithful through every change of wo,
My heart still flies to meet thee there"—that is,

some where next summer.

We all participate in your joy at hearing from the California friends; we had letters also from Dr Neilson and his company at the same time—The Drs letters gave me a very severe attack of the California Fever. Indeed I scarcely slept any for a night or two in consequence. If I were there, O how I could labour to get wealth for you! But I could not think of leaving you behind and of course you would not want to go, and so I trying to quit thinking of it altogether. Excuse me Harriet, if the thought of obtaining gold led me astray even for the moment. To a poor young man like me, it is a great temptation indeed, but there is still a *greater* one for me to stay at home—

You say you want me to gratify your curiosity by telling you what it is that I had to talk to you about. I am sorry that I excited any curiosity in you for I assure you I have nothing of any importance to tell. I believe I only thought of talking some more upon my future prospects and getting ready to get married. In other words, I want to talk to you plainly, the next time we meet, as to how we are to get along in this world after we get married. I really get very much distressed when I think of our approaching union, and my poverty. I can not help feeling so, notwithstanding your earnest wishes to the contrary—But "hope springs eternal in the human breast", and I hope on hope ever. Since I commenced writing this letter I have been to that dance I spoke of at the Eagle Hotel where I had the pleasure of seeing and conversing with Miss Clara considerably. I obtained an introduction then to Miss Muff McEntire[29] from Rutherfordton, one of Jim McDowells "old flames"—I called upon them at home yesterday evening again, so you see that I am fulfilling your behests rapidly—I saw also Miss

---

29. Martha McEntire was a daughter of Dr. John McEntire, successful physician and prominent citizen of Rutherfordton. *Census* of Rutherford County, 1850; Clarence W. Griffin, *History of Old Tryon and Rutherford Counties, North Carolina, 1730-1936* (Asheville, N.C.: The Miller Printing Co., 1937), p. 191.

Mary Ann William's brother, but nothing of Miss Mary Ann[30] herself as she has not yet got here.

We had a considerable party among the juvenile portion of the villagers on Friday night given by the cadets of Temperance. I did not attend it, but understand that it was "some". I think I will go to Yancey very soon after the election, as I am anxious to get the favour of the good folks over there. Since I got home I have had the auspicious luck (?) of getting two suits entrusted to my management in the next county court. Huzza for me: "Large streams from little fountains flow" &c, and may not this be the beginning of great streams of practice?

I bought a lot the other day at public sale but dont like my bargain and as a gentleman offers to take it off my hands at the same price, I think I shall let him have it—It was Lochers lot on the hill between Edneys and Atkins—It is a beautiful place with a little house upon it, but there can be no water obtained on it—How would you like it?

Dont you think you could get over to Asheville about the time the Methodist Conference will be holden here? I would suppose some of the Burke folks would come then, and could you not come with propriety? But I'll talk of that when the Dr (Lester) and I go over, to Morganton. Tell Cousin Mary Jo something for me will you—How is Mrs McKessons's health? Sister has been improving all the time untill yesterday; she was quite unwell then and is to day, but not seriously I hope—I almost forgot to tell you something with which to teaze Miss Ann Happoldt. When I lifted your last letter from the P. O. I saw Dr Lester get one also from M—— backed in a delicate female hand, containing some six or eight pages—I suppose of course it was from Miss Ann but the Dr would not say—He seems in such fine spirits and talks so pleasantly about it, that I am inclined to think he will succeed—That letter must have contained something good, for of course it would not take a lady six or eight pages to reject a gentleman. If you recollect you disposed of me once in a few lines—The long letters never come untill after the engagement—

Of course you will not let her know how you got word of that long epistle—My dear, sweet, Hattie I shall have to bid you adieu once again for a short time—I will write again soon and shall

---

30. Mary Ann Williams, daughter of well-to-do Charlotte merchant H. B. Williams. Mary Ann was evidently a former schoolmate of Harriett's. Her name is written in HNE's geometry book, which can be seen at the museum, Vance Birthplace Historic Site, on the Reems Creek Road near Asheville. *Census* of Mecklenburg County, 1850.

give you some information which I know will be gratifying to your noble heart—Dont let that excite your curiosity again, for it is something which few young ladies beside you would regard as worthy of her turning to—But thank God, I know it will please you. Farewell, Harriet; write when you can, and may the guardian Angels of the good hover around you as close as the ever devoted heart of your

Zebulon.

[1852]

My dear Harriet,

I sit down again this evening to write you a letter in accordance with the promise I gave you, that I would write without waiting for your answer—It is always a pleasure for me to sit down thus and commune with you, but on this occasion it is an especial pleasure, inasmuch as it relieves me temporarily from the angry whirlpool of political strife in which I have been tossing and whirling for the last week.

I, at first, adopted a policy in regard to the past elections [on August 5] which prudence suggested I should rigidly adhere to: I intended keeping aloof from politics altogether and do nothing but vote silently, which course for a young man in my situation would have been far preferable to any other. But I could not, to save my life keep silent, when the crisis approached. When all around me became uproar and confusion, I became noisy too, and when I heard my friends being abused, I was affected like human nature generally is on such occasions, and I defended them. Once embarked but in the slightest degree, and I had to go the whole figure; I can never be only half a friend to a man or measure; my disposition on the contrary is thorough going and ardent in everything when aroused. I do not think I am disposed to *sham* in anything at least I hope I am not. I have thus been in a state of unpleasant excitement for several days and am extremely glad that it has partialy subsided. I am in hopes I shall be able to sit down quietly tomorrow morning to my law books again—I suppose you have heard of the result of the elections—Woodfins majority over Erwin is 537 in the four Counties. Messrs [John A.] Fagg and [James] Lowry are elected to the Commons by a large vote— West of this, Col [Robert G. A.] Love is reelected in Havwood and Capt [Stephen] Munday in Macon. Bird [Cornelius R. Byrd] is elected over [Bayles] Edney in Yancey &c. Kerr[31] has fallen off from the Whig vote in this county and West of this, considerably. I offended a great many of my pseudo friends here by voting for D. Coleman[32] for the Commons. He is a democrat and hence the offence. I can only say in justification, to all who may take it upon themselvs to question me about it, that I voted for him because it was my own soverign will and pleasure—I scorn to assign any other reason when the propriety of my voting as a freeman is called in question. This is all doubtless of very little interest to you, but I felt so indignant at my friends (?) for wishing to dictate to me in voting that I can not forget it soon or refrain from talking of it. What a world this is! I learn surprising and I hope not uninstructive lessons of human nature every day—I shall lay them all up against a rainy day—But I know you are tired of politics and so I'll get on to something else—

I do not know when I shall start to Yancey; it will probably be some month or more yet. I have pretty much got over my attack of the California fever, and begin to feel as if I could live in Buncombe very well contented—provided you were with me; then the golden land could not offer temptations sufficient to draw me away— I attended yesterday a pic-nic out at Mr William Pattons[33] farm on Swannanoa—There was quite a crowd in attendance and everything passed off in splendid style—I had the *exquisite* pleasure of making the acquaintance of Miss Mary Ann Williams of Charlotte—I was introduced to her at the Hotel and rode out with her to the pic-nic

---

31. John Kerr of Caswell County, the Whig candidate for governor, was defeated by the Democratic incumbent, David S. Reid of Rockingham County. *The Raleigh Register*, September 18, 1852.

32. David Coleman, a nephew of David L. Swain, was a son of William and Cynthia Swain Coleman of Buncombe County. David Coleman practiced law in Asheville. ZBV's espousal of Coleman's candidacy in defiance of his own Whig party makes their subsequent political relationship worthy of note: In 1856 when Coleman sought re-election to the North Carolina Senate, he was opposed by Vance. Vance lost. This was the only defeat by the people he ever sustained. In 1859 Coleman tried to deprive Vance of his seat in Congress. This time Vance won. During the latter campaign some remarks and gestures of Vance offended Coleman, who, after the election, challenged him to a duel. The intervention of mutual friends prevented the duel, however. Arthur, *Western North Carolina*, p. 403; Johnston, *Papers of ZBV*, 1: xxxiii, xxxvi, 19, n. 91, 42-53.

33. William Patton of Charleston, S.C., was a cousin of the Asheville Pattons. Azalea, his summer home on the Swannanoa, was only a part of his extensive real estate holdings in the area. Arthur, *Western North Carolina*, p. 425; information furnished by Miss Edith Holmes of Asheville, great-granddaughter of William Patton.

and back. I found her not so pretty as report led me to expect, but still quite pretty and *very* interesting. I enjoyed myself very much indeed in her company. Miss Graham[34] from Charlotte I was also introduced to. Do you know her? Mr. McEntire[35] of Rutherfordton was there—Do tell Jim McDowell to come over—I know there is sufficient to induce him to come; Miss Mary Ann and Miss Muff are sufficient to make any *unengaged* young man cross the mountains, aint they? Miss Mary Boyd[36] has returned to Asheville also, so you see our village has charms in abundance for young gentleman at this time. I hope Jim McD——will come over. Tell him to come soon—If I had the time to spare I could enjoy myself visiting the ladies wonderfully. I intend calling on Miss Williams tomorrow for the purpose of getting her to play "When other friends around thee" for Jim's sake.

My dear Harriet will you write soon? You say you do not expect to write so often yourself but hope I will write more than ever—Anglicised that would read about thus: "I am going to neglect my duty in future but I expect you to be still more punctual in the discharge of yours"—I do not want you to inconvenience yourself, My dearest, in writing to me, but you know my greatest pleasure is hearing from you frequently—My sheet is filled and I have yet a great deal to say—Another time will do. May God protect you my own beloved Hattie is the sincere prayer of your still devoted

Zebulon—

I realy ought to take another sheet and write some more but will not this evening. Have you seen the August number of the University Magazine? There is an amusing criticism in it upon several productions in former numbers, my piece of poetry among the rest—It is very amusing indeed—I think I know the author. I will look for a letter from you by next Sundays mail at all events. I yield in all things to your wishes of course, but I do hope you will not be much remiss in writing to me in future. When I agreed to let you off from writing so much I did not know it would go so hard with me to do without hearing from you so often. I hope

34. Harriett Graham was a daughter of the prosperous Charlotte merchant Alexander Graham. *Census* of Mecklenburg County, 1850.

35. Thomas McEntire, brother of "Miss Muff." *Census* of Rutherford County, 1850.

36. Mary Boyd, daughter of James P. and Annis Boyd of Buncombe County. *Census* of Buncombe County, 1850; Minutes, Buncombe County Court, October 9, 1849, p. 547.

however that you will do that which tends most to your own happiness, without reference to my preferences. That is all I ask. God bless you again, and preserve your health and happiness, both now and forever.

>Zeb—

>Asheville
>16th August, '52

Dearest Harriet,

Another week has rolled round and the ever pleasant task of writing to you is again mine. I wait each week for the time of writing to come with an impatience only exceeded by the impatience with which I look for your reply—I feel when I seat myself in my room, with the door and blinds closed, and take up my pen to write to you in unchanging and unmistakeable characters of my undying affection, as if I were stepping into your presence and face to face pouring my assurances into your ear. Hence as you will imagine, the pleasure I receive even in writing to you, tho' you may not see it in two or three days. But enough of this. My frequent letters furnish you undoubted evidence of the cheerfulness with which I do this which love has made a duty—
You can scarcely imagine the disappointment I felt last evening when the mail came without a letter for me. It is now nearly three weeks since I heard from you, and I really feel some uneasiness—not only on account of your health but also ———. The fact is my dear Harriet I am by you as a miser by his gold, ever jealous and timorous lest something should be wrong. I can never feel that my treasure is safe unless within my sight or where I can from time to time hear of its safety—When I fail therefore to hear from you at the expected time, I can not prevent my foolish heart from entertaining unfounded fears. I can not help it Harriet—It is the natural disposition of one whose *all* depends upon a single chance—I have often trembled at that thought which my observation has forced upon me, of which you have so often reminded me, that it is dangerous to fix our whole affections upon any one object of earth, and that Heaven often snatches those objects from our embrace which we are disposed to love too much—Do you believe so? If this is true, it is probably one cause of the great anxiety with which I look for the arrival of your letters, to learn if you are safe,

and still devoted—While in the P. Office yesterday gazing abstractedly over the pile of letters from Morganton, my eye fell upon one backed in your hand to Cousin Mary Henson[37] in Tuscaloosa— This assured me at any rate of your being alive and in some degree of health. Well, well, I'll speak of something else.

Our village is very gay indeed at this time. The S. Carolinians are crowding both our Hotels to over flowing—The streets resound with the noise of carriage wheels from morning untill night—The Warm Springs have a large crowd of visitors also—There are several ladies at the Eagle Hotel from Charlotte and I have been enjoying myself very much in visiting them. Miss Williams, Miss Roberson, Miss Graham and Miss Alexander[38] from that quarter I have become acquainted with—We have had dancing at the Hotel incessantly for the last two weeks. I was strongly solicited to join a large party which starts for the Springs in the morning but I refused, thinking very justly that I had spent already too much time with them to the neglect of study—Miss Roberson I think knows you, for she told me yesterday that she attended a party given to Mr [Victor] Barringer in Charlotte where she got acquainted with a great many of the Morganton ladies, at the same time looking at me very wisely and laughing—Do you know her? On a better acquaintance with Miss Williams, I dont admire her very much—I think her extremely vain and affected; but dont tell Jim so if you please.

Miss Clara is quite well; she has some visitors from Burke. Miss McEntire is still with them. I would reccommend her to my friend James as the preferable of the two, I mean of her or Miss Williams— I dreamed last night that you came to Asheville with Mrs Woodfin. Is there anything in dreams? But you dont have much idea of dreams and so there is nothing significant in mine—Well, I can wait untill September—Dr Lester has bought a new buggy expressly he says, for him and I to ride in across the Ridge, so there is no doubt about our coming—Inform Miss Ann of these particulars will you! We will have three weddings in this country in September—"Branch"[39] and Cousin Magie, Miss Garret at the

37. Mary M. Henson was a daughter of Freeland Henson and Sara Myra Erwin Henson. McDowell, *McDowells, Erwins, Irwins*, p. 195.

38. Probably Jane Alexander, daughter of Thomas Alexander of Charlotte. Salem College Alumnae Records in the library of Salem College, Winston-Salem, N.C.

39. Surely this should read "Gus and Cousin Magie," for Augustus Summerfield Merrimon and Mary Jane Baird were married within a month. Perhaps the slip of the pen was caused by the fact that A. S. Merrimon's younger brother Branch and Zeb's "Cousin Magie" had been sweethearts. In a letter to "Cousin

Springs and another one of which I am not allowed to speak. I am to be one of the attendants at the last mentioned one. I think it right that I should practise that ceremony as well as you.

And now my task is again almost ended. Shall I close this as I close all my letters to you? Shall I repeat again & again those vows of eternal love and devotion I have so often made? I conceive my own sweet Harriet, they are needless though I never tire of uttering them—With the full assurance that you will write when you get ready, I can only beg you to accept the affectionate adieus of your devoted

Zebulon

Gen. Burgins,[40] Near the Old Fort.
August 29th 1852

My dear Harriet,

I take my pen to write to you this evening in the most distracted state of mind that I ever experienced in my life. I hope soon to be rid of my present horrid feelings, never to feel such again. I left Asheville on friday morning to go to Morganton to see you. The rain was pouring down in perfect torrents and had been all night previous and all my friends begged me not to start, saying the streams would all be swollen, but I was determined to start even at the risk of my life. I travelled all day yesterday through the rain and came very near being drowned in some of those mountain streams on this side the Ridge. To day I came on safely untill I got to a small creek in Gen. Burgins lane—This creek was considerably swollen but from appearances I could not perceive it and as soon as I got into it I was immediately swept off headlong down the roaring torrent—Henry Dickson[41] who was in the buggy

---

Matt" dated August 12, 1851, Zeb says, "I should like to hear how my fair Cousin M.J.B. is getting along with Branch." Johnston, *Papers of ZBV*, 1: 6.

40. General Alney Burgin was a social and political leader of Burke, later McDowell, County. Burgin ran a stage stop near Old Fort. Arthur, *Western North Carolina*, p. 36; Henry E. Colton, *The Scenery of the Mountains of Western North Carolina and Northwestern South Carolina* (Raleigh, N.C.: W. L. Pomeroy, 1850), p. 83.

41. Henry Robertson Dickson, of Charleston, S.C., was a son of Dr. John Dickson, pastor of the Presbyterian Church in Asheville from 1843 to 1847. Henry Dickson's letter to ZBV, October 26, 1852, refers to this mishap. Johnston, *Papers of ZBV*, 1: 17-20.

with me jumped out before we got far from the bank and saved part of our baggage but I sat in the buggy endeavering to save the horse and buggy—About fifty yards down the stream the buggy turned over, when I sprang out and caught by a limb and thus narrowly saved a life which seems now scarcely worth preserving. Some quarter of a mile lower the horse and buggy lodged against some trees and on the arrival of help we got them out; the horse dreadfully injured and the buggy broken into almost a thousand pieces—It was truly a frightful adventure. I am thus compelled in spite of my earnest efforts, to defer visiting you for the present.

Dont you know Harriet the object of my visit? Do you know what it was that induced me thus to risk my life to see you? O you *can not* be ignorant of it! I had been fearful that something was wrong for the last few weeks past, from the fact of your not answering my letters, and this fearful presentiment was converted into truth by some news, or rather suggestions which came to my notice rather accidentally last wednesday evening—I have heard, that some friends of yours and as I once thought friends of mine also, have been advising you and your uncle to break off with me— The arguments they made use of it is not necessary to recapitulate even if I knew them, but I have indisputable facts in my possession to prove that they have been making efforts to my prejudice. Those arguments I understand also had made an impression on your Uncle and also to some extent upon you, tho' how much you were affected I know not. This is all true, most true, and I feel confident you will not deny it to me whom it concerns so vitally. Farther than these hints it would be of no use to go at present— Suffice it to say that I *know* these things to be substantially true. Now my Dearest noblest Harriet, whom I love as never man loved woman, I beg you to reccollect that when I was sitting by your side during my last visit you gave me your solemn promise that if anything should occur to interrupt the course of our love *you would never condemn me unheard*. I now, in this my hour of bitterness and trial, call upon you to redeem that promise. Will you fail me? If the Angel of Truth were to tell me you would refuse to make good your promise I could scarcely believe it! I call upon you then for the cause of your dissatisfaction if any exist in your mind, and for the things which have been urged against me, so if they be true I may acknowledge them and if they be false that I may refute them. You need name no person as engaged in this business if you do not wish to, for I *know* my accusers—O, how I want to see you! There is an almost irresistable force in the pleadings of an injured man when face to face with an honest and equitable Judge, such as I have ever known you. I have thought that probably you felt your situation very unfortunate and embarassing, inasmuch as your engagement bound you to me and the wishes of your friends was inclining you against me, hence thought I, probably your silence. Is this true? I have often heard you say that you would not marry anybody without the consent of your Uncle & Aunt, and if you still adhere to that and they have become unwilling for you to marry me as I fear they have, there is reason for me to believe your situation embarassing enough—I never have thought that you were persuaded by them to entertain my addresses, I flatter myself that it was entirely of your choice. Your Uncle & Aunt were once willing, and what I have done to cause them to revoke that consent I cant imagine. I presume they were always aware of my poverty and as to my conduct since, I can but believe it has been such as to raise me in the community. But I will not defend myself untill I know what are the precise accusations against me. The object of this letter is therefore to know what you will do with me and what has been told you. I hope you will let me know immediately. I invoke you, my noblest Harriet, by all the affectionate love that you once at least entertained for me, by the deep and true, and devoted and holy and undying love, I now and forever shall entertain for you, by the mortified pride which I experianced when I heard of those slanders against me, by the keen anguish and suffering I have undergone in the fear of losing you, and lastly, by your sacred word to that effect, to answer me soon and give me the whole of this affair. I shall return home tomorrow by the stage and I hope by next mail to have a letter from you. In the meantime believe me to be toward you, all that I have so often sworn myself to be, and ever shall be if such be your wish.

Zebulon B. Vance

ZBV visited HNE in September, 1852.

Asheville,
11th Sep. 1852

My dear Harriet,

According to the promise I gave you I sit down to write to you immediately on my arrival home. I waited wednesday as you reccollect for it to quit raining, and Thursday was still worse but I thought I was compelled to start, as I had staid so much longer than I anticipated. My horse would not suffer me to carry an umbrella and the consequence was I got thoroughly wet during the day, on two occasions—The rain came upon me some distance from any house and I was compelled to take it. I staid at Gen. Burgins on Thursday night and got home at 2 O'clk on Friday— I found my Mother so extremely uneasy at my long delay that she was on the point of starting Brother[42] after me. I told you that I was doing wrong in staying so long, but I had been so late in getting to see you that I could not think of leaving sooner. I have suffered my Dear Harriet in this unfortunate difficulty, an exceedingly great degree of mortification and mental anguish, for which I could only be repaid in the great and exceeding gratification I experianced when I saw the nobleness of your high toned and independent conduct to me. I thought however when I left you that the mortification I was to feel from the opposition of your relations was at an end, and that the many bitter things which I had endured so tamely on your account would never be repeated. But it seems I was mistaken. I had scarcely arrived in town before I was met with the report that your relations in this place had said publicly that I was reporting through the village I was engaged to you when I knew there was nothing of it, and that I was only spreading that report to give myself some importance. This report I had on the authority of Mr T. T. Patton who told it in the presence of several ladies and gentlemen. You can have no adequate idea my dearest One of the extreme mortification I felt on hearing of this new unkindness on the part of your relations here. I know not of its truth but if it is true (and it came by respectable authority) it is the most cruel and unjust remark which has been yet levelled at my persecuted head—Just think now that I should for the sake of giving myself importance, be such [an] unbred villain as to couple a young Lady's name with mine in that way with-

---

42. This is one of only two references in these letters to ZBV's older brother Robert Brank Vance, twenty-four. Zeb and his brother had a close relationship, however. Robert Brank Vance was at this time clerk of the county court and already a devoted Methodist layman and worker for temperance. Ashe, *Biographical History*, 6: 469-77.

out foundation and that I took particular pains to tell the villagers of that thing! Indeed Harriet, I could scarcely contain myself. My only hope was that it was not true, that your relations had never said it; and yet the report is prevalent in town and how did it get started? I can bear all these persecutions, however, for your sake; in fact, I can bear anything so long as I am supported by the love which I am more than ever convinced you have for me. What my enemies say of me shall pass as idle winds, so long as I know there is one pure and generous heart that does me and my character justice. God bless you, you have done so hitherto, and I am convinced you ever will—I have no fears of suffering from the injustice of any one hereafter. No one but myself can blast my hopes with you, and whilst I conduct myself according to the dictates of honour and principle I know you will judge accordingly. In the meantime, as I said before, I intend to double my exertions to convince my enemies of the injustice they have done me, by the correctness of my conduct in future. Excuse me for dwelling on this unpleasant subject. I thought to have mentioned it no more but I was forced to say something of this. God knows I have been so hurt with the many things said about me that I would willingly if possible forget the whole matter.

Miss Garrett who as I told you was to have been married on the 2nd inst. was taken sick on the day before her wedding day and when her intended came the Drs were despairing of her life. She is scarcely thought likely to live yet. Truly "in the midst of life we are in death". Hers was truly a distressing case, was it not? Those other weddings in this place will come off, the one on the 14th the other on the 23rd. I have not space here to express my dear Harriet the gratification I felt during my recent visit to you. I expressed that in as warm a manner as possible when with you. O how proud I feel, and what a thrill pervades my boosom when I think of the severe test which your love for me has undergone! And you sustained it so nobly! O, I thank thee my own noble Harriet! Do write me soon if tis but a line. You know you was unwell when I left you, do let me know of your health; I assure you I will be quite uneasy until I hear. For the present then adieu Harriet and God bless you.

Zebulon

Morganton September 14th '52

My beloved Zebulon;

I know you dearest, will excuse me for writing only a few lines in reply to your highly appreciated letter, that I did not receive until this morning & this is Tuesday evening—I wish very much I had time to write a long letter, but I am in the Village with Mollie Jo—I inquired yesterday morning at the Office for letters but Brother Will had taken my letters out, so you see why it is that I did not write before this afternoon. I have just returned from the mass meeting & was highly amused for a while with Mr James Edney—he was the only speaker this afternoon—tomorrow I guess we will have a "feast of reason"—*it* will be a great day in our Village—how much I wish you were here, but I will enjoy your company much more at another time.

I was quite unwell for a day or two after you left, but I am now in my usual health I hope My dearest one is in both fine health & spirits—I was truly sorry to learn from your letter, that my relations are still making unkind & uncharitable remarks about you—Do dearest dont allow them to excite you—I dont think it can be true that they are talking in this way—please dont speak of them disrespectfully—nothing of the kind that may be said will change the feelings of your devoted Harriett.

While I was writing Mollie Jo came in & insisted that I go to ride with her, so I went & have just returned—I enjoyed the ride very much, but how much my pleasure would have been enhanced by your company—Oh! that I could have you with me always but this cant be for some time.—My heart be assured is ever with you & should this not be sufficient to prevent you from regarding the abuse of my friends in Asheville [?]—I fear you will become angry with them & make remarks that you will regret afterwards—do dont —I have confidence in you—I believe that they will change their opinion before long;—I am truly sorry that you ever learned who told me the things that I heard concearning my own one—I really must close my letter as it is time to go to the court house—I would greatly prefer writing to you, but every one is preparing to go & insist upon me going & beside I am one of the singers—Scotts[43] songs, of course. I will be at home alone for the next three or four weeks—Aunt left this morning for Rutherfordton, will go from there to your Village—I will write to you very frequently during

---

43. General Winfield Scott, hero of the War of 1812 and the Mexican War, was the Whig candidate for president of the United States, running against Democrat Franklin Pierce.

her absence. Mollie Jo & I will be together much of the time. She sends her love to her cousin Zeb—Now My own beloved one farewell—Do remember your promis to her who has at all times your interest at heart—God guard you dearest is the sincere prayer of her who will ever be true to you—. Do excuse great haste & write soon—I will write again very soon—My love to your good Mother Sisters & Aunt Mary—I have much to say in my next & I am, as ever your own devoted

Harriett.

Quaker Meadows September 20th 1852

My beloved Zebulon;

 Imagine my extreme disappointment today, when the servant returned from the Office without a letter for me from you & I know you will reproach yourself for not writing—Why is it, dearest, that you did not write me a few lines at-any-rate? It is so seldom that you ever fail to let me hear from you at the expected time, that I cant avoid feeling a little uneasy when I dont hear; you know you had been suffering a great deal with tooth ache when you were to see me last & then you traveled most of the way home in the rain—from this, I very much fear, indisposition has prevented you from writing. Do let me know immediately, if such is the case; I hope next mail will certainly bring me a letter from him in whom (above all others) I feel most interested—you occupy my almost every thought My dear Zebulon & you dont know how it disappoints me when I dont receive your frequent assurance that I am always remembered by you, not that I doubt it at all—but it affords me so much pleasure to peruse your epistles as I can enjoy so little of your company—I frequently ask myself if the time is not very near, when I shall have you with me again—& then I remember that it has only been two weeks since you were to see me & that it will perhaps be several weeks longer before you repeat your visit—I endeavor to bear these long separations with patience but some times I fear, I become a little impatient. I think though, that if I do get a little anxious to see you now I ought to be excused as I am at home with only Uncle for company & he not in the house half the time. I believe I wrote you in my hastily written letter of last week that Aunt had gone to Rutherfordton; she I presume is in your Village by this time, as she expected to leave

Rutherfordton this morning. When she left home; I came very near going to Asheville this morning myself, with the company that left Morganton—Ephream was anxious for me to accompany him but I disliked the thought of being in Asheville & not getting to see you. I suppose this will be a gay week there as the Examination, Dr Whitsons[44] wedding & Mass Meeting all come off; I hope dearest you are not too much indisposed to enjoy the festivities of the week—for I am almost confident that you are not altogether well or you would not have neglected her who never intentionally neglects her dearest earthly treasure. I met with an acquaintance of yours yesterday—Mr Everet [James Battle Avirett] —when I came home from church I found he & William Gaither[45] spending the day with Brother James—William began to tease me directly after my entrance in to the house & in this way I found Mr Everet to be a friend of yours—I think he intended going on to Asheville this morning—It was very gratifying to me I can assure you to hear him speak in such high terms of you as he did; I find you have many friends, if you do have enemies & how sorry am I to know that some of your enemies are my relations—I hope this will not always be the case, nor do I think it will—I regret exceedingly (as I have told you before) that you are aware that my relations in Asheville are not friends of yours—& I also regret that they continue to make unkind remarks about you as you wrote me in your last that you understood they did—I cant believe that they would speak publicly in the manner that Mr Patton said—it is not only calculated to mortify you, but wounds my feelings very much indeed—I hope dearest you will not listen, or at least, treat with silent contempt all such rumors—I know you will hear that cousins should have said a great many things that perhaps they would not think of saying—Do my own one, bear in mind what I have said to you on the subject—You ought to be convinced by this time that your devoted Harriett will not be influenced by such things—

I was truly grieved to learn that Miss Garret was so very ill—do write me particularly about her health in your next—she has been an invalid for some time has she not? How uncertain is life —This to us is a call, "be ye also ready." I suppose Cousin Maggie

44. Dr. George W. Whitsun, dentist, of Asheville, married Jane Roberts, daughter of the Asheville attorney Joshua Roberts, *Asheville News*, July 24, 1850; Arthur, *Western North Carolina*, pp. 391, 392.

45. William E. Gaither, eighteen, was a son of Burgess Sidney Gaither, Morganton lawyer and Whig politician, and Elizabeth Erwin Gaither, a "Belvidere Erwin." Ashe, *Biographical History*, 2: 96, 97; McDowell, *McDowells, Erwins, Irwins*, p. 212.

is now Mrs Merrimon—did you attend her wedding? Were the Asheville people generally invited &c—Dr Whitson, I presume, by the time this reaches you, will be united forever to the idol of his heart— what does he think of the female character since your return home? I hope he makes me one of the exceptions to the sex in general as you say he thinks the ladies are generally, *so fickle*; but dear Zebulon, whether he does or not I know you do & that is sufficient. I hope dearest you have succeeded in keeping your promis with regard to that awful habit that you were so noble as to confess you were guilty of—it certainly was magnanimus in you & do now abandon it—I believe that you will & Oh that I could be the means of your giving up all of your other sins—I trust you do not think I am rong in alluding to your souls salvation—it is a subject that dwells nearest my heart my own one & I can't refrain from speaking to you about it—my constant prayer is that you may be converted— I hope I am not alone in offering up this prayer—I know I am not.

When may I expect another visit from you? Do dont put it off too long, but need I urge that? I know you will come as soon as possible; I am sorry your mother was so extremely uneasy about you during our last visit—tell her she should not allow herself to be uneasy about you, when you are with one that will take such good care of you as you know I will; you must not appoint a time to be at home when you come again. It is very late & my sheet is full, so I must close, not that I have said all I have to say—for I verily believe I could fill another sheet this night but dearest one I would suffer for it tomorrow & I know you would not have me be made sick for a number of such species of composition as this; it is already some time past my hour for retiring—Now will I be disappointed again next mail? I cant think so—you must write to me every week. I don't think you ought to think that too often to write to one who you love so devotedly as I am sure you do me & I know you are not more devotedly attached to me than I am to you. I must bid you good night—May you have sweet dreams—I will write you very soon again—God bless you my love—your own devoted

Harriett—

Quaker Meadows September 25th 1852

My beloved Zebulon;—
Another mail has come & brought no communication to me

from you—Now is this the reward that my constancy to you under all circumstances is to meet with? I have written you, this is the third letter since I have had one now from you—can it be, that you are treating me in this manner by way of retaliation—? if you are you must pardon me for considering it very unkind—I acknowledged to you that I did rong in not writing to you before you came over—you said you forgave me—I will not ask your forgiveness for the same thing again—I dont remember ever before to have had cause to charge you with unkindness & I cant avoid feeling hurt, that you would act so at this time, especially—your last promis to me was that I should hear often from you & I have only received one letter from you since your return home—I cant excuse this in you unless you offer the best of reasons—Would I have believed any one if they had told me, that you would have acted so indifferently towards one who has been so lavish in her devotion to you?—I assure you I would not—Such conduct as this, would go to confirm the statement of some of my friends if I had not the utmost confidence in your truthfulness. Is it possible that I have been deceived in you?—It cant be—have I bestowed that ardent devotion, which should ever characterise the love of women, upon one that I can not longer trust—? the answer instantly arises in my heart—No, this cannot be! Well, why is it that you have not written? Are you not well, as I asked you in my last? it really appears to me that sickness is the only thing you would allow to prevent you from gratifying me, particularly at this time, as I have not been influenced by some of my friends to desert you—but have turned from them & prefered you—"If this be not loving you have not been loved." When Aunt left home I thought my greatest enjoyment during my hours of lonelyness would be in writing to & receiving letters from, you. you have surely forgotten that I am at home alone—I want you My much loved one to reflect upon the treatment that I have received from you & ask yourself if you think you are excusable—It is probable that you have written to me & that this letter is entirely unnecessary; if such is the case I sincerely ask pardon. I could fill this whole sheet in my complaints but I know it would not be interesting so I will desist from saying more on the subject of my disappointments. I hope you are in the enjoyment of your usual health—I think I would have heard from some sorce if you are not; I received a letter from Clara by last Mail, in which she mentioned you, but said nothing about your being unwell so I dont think you can offer indisposition as an excuse for negligence. I would have written you quite a different letter, to day, from this, if I had received one from you by last Mail. I feel quite in the humor of writing you often lately & long & affectionate letters but I cannot write you such letters until I have an explanation of your conduct & hoping to have that soon I am yours truly

Harriett.

Sep. 25th 1852

My Noblest Harriett,

    I am afraid you will censure me for my long delay and I must confess it has been longer since I last wrote than has been my custom, but I assure you I am not without a valid excuse. I intended writing by last Thursday's mail but on Tuesday night I met with a college mate from Chapel Hill and he hung to me so closely untill he left that I had no chance to write or to do anything else scarcely. On Thursday night I attended my friend Whitsons wedding, friday went with him to his Fathers and arrived in town this (Saturday) morning. To day is the time of our great Scott barbacue. I heard several speeches to day and have just returned from the grove where the dinner was served. We had quite a fine time, but the rain was pouring down in torrents all the time we were eating. The streets are now crowded and it is with great difficulty that I can get to write to you this evening; but I have locked my door and shut the window blinds & hope I may pen you a short and imperfect letter without interruption.

I was made very happy by the reception of your letter. I promise to comply with all your requests in regard to your friends here. I shall speak of them respectfully and treat them politely. I wish to show you my dear Harriet, that I can suffer mortification and every thing to which an honorable man can submit for your sake. Especially can I do this when I have such assurances of fidelity from you. Be assured my noblest of women, that I shall appreciate your goodness both in speech and actions. There are daily calls upon my patience in regard to this matter to which I can scarcely submit. I hear it all over the Village that your relations are opposed to me, and am frequently asked if such is not the case. I suppose Mr J. W. Woodfin has told it, I dont know how else every body could have heard it—But I will not dwell any longer upon this to me, painful subject—it is enough for me to know that your feelings for me remain unchanged. I intend to try to conduct myself so as to give persons as little chance to make remarks about me as possible treating all respectfully and politely. I saw a great many of the Burke people lately. Eph & S. Greenlee left this morning Wm McKesson is still here. I spoke to Mrs McDowell on Thursday and Mrs McKesson at Merrimons wedding. I would like very much to visit them, but I can not do so while they are at Mr Woodfins. I need friends among your relations and sincerely regret that I am not in the proper situation to try to make them. I do hope they will both excuse me for not visiting them. I should like exceedingly to have the good opinion of Mrs McKesson, and I hope her relations will not try to lower me in her esteem while she is here. I have seen Miss Clara only for a few moments since my return, and she wished to know of me what was the matter. She knew from your letter that something was wrong. I hardly speak to Miss Clara confidentially; are you willing that I should? She seems to be very much in your confidence. Miss Williams will leave on Monday I hear. That friend of mine from Chapel Hill Mr Avirett[46] said he dined at your uncles and made your acquaintance. Dr Whitson is I think the happiest man alive; I never saw anybody so devoted, always excepting myself. I envied the happy fellow and thought of the long, long weary months between me and a similar bliss—I could not keep from sighing over the prospect of such a long separation from the loved one of my heart. But patience, patience. A great many little items of gossip that you may learn from Mr & Mrs Greenlee I will not write to you now, and besides I have met with a half dozen interruptions since I began to write and I scarcely know what to say, my ideas are so badly arranged. Do write to me often during your Aunts absence as you promised. I have a long *long* letter in store for you before long. I promise you I will not be silent so long again if I can possibly help it. I shall attend but few of the courts, probably Madison & Yancey, as I am doing better when reading. Do give my love to Cousin Mollie Joe, and James McD—— Aunt Mary[47] was extremely obliged to you for your love, and desires to be kindly remembered to you, as also does Mother; Sister Laura is not at home. Next time I will do better than this imperfect letter, its almost impossible for

---

46. James Battle Avirett of Onslow County, who was a student at the University of North Carolina with ZBV. Grant, *Alumni History*, p. 25.

47. Mary Adelaide Baird, older sister of ZBV's mother, never married. She lived in Asheville with her first cousin William Baird and his wife, Christiana Weaver Baird. Dowd, *Life of Vance*, pp. 5, 7; *Census* of Buncombe County, 1850.

me to write now. May God protect you my own noble Harriet is ever the sincere prayer of your truly devoted

Zebulon.

You remind me of my promise to you, God bless you for your interest in my welfare. I am ever mindful of my promise & shall try and have been trying to observe it. So far I have been remarkably successful and find that it only requires a determined will to conquer bad habits. Keep on reminding me of it, and I will be greatly aided by you in doing better The bells are ringing for supper and I must go home. Farewell again and Heaven protect you.

Zebulon

Letter from HNE missing.

Asheville, Oct. 7, '52

My own dear Hattie,

I recd your last blessed letter containing my forgiveness, and regret that it was out of my power to answer it by last nights mail. This evening is the only time I have had an opportunity to write this week, and as I have to go to the country tomorrow on business which may detain me all day and then the next day (Saturday) start to Madison Court, I hasten to write this evening though several days in advance of the mail, lest I might again make you uneasy at my silence—Since the first of last week I have been in one continued scene of excitement and bustle—Conference[48] and court going on together, our house full of company, the streets lined with carriages and a miscellaneous concourse of horse & foot passengers thronging the streets & avenues made our little village for the time quite noisy & exciting, and has prevented me from writing to you as I should have wished. But to the point—You can imagine something of my feelings Harriet, when I read your affectionate and for-

---

48. The twenty-ninth session of the Holston Annual Conference of the Methodist Episcopal Church, South began in Asheville September 29, 1852, with Bishop William Capers, D.D., of South Carolina presiding. Price, *Holston Methodism*, 4: 113.

giving letter. I measure your feelings by those which pervade my own boosom in regards to our love and I know you can well imagine what a burden was lifted from my soul when I knew you forgave me. The course of true love never did run smooth, but O Harriet, has not ours been rough long enough! When shall it be that we shall have no more difficulties and misunderstandings, but trust and confide in each other with a holy and abiding faith? Situated as I am in regard to you, I am ever tormented with fears, and ever ready to look upon your slightest displeasure as fatal to myself. I cant help this feeling Harriet although I know it does you injustice; I am not afraid of your forsaking me of your own free will so long as I act properly, for I believe you to be most sincerely and devotedly mine as you profess but there is no knowing what my enemies may tell you—But if the heavens will but be propitious a little while longer I will put it out of the power of any one to blast my happiness—For the present however, I am extremely happy in being restored to your favour and beg pardon for troubling you with vague fears & forboding of future evil when I should be rejoicing—Considered apart from those foolish fears, the future begins to brighten considerably—I think I can see light gleaming ahead upon my path in relation to my professional prospects. I feel more in high spirits since this weeks transactions than I have in a long time—I am more and more convinced that I only need to have industry and sobriety to succeed. With you for my friend, my councillor and my guardian Angel, how can I fail in either? O Harriet, I look forward to the time when I shall be guided by your affectionate councils and stimulated by your holy influence to labour and exertions, with an impatience which I can hardly restrain within the bounds of prudence! I know, if God grants me health that I *can not* fail while you are near me.

Next week I go to Madison Court, the week following to Yancey so you must not think anything to be wrong if I do not write to you before I get back home. I will write however if I can from one of those places. You will not I suppose expect me to give you an account of the conference which has just closed its session at this place. You will learn all about it from Mrs McDowell who leaves on Monday as I hear. We had a great deal of very good preaching and a great chance of noise & confusion. I attended allmost all of the preaching untill Court began but cant say that I was particularly benefited—There is one thing which I regret exceedingly—and that is that I could not pay more attention to your good Aunt while she was here. I spoke to her several times and escorted her home once but I could not call upon her at Mr Woodfins while feeling towards them as I do. I can not be a hypocrite Harriet, and treat people kindly when I dont feel it in my heart— Your Aunts treatment of me at her house has been such as to win my entire esteem and I deplore sincerely my unfortunate situation which prevents me from reciprocating as far as is in my power— But let us trust in God Harriet, that time will heal all ill feeling between me and your relations and that we may yet live as it becomes us—I am determined that it shall not be my fault if we do not. I think I will be to see you shortly after my return from Yancey Court, as I am getting so that I cant stay away from you long. Write to me as soon as you can, I may get it the last of next week. There is an interesting meeting going on in the Presbyterian Church and I am sorry that my business will not let me attend only during the evenings. Rev Mr [Robert Hett] Chapman from Ala[bama] is here. When are you going to Rutherford? I do hope the next time I write that I will have leisure to write you a very long letter. I must close this one and implore the protection of Heaven upon you untill I write again—

       Yours truly & devotedly
       Zebulon

      Quaker Meadows Oct 9th 1852

  I hope Dearest you have ere this recovered from the distracted state of mind in which you were plunged by my cruel letters—I wrote you a hurried letter this day week acknowledging that I was wrong in imputing such unworthy conduct to my faithful Zebulon, as negligence & retalliation, though I still think you should not have allowed so long to pass without writing me at least a few lines & you must remember my love, that you confess to this—but I have truly forgiven you—I know it was not intentional; you say that you intend in future to neglect business, treat your friends impolitely & do almost anything else in order that I may be gratified in receiving letters from you—Now dearest I hope you will retract that for I am not as exacting as to require you to write to me if you should have to neglect all other things to do so— It is not right to require of you more than I perform myself. I am fully convinced that you will write when ever you possibly can— this is all I desire—At any other times I dont think I would have thought for a moment that your silence was intended—but you know I had heard *my friends* say that they believed you were untrue to me or at least one of them & I think it was but natural that I should have some fears, as I never before remember of your having delayed replying to my letters so long, unless I had been remiss in answering yours—but I must change this unpleasant subject not without telling you, though, how much I regret having caused you so much unhappiness—I reproach myself no little my own one for writing you (who have ever proved so faithful & true to me) such a letter as the last but one—I must ask your forgiveness—I know your forgiving heart will not refuse your devoted Harriett such a request—No dearest, I know that you love me & as you say the heart that loves can forgive again & again; then you will I am sure forgive your own Harriett. I promis for the future to write you no more such epistles.

I thought I would have received a letter from you by last Mail acknowledging the receipt of my last, but Brother Will has sent none so I suppose none came; he may though have neglected sending it, as he frequently does—I am going to the Village this afternoon & would wait to close my letter till after I go in, but fear it will be too late for me to write much, even if I find a letter there from you—I believe I have not permited longer than a week to pass without writing to you since you were to see me last, so I must not allow this Mail to return without a letter for you & unless I finish it before knowing whether there is a letter in the Village for me, you will not receive a word from me until Wednesday—I hope I will find a letter this afternoon, but if I should not I will certainly expect one by next mail—Is not the time drawing near when I may expect another visit from you? Do reply to this question in the affirmative—I am so anxious to see you—Do come as soon as convenient—but I need not urge this upon you—I know you will visit me as often as possible. I received a letter this morning from my dear friend Mary Wilson[49] in which she desired to be particularly remembered to you—I have a secret to tell you concearning her when we meet—I expect you can guess what it is.

49. Mary Lizzie Wilson, daughter of the Reverend John McKamie Wilson, Jr., of Missouri. He was a first cousin of Mira M. Vance and pastor of the Morganton Presbyterian Church from 1846 until 1851. HNE joined this church during his ministry. The "secret" probably concerned Mary's engagement to Dr. Robert N. C. Tate, son of Dr. Samuel Tate of Morganton, whom she subsequently married. Avery, *Presbyterian Churches*, p. 33; McDowell, *McDowells, Erwins, Irwins*, p. 229; *In Memory of Mrs. Margarett M. Vance and Mrs. Harriette Espy Vance* (Raleigh, N.C.: Edwards, Broughton & Co., 1878), p. 31.

In one of your letters you ask me if I object to your speaking confidentially to Clara Patton—I am very willing that you should dearest if you wish—she appears to be a friend of yours—you say she seems very much in my confidence; I have not made a confident of Clara though I have great confidence in her friendship towards both of us—she says in her last letter to me that she hopes I have not treated her highly esteemed friend unkindly & asks me if I have. I trust you have not been mortified by any more unkind remarks of my relations—I dont think they will say anything more about you. I asked Sister on her return, if Cousins had made that last unkind remark that you heard they did & she says she thinks not.

I suppose you attended Cousin Augustus's wedding—Mr James Patton[50] was telling me that he appeared very happy & no doubt he feels so for he has a very lovely Bride—Did you attend the party given to them at Cousin Eliza Woodfins? You must write to me if Miss Garrett has entirely recovered—I have heard nothing of her since you wrote me she was so very ill—I feel anxious to know something about her.

Our first meeting of the Reading society, is to day I am so delighted to have it in operation again—I enjoy it so much—It is a great sorce of pleasure to us during the dreary winter, besides being very imposing—I am very much interested in the books that you sent me by J Patton—tell Miss Mary I have thought of her frequently while reading several things—I have never read many of Hannah More's[51] peaces until you sent me her works—I expect now to read them almost constantly until I get through. I have not received the Oct. number of Harpers yet—I found the September number of it very entertaining—I was also pleased with several peaces in the September number of the University Magazine among others "Carolina claims her children"—I agree with the auther of it, who ever he may be—was it not your noble self? I suspect it was.

I have many more things to say—but have neither time nor space—I suppose the excitement of Conference is over—May I hope dearest that you were much profited by the preaching of at least the good Bishop Capers—I trust you have succeeded in keeping your promis to me with regard to your wicked remarks—you ask

50. James Alfred Patton of Asheville was a son of James W. Patton. He had been valedictorian of the Class of 1851 at the University of North Carolina. Johnston, *Papers of ZBV*, p. 19, n. 88.

51. Hannah More (1745-1833), popular English playwright, novelist, and writer of religious tracts.

me to remind you of it often—& you must expect me to do so for my much loved one I am truly interested in you and I am anxious that you should give up all your bad habits & especially that one, for above everything, profanity is to me the least to be admired & the most to be abhored & my dear, it is not only on my own account that I desire you to quit it but more especially upon your own. I really must close though I could write as much more if I had time—but I must go to the Village—I will write soon again—Remember me to your Mother, Aunt Mary & sisters—Do write very soon & very frequently—I have quite a lonely time & your letters are more welcome than ever, on that account—I am becoming anxious for Aunts return—"Home is not home without her", I hope she will return soon—I have read a letter from you every Mail for the three last. I trust you will continue to write as frequently & you must certainly write every week. I hope to receive you before very long—May the Lord watch between me & thee while we are absent from each other is the sincere wish of your truly devoted

Harriett

Mollie Jo's love to you—she is still as enthusiastic about you as ever.—In haste
Harriett

Oct 15th 1852

My own sweet Hattie,

I returned this (Thursday) evening from Madison Court and found a letter from you in the office which I sit down to answer tonight as I expect to be extremely busy tomorrow and Saturday and I might not find so much time to write as I should wish if I were not to write to night. I was extremely gratified with your letter Harriet; it was such as I delight to receive, long, loving and affectionate. I perceive in every letter I receive an additional evidence of the sincerity of your attachment for me: a thousand little things which you would not think of as conveying any meaning in particular furnish me with the strongest and most indubitable proofs that my noble Harriet really loves me. I have never doubted this, since you first told me so, but if I had I must long since have been ashamed of my skepticism from reading your affectionate and confiding letters. I thank you Harriet; with all the warmth of a lovers devoted heart I pour out my gratitude toward you. Nay, I do more, I love you for it which is something warmer than thanks as I take it. I shall endeavor to thank you Harriet, not only with my lips, but with all the warm feelings of my heart and soul and a life devoted loyally to you which only our common enemy can destroy—May God grant me health and strength to give you such evidence of my love that the world shall see and admire. Your nobleness as evinced in your conduct to me sometimes makes me melancholy despite myself. What if I should prove incapable of appreciating rightly so much goodness? What if I should prove unworthy of so much purity and abuse that generous confidence which your young heart reposes in a poor adventurer as I might well term myself? O, I think often, very often of this and the bare thought makes me shudder. I do not flatter you Harriet; I scorn to use flattery to *you* but speak truly when I say I feel myself to be wholly unworthy of such a noble woman as you are. My only recommendation as I told you I believe in the first letter I ever wrote you, is my violent and faithful love for you and admiration of your character and many virtues. This furnishes a link which connects us to each other, and deserves as my heart tells me something at your hands in return. With this I first threw myself at your feet and slight as the offering was it was well received and found favour in your eyes, because like Abels sacrifices to his God it was offered with a sincere and devoted unity of heart. And while asking a continuance of your love Harriet I can only urge that mine has so grown with my growth and strengthened with my strength that the pulsations of my heart must cease when it ceases to lay its morning and evening and miday tribute of affection upon your Altar which love has erected in my breast. But I am getting prosaic. Dont you frequently grow tired of my love-sick digressions? No you dont either, but anybody else would. In fact I know that at times (and tonight is one of them) I am incapable of writing a letter of any general interest; I can then speak of nothing else but of my love and the various reflections that arise in my mind concerning it. I forget that I am *replying* to your letter and the word reply indicates something said in answer to a question and must be relevant to that question. Now you asked me several plain questions as to when I was coming to see you &c, but you did not ask me how much I loved you and what effect the reading of your letters had upon me. To these latter, imaginary interrogatories I have been replying, when perhaps I should have been acting the part of a good correspondent by answering your questions, giving you all the news topics &c. But of that matter which most occupies my thoughts will I speak most and I will continue to write this style untill that time shall come when we shall ever be so close together as not to require writing and even then Hattie I cant promise that I will reform. But let me come to earth a while like a terrestial body.

In my last letter which I hope was in the office waiting for you as you expected I told you I should not attempt a description of the Conference which sat here lately, knowing you would hear more minutely from others. My favorite preachers were the Bishop & Dr [William M.] Wightman of Charleston. The latter gentleman is a divine of a high order of talents and education and possesses in an eminent degree the essential character of an orator. A fine person, chaste and beautiful language nervous and vigorous gesticulation and splendid classic & expressive tropes and figures completely captivated me and made me one of his most delighted listenors. Our Court was uninteresting, not much done in consequence of most of the prominent lawyers being in Raleigh. I attended Madison and intended going from there to Yancey but court did not last but a few days at Madison and I returned home and will start to Yancey on Saturday if I can, if not Saturday then on Sunday. Miss Garrett I am happy to say has nearly entirely recovered; at any rate she got married[52] on last Thursday—I am glad that her fate has turned out so pleasantly. After I get back from Yancey I think I shall go to see you within a week or ten days. I have some business on hand as guardian for a lunatic which can not possibly be neglected. I met with some little encouragement at Madison Court and hope to meet with more in Yancey. I have not seen any of the ladies lately & can say nothing of them. I suppose tho' your friends among them are well. I thank you for reminding me of my promise. I am doing better than you would think in that respect. In respect to that "cruel letter" you are most fully and freely forgiven Harriet so make yourself easy on that head. Do remember me most affectionately to Cousin Mary Lizie when you write and kiss Cousin Mollie Jo for me. I will return from

52. On October 7, 1852, Sara L. Garrett married James Jones, second son of George Jones, a merchant in Greenville, Tennessee, and his wife, the former Kesiah Sevier. Marriage certificate on record in Madison County Courthouse; Cora Bales Sevier and Nancy S. Madden, *Sevier Family History* (Washington, D.C.: Kaufman Printing Co., Inc., 1961), p. 442.

Yancey early next week, so write again soon, dont be afraid I wont get it. Please remember me to Mr & Mrs McDowell. I am sincerely

Your affectionate Zebulon

I forgot to answer several of your questions among others was I at the party given to Merrimon at Mrs Woodfins—I was not. I am not the author of that piece in the Magazine which you admire &c. I will see you by at farthest the 1st of Nov.; in the meantime write to me as often as ever. May God protect one of his noblest children from harm is the constant prayer of Zeb.

Rutherfordton Oct 21st 1852

My beloved Zebulon;

I have only time to write you a few lines this morning. I arrived at this place on Monday evening. I left home very unexpectedly or I would have written to you before leaving—I new nothing of it until about nine O'clock on Saturday evening. I requested Brother William to tell you that I would come here on Monday, which I hope he did—I should have written you a few lines at-any-rate by him but did not know he intend[ed] going to Yancy until a few moments before his departure—I hope however, you were not disappointed at not receiving a letter before this— it is as early as I could possibly write & I now write in haste. I wish I had time to write more lengthily but I have not. I will expect you to see me certainly next week & will look, a little, for you the last of this. I have enjoyed my visit to this place, thus far very much—your presence dearest one will greatly enhance my pleasure— I am so anxious to see you, the time appears long since I enjoyed that privilege. Do come as soon as possible, which I know you will do. Write to me immediately when I may expect you—I have many things to talk with my own dear one about,—so do come soon. God bless you dearest. In haste your own devoted Harriett.

Asheville Oct 23—'52

My own dear Hattie,

I came home on Thursday night from Yancey Court and

was surprised at not finding a letter in the office from you—I heard by Mr McKesson that you were to leave on Monday morning for Rutherfordton and I thought you would have written informing me of the fact, so that I might know where to write, and it may be (I hope soon) go to see you. But getting no letter and feeling uncertain as to whether you have gone or not to R—— I shall write to Morganton so that if you be there you may get it, if not, then trusting you have left orders for your letters to be sent forward to R——.

I am heartily tired of following the courts and am not going to attend any more this fall. With such a small share of business as I have in the Superior Courts it becomes exceedingly tiresome to travel round the circuit and hang about the courts like a loafer. I only do so for the sake of learning the minutia of the practice, and in doing that I make the acquaintance of numbers of the coperas-trousered sovereigns of this great and growing Republic. This all has to be done sometime before one can get into practice and it is as well done now as at any other time. The people of Yancey are still very solicitous for me to give *dignity and character* to this county by *making myself a citizen* of it and having promised while I was a candidate to settle there, I scarcely know how to neglect my promise with honor—Inasmuch as my promise was then a *bona fide* one I think I will compromise by spending the winter with them.

We had a runaway match among us on last Tuesday. Miss Emily Blackstock[53] of this county ran off with a rather triffling fellow, as I think by the name of Dickinson—They have gone to Virginia, where the young gentleman has heretofore had his washing done. May happiness attend them—if possible. I hope you got my last letter before leaving Morganton. I wrote you that you might look for me shortly after I got back from Yancey and I think now I shall be able to visit you in a week or ten days from this time. My business is such however that I shall be compelled to stay with you only a short time. I hope to be able to make up for the brevity of my visits in future by their frequency. One thing only will prevent

53. Emily Blackstock married William T. Dickinson. She was a daughter of Squire Nehemiah Blackstock, who lived near Reems Creek. When Zeb was five years old and Robert Brank was seven, they were boarded in Blackstock's home in order to be near a school after the Vance family had moved to Lapland on the French Broad River, Buncombe County Marriage Register No. 91, Buncombe County Courthouse, Asheville, N.C.; *Census* of Buncombe County, 1850; David Vance II to his sister, Mrs. Jane Davidson, February 3, 1836, Z. B. Vance Papers, State Department of Archives and History, Raleigh, N.C.

me from seeing you often, that is the necessity of reading more than I have been doing. For more than six weeks past I have scarcely read any law at all. The courts are past now and it is time to stir up. I hope to read a great deal this winter. I am happy to state my Dear Hattie, that I have met with nothing more lately of a disagreeable nature from your friends in this place. I have been with Mr J. W. Woodfin for two weeks past on the circuit and having adopted the plan of not speaking to him at all when it could be avoided we got along much better than I could have expected; he attending to his own business and I to mine. He treats me politely and I return the same. But to forgive such an injury as he attempted upon me, and seek his friendship, is more I know than you could ask or I think of doing. But enough of this, I am still indulging the hope that time will heal all these unpleasant things and that you and I may be happy without any enemies amongst our relations. The love which we have pledged each other Harriet, is on my part amply sufficient to buoy me up under all circumstances of adversity and to that I surrender every thing but my honor, when necessary. Dr Lester said he saw you when he was last over, and pronounced your health good. I think, between you and I, that the Dr has made his arrangements for a wedding to come off shortly. At any rate he said that Miss Ann spoke of asking you to wait upon her and asked me if I would go with him over there shortly as groomsman. The Dr might have been premature in speaking to me in this way so please do not mention it to any one. How would you like an affair of this kind? Would it not be somewhat embarrassing to you? I withheld my answer to him untill I could ask you about your wishes in the matter. Perhaps I am also premature. Has Miss Ann said aught to you upon the subject?

In my confusion of late, I have failed to visit any of the ladies—Miss Clara I have not seen in two or three weeks; Miss Williams left this week in my absence and the town is now most exceedingly dull. Rutherfordton will I suppose be very gay this winter; thither will I go—that is—if—if—"you know the rest." Write to me soon Harriet, it seems long since I heard from you. My love is still as glowing and devoted as ever—indeed I can not but think it grows stronger and more violent every day. How slowly the sluggard hours roll round towards that great and *happy period* when we shall be united! Mother and Sister Laura beg to be remembered to you respectfully—I am going to call on Aunt Mary this evening, she would probably send a message if she knew I was writing. Excuse me for not writing another sheet. I really feel very much like it, but have some writing in the clerks office to do this evening. I thank you again for reminding me of my promise; I am doing very well in regard to it, so much so that it has been observed by some of my friends. I am almost ashamed to think, however that I refrain from committing a great sin from a motive which has so little religion in it. But better that way than not at all, yes infinitely better. I hope in my soul Hattie that this is only the beginning of the good you will accomplish in making me as I should be. In those matters I surrender myself to your guidance and trust in God that you may be successful in your noble efforts. May heaven protect you Hattie and keep you from all harm is the sincere petition of your still true and ever devoted

        Zebulon

Part III

November 2, 1852, to March 14, 1853

ZBV visited HNE in Rutherfordton the latter part of October, 1852. His letter of November 1, 1852, is missing.

Asheville Nov 2d—[1852]

My dearest Hattie,

 I have just got partly through quite a busy and exciting day, and as the polls of election have just closed I sit down to write you a hasty line. I got home safely last night after a pleasand days ride in company with Dr Boyd[1] and little daughter, Miss Twitty[2] and Mr Edney & Lady—You see how I was rewarded for keeping the Sabbath!

 This morning I had business on hand with men from the country and was so engaged with them that I did not get time to electioneer much for the Old Hero [General Winfield Scott]. But I did something for him beside voting myself and the result as to this precinct is quite satisfactory, showing a gain over the Whig vote in August although there is a falling-off in the whole number of votes cast. The vote stands here; Scott 185 Pierce 67; in August it stood in this precinct; Kerr 190, Reid 83; on the whole a Whig gain of 77 votes. This argues well for the whole county. Huza for Scott!!! The returns from the other precincts will be coming directly—I am very much excited and wish I had more returns to send you. I didn't think I should become so much excited as I am at present and have been ever since morning, as you recollect I told you I felt quite lukewarm on the subject.

 But notwithstanding all my anxiety about the election I did [not] forget you, and I stole away into my office as soon as possible and locked the door to not only inform you of my safe arrival, the news &c, but to show you my Own beloved Hattie that you *can not* be forgotten or neglected by your truly devoted lover and that I am ever mindful of you whatever may be going on around me. I wish I did have time to give you a long letter this evening: I had so many of those wild lover-dreams of you as I came on home yesterday—I enjoyed my last visit far more than any I have ever

---

 1. Dr. J. D. Boyd had moved with his family from Charleston, South Carolina, to Asheville in 1851 to run the Eagle Hotel. Later he opened an office at the Eagle for the practice of medicine. *Asheville Messenger*, August 27, 1851; *Asheville News*, February 23, 1854.

 2. Penelope Twitty was assistant teacher of music at Holston Conference Female College in 1854. *Asheville News*, February 23, 1854.

paid you. Oh, yes, indeed Hattie it was almost paradise to me to sit by your side and receive so many repeated and unmistakeable evidences of your devotion to me! I hope you got a note I gave the boy at the Hotel for you on Monday morning. I was quite uneasy all the day yesterday and am quite as much so yet about your health—I was afraid you had taken a cold by sitting in that cold room with me on Sabbath evening. That thought detracted much from my pleasure all the time we were sitting there. I knew, or at least I feared, that you would suffer much with the cold rather than have me leave. I hope however for the best. I would never forgive myself for keeping you in the room if you have suffered from it on my account. Do please Hattie write me a line by the next mail and relieve my anxiety for your precious health.

I found my Mother and Sisters all quite well and return to you their thanks for your kind message to them. Mother and Aunt Mary left this morning on a visit down on the River. I met Mr Woodfin in the street this morning and gave him Mrs Bynums letter—I have not time to write any more as it is getting too dark to see the lines upon the paper and the mail will be closed in a few minutes. Please mention me most respectfully to Mrs B——, I was quite pleased with her, and her treatment of me was so kind. I would like very much to possess her good will in relation to our union—I concieved her to be a most estimable Lady—God bless you my sweet Hattie and may His good spirit watch over you—O, that I had the power to do so myself during the long and weary months which must intervene between our happiness:

Do write by next mail.

Your own devoted
Zebulon

Rutherfordton Nov 3rd 1852

My beloved Zebulon;

I was truly delighted to see your letter this afternoon & as you appear to be so anxious to hear about my health, I cant allow the Mail to leave without assuring you that I have suffered none at all from sitting with you in *"that cold room,"* on Sabbath evening—you know I had a slight cold before that evening but I dont think, that increased it, at any rate I have felt quite as well since as before. Do dearest dont be uneasy about me any longer—I will be prudent & take care of (as you say) my precious health. But enough of this, you must remember that it is a subject with which I soon become wearied.

I received your note the morning you left—was much pleased to learn that you had such good company—A person is always rewarded for doing what is right & may my own beloved one ever be mindful of this;—I was truly gratified to see you so willing to keep holy the Sabbath—I hope dearest you will continue to do so.

I can say but little about the election over here—I understand Scotts majority is three to one at this place—I dont know that this correct—I hope it is—I was much obliged to you for the information you gave me concearning the election with you, & I was also pleased to learn that you did all you could for the Old Hero—but it is quite late & I must close—I wish I could write you a long letter—I only write these few lines to assure you that I am as well as usual.—be assured my dear one I will never deceive you about my health, but [will] let you know whenever I am the least unwell. I will expect another letter from you very soon & will also write again before long—I dont think I shall remain here longer than two weeks, I will write you in my next, I think when I shall leave for home—I am anticipating much pleasure the remainder of my visit here as I hear our friend Clara is to be over tomorrow. Muff came over & spent the evening you left with me; we spent the time very pleasantly—she had much to say about you & so has every one I have meet since you left—but I have not time to write more at present.

Cousin Mary desires her respects & appears equally as much pleased with you as you were with her—she says you certainly have her good will in relation to our Union.

You see dearest that I am writing in haste; this should prove to you that you are no more forgotten by me than I am by you. I know though that you certainly had to write in great confusion & excitement—I assure you I prized your letter very highly & wish I could send you a more interesting one in reply but you must excuse me this time—I will write again soon. May heavens blessings attend you, My dearest Zebulon is the sincere prayer of your more than ever devoted

          Harriett

Asheville. Nov 6 1852

My Own dear Hattie,

 I was not able to write to you by the last mail as I wished to do but I hope you were not disappointed. On Thursday morning I went some twelve miles into the country on business and did not get into town untill it was too late to answer your letter. I was happy to learn by your last that you was in health, for I was really quite uneasy until I heard from you. But I will say nothing more upon the subject now as you say it wearies you. I would ask pardon for wearying you in my last but that I feel it needless as you are fully aware of my motive in asking so anxiously after your health; its only my everwatchful devotion prompts me to it. Have'nt I a right to do so Hattie? Well now I'l hush.

 I hope my Dear, that you have enjoyed yourself since I left. I was truly glad to hear that Miss Clara and Miss Lou[3] had gone over there: I knew they would add so much to your pleasure. I hope they have kept you entirely from getting lonely or taking the "blues" or anything of that kind. I dont think any one could take the blues in Miss Clara's company, except perhaps it were some unfortunate youth desperately smitten with her innumerable charms, and at the same time haunted with the consciousness that it was "no use knocking at the door." That would be enough to give the "blues" indeed; worse in her presence than away from her. I have been so engaged with business and the election that I have not had time to get lonely since I came home, besides the fact that I am constitutionly very little subject to low spirits, and besides all this, when I look a few months ahead into the future I see so much thats bright, and beautiful and happy in store for me, that the demon of melancholy dares not show his weeping visage near me. My only unhappy hours are those which I spend in brooding over some things which I have often mentioned before and therefore will not speak of now. I drive them from me whenever I can and endeavor to think only of you Hattie, in connection with happiness and love alone. I bring my philosophy to bear upon my troubles and seldom fail of experiencing relief. This philosophy I am endowed pretty richly of and I hold it in considerable esteem for which you have sometimes chided me. It is indeed Hattie as nothing when compared with the great theory of philosophy which

---

 3. Louisa Patton (Lou), younger sister of Clara Patton and daughter of Thomas Taylor Patton and Louisa Walton Patton. Frontis W. Johnston, ed., *The Papers of Zebulon Baird Vance, 1843-62* (Raleigh, N.C.: State Department of Archives and History, 1963), 1: 56, n. 205.

you profess whose Author and Founder is Jesus Christ; I own and confess it and would to God I was a participator in its blessings! I hope for better things Hattie, and feel that I shall become a better and a worthier man when brought under the sacred and almost irresistible influence of a pius wife such as you will make. I feel a deep consciousness of my unworthiness when I find that so many actions of my life do not meet with your approbation. But we have talked this subject over frequently and I fear of becoming tedious—

Cousin Julia Tate and Cousin Wistar[4] are in town. They got in last night and are spending the day here. I have only just spoken to Cousin Julia and intend calling on her as soon as I finish this letter. I hope Miss Muff is quite well. As you know she is a favorite of mine. You said in your next you would probably tell me when you should leave Rutherford, do you think of going sure enough by Burke Court? Dr Lester told me he was going to Burke then and wished me to go with him. I would like to do so, but it is absolutely impossible. I have indeed a great deal to do and I really fear its going to be a great while before I do get to see you again. I shall endeavor to fix my business so that I can visit you before I start upon the circuit in December, but is really somewhat doubtful—The defeat of Gen Scott I suppose is most undoubtedly true and if our advices are correct he is not only beaten but *badly, wretchedly* beaten. I have been mad, almost to the fighting point, ever since I heard it—But there is no earthly use fretting about it and so I am preparing to submit, not *cheerfully* its true, but resignedly, composedly, like a *martyr*—in other words like a sensible man has to do when he cant help himself. Let me reccommend that sort of spirit to you: acquiesce but enter your solemn protest on the record. Have you heard lately from Gen. [John Gray] Bynum? I hope he is in health. Write to me soon Harriet, I am always so happy to get a line from you, that, although I know its getting irksome to you to write so much, yet I hope you will remember me in that way as often as possible. I will not write again untill I get an answer lest you should have left there. God bless you my own sweet love—Adieu.

Zebulon.

4. Julia and Samuel Caspar Wistar Tate of Morganton were the daughter and son of Dr. Samuel Tate and his wife, the former Mrs. Elizabeth Tate Gilliland. Wistar Tate was a lawyer. Sam J. Ervin, "The Tates of Burke County, N.C.," unpublished manuscript supplied by Samuel McDowell Tate of Morganton, N.C.

Rutherfordton Nov. 10th 1852

My beloved Zebulon;

As has been my custom for some time past, I have to write you only a few lines this afternoon & in great haste—I expect to leave here tomorrow or next day for home—Cousin has just left for Raleigh (in the stage) so you know I am anxious to leave as soon as possible—Cousin Gray[5] has been very ill—Cousin Mary has not received a letter from him since you were here—Cousin Woodfin has written frequently that he was improving slowly, but Cousin was so uneasy that she as well as myself thought it much the best that she should go down—I will stay with Muff & Clara until I leave for home. I have no doubt but that I will enjoy myself very much. They are going up to Morganton on Monday or Tuesday, will only stay a day or two—They are going up only to attend the *Odd Fellows* party—You spoke something of going to Morganton next week with Dr Lester—How delighted my dearest, one should be to see you then—I know you will go if you possibly can—Do dont write me again, that it is doubtful whether you can visit me before going on the Circuit—I think you *ought* to come before then,—but it is getting late & I must close; I have a great many more things to say & wish I had time to write them but have not; I promis you a long letter when I get home—& will also expect one from you very soon after my arrival—Do dearest come to see me next week if you possibly can though I would enjoy a visit much more at a private time but come then if you can—you know I enjoy your company at all times—Really dearest I must say farewell—Muff is now waiting for me—Do excuse this half sheet of paper as well as what is on it—God bless you my dearest. In great haste—Your own

Harriett

Asheville Nov. 14 '52

My dear, Noble Harriet,

I am writing to you on the Sabbath as you will see by the date of this, but I hope I am excusable for it under all the circumstances.

---

5. John Gray Bynum and Nicholas W. Woodfin were members of the state Senate in session at Raleigh. R. D. W. Connor, comp., *A Manual of North Carolina Issued by the North Carolina Historical Commission for the Use of the Members of the General Assembly Session 1913* (Raleigh, N.C.: E. M. Uzzell and Co., State Printers, 1913), pp. 517, 799.

I have since last monday morning, been on horseback and away from home every day, and only got in home, last night quite late, quite "*8 O'clk*" sure enough this time. The business I have undertaken is extremely tedious and troublesome and requires my almost constant attention. Withal it is not very proffitable, so that I am becoming sick of it, but am compelled to hold on at this stage of the game. I could not possibly have written to you at any other time during the past week, and fearful of making you uneasy by delaying farther, as I have to start again in the morning, I determined to write to day at all events. It is bitter cold weather this morning; the villagers are attending church and I should be there myself, but the temptation to enjoy a good fire in the silence of my room and a communion with you by letter, overcame my ideas of duty and I am not there. Besides the church is but poorly warmed and from riding in the cold wind last night I have a slight touch of the toothache.

So you are back at home again! I do wish I could go to the Odd Fellows Celebration on the 17th. I recd. an invitation, but it is entirely impossible for me to attend. And Mrs Bynum has gone to Raleigh to attend her husband in his illness; I can not but admire her devotion, at the same time I am sorry to hear of the Generals [John Gray Bynum's] continued ill-health. You spent the time after her departure I suppose, with my fairest of friends Miss Clara and Miss Muff. I almost envied you the pleasure which I know you must have enjoyed in the company of two such charming young Ladies. I hope you may have equally as much enjoyment while they are in M—— and especially at the party. After it is over I hope you will write me a long letter giving me a description of your amusements &c since I left you. It has been so long since I enjoyed one of those lengthy and affectionate letters which you used to write me, that I am getting quite impatient for one of them. I will not expect it though, untill you have sufficient time, and am quite happy to receive your short ones, as they are weekly assurances of your health and continuing affection. I hope mine have the effect of giving the same comfortable assurances to you; they possess no interest otherwise I am certain, for I have really exhausted every topic pertinent to our correspondence, except the *one glowing theme:* that I consider inexhaustible, and yet I have written so much upon it and raved so passionately in your presence that I begin to grow almost ashamed to fill my letters intirely with it. Yet I do assure you Hattie, that it is almost an impossibility for me to write any other kind of a letter to you. When ever I leave that subject to speak of anything else, it seems as if I were digressing most unpardonably from the object proper of my letter, and feel like hastening back to it, and begging the reader's (which of course is you) pardon—But here goes for a slight digression, which I hope you will be good enough to forgive.

I recd—a letter this week from a friend of mine in Charleston, Murdock,[6] from whom I scarcely ever expected to hear again. Some few weeks ago he was taken with the yellow fever and lay for a considerable time in the Hospital given up by the physicians for lost. But after considerable suffering he got up and has given me a long description of his misfortunes. He was out of employment and consequently out of money when taken sick and his father here was unable to go to his relief—He was consequently left to the care of the keepers of the Hospital, quite a cheerless place for a man on a death-bed. A slight extract from his letter may not prove uninteresting—After speaking of tossing and turning consumed with a burning fever and dreaming of the clear and cool mountain rills of Buncombe, he speaks of the force with which the mind on a death-bed flies back to the early scenes of home and childhood and adds— "I have had many opportunities of observing it. I have sat up many nights in the Hospital and heard the last words of men of different nations. I heard the dying German rave wildly of the blue waters of the Rhine and the vine covered hills of his Fatherland; the Swiss call the cattle among his dear native mountains, and the Scott remembering with love when dying, what he never did in health, the bonny heather crowned hills of Caledonia; and 'mine goot Mutter' and the 'Auld Mon' quiver on their lips while the vital spark was burning low & the horrid black vomit was choking their utterances." He is quite well now and doing well enough. We had a letter quite lately from Dr Neilson—his health is very bad indeed but is much better than it had been as he was once nearly dead. He says he will come home next summer. I will look for a letter before long from you and shall write frequently myself. Our friends here all quite well. I have nothing more to add Hattie, but my blessing; you have that with all the warmth of an affectionate heart, and may God add His also upon you is my prayer.

Your own devoted Zebulon.

6. Robert J. Murdoch, son of William and Margaret Murdoch. He and his father were farmers in Buncombe County. Johnston, *Papers of ZBV*, 1: 20, 94 n.

Asheville—
19 Nov. 1852

My dear Harriet,

Again I sit down to write you yet another letter. It is now almost a week since I wrote to you last and I consider it a long while to do without hearing from you and I suppose your feelings must be the same. I should have written last mail, but was looking for a letter in it from you and thought I would wait and answer it. But none came, and I write by this mail to let you know of my health and ever constant devotion, thinking that you may have been so much engaged with the party on the 17—&c that you could not well write. It has been so very cold this week that I have not been from home as I anticipated when I last wrote. We have had some severe weather indeed. I thought pretty strongly of attending the Celebration and would have been exceedingly pleased if I could have been there, but I thought if the weather was too cold and disagreeable to attend to business *a for[t]iori* it must be too cold to seek pleasure and at that distance from home. And now Hattie I will be compelled to repeat those words which you begged me not to say again, for I do think it almost impossible for me to see you before going upon the circuit. Cherokee Court begins on Monday week from this time, and being so close at hand if I go to see you I will have to defer visiting that court. I have some business there too, but none of any considerable importance its true. There is a probability of my being benefited by going out that way this time, tho' it is only a probability. Anticipating as I do a long and *very pleasant* visit to Morganton in company with Dr Lester very soon could you my dear Hattie suffer me to delay my visit untill that time? if I am rightly informed as to the time when the Dr will make his *grand visit* it will not be so very long to wait. If it should be farther off than I expect I promise you to be with you as soon as I get back from the courts. Nothing but a sense of duty could induce me to undergo such a great self denial of pleasure as visiting you affords me. Besides my Dear Hattie you know that to some extent the eyes of the community are upon me, watching my conduct, and I must exhibit at least a seeming of attention to business if nothing more. I am very anxious to establish the character of an attentive man to my business and having a little entrusted to my hands already I must make it the means of getting more and that which is more proffitable. Your good sense will readily acquiesce in the justice of my remarks I am certain, tho' your love for me (for which may Heaven bless you) may wish it otherwise. Please write me upon the subject. I must own Hattie that I am so proud of your affections for your unworthy Zebulon, that I can scarcely find it within my boosom to deny your request of visiting you no matter what kind of business I have on hand. Indeed Hattie I could refuse you nothing of that, if I did not think upon the future, and how much I have to do both for you and myself, to establish a character and earn a competency for us. I do hope you may appreciate my motives. God knows Hattie, if it were possible I would desire to be with [you] always———.

Dr Lester has gone over, as he intimated to me, to make his arrangements for a wedding. He wished to take a message for me, and I told him he could deliver *my respects* if he saw you. Mrs Chunn[7] is also there and requested to bear some message to you but of course I could give her none. She is, and always has been my favorite female acquaintance among the married ladies of this place. I hope you like her too. Aunt Mary has been up in my room since I began to write and desires to be remembered kindly to you. Mother has been quite unwell for a day or two but is now better. Sister's health has improved beyond our most sanguine expectations. Sister Ann[8] is in Yancey teaching school. Do kiss my lovely cousin Mary Jo for me, I am almost afraid to tell you how much I love—no—*like* her. Please write to me soon as you can conveniently and believe me to be the same faithful, constant, and affectionate Zebulon.

Letter of HNE missing.

Asheville, 25—Nov. 52 [1852]

My dear, *dear* Harriet,

I have just returned from a little excursion into the coun-

7. Sarah M. Chunn, thirty-five, a native of Pennsylvania, was the wife of Alfred B. Chunn, prosperous farmer and politician of Asheville. *Census* of Buncombe County, 1850; Foster Alexander Sondley, *Asheville and Buncombe County* (Asheville, N.C.: The Citizen Co., 1922), p. 199.

8. Ann Edgeworth Vance, a graduate of Holston Conference Female College, was teaching at Burnsville in Yancey County, N.C. Clement Dowd, *Life of Zebulon B. Vance* (Charlotte, N.C.: Observer Printing and Publishing House, 1897), p. 7; *Asheville News*, October 28, 1852.

try where I had the pleasure of getting a pretty severe wetting, as it has been quite a disagreeable, rainy day, and having seated myself before a cheerful fire I take up my writing implements to give you my usual letter for the week. I am in my usual health and spirits this evening, but we have had for some days past such gloomy and disagreeable weather that it is almost impossible to keep from being infected with the blues since all nature seems afflicted with them. The rain continues to fall, and our streets are almost impassable with the mud, and thousands upon thousands of hogs pouring through the town adds to the general filthyness of every thing around. This is the time for self-communion, when the mind debarred of impressions from the external world, falls back upon its own resources for nutriment for its unceasing activity; and if ones mind in this situation be accustomed as mine is to secret and self cognizant thought, then it can find amusement enough to drive the flying hours past without suffering them to lag so as to become tedious. This is the time above all others when the inestimable riches of the Social circle where *love* is predominant are felt and appreciated, when happiness will be doubly felt when the tempests assail the roof over our heads and we feel that it can not reach us. In such a situation as this, in which I now am what so natural as that my heart should turn with softest emotion to its idol and throb with wild desire for your presence to dispel the sense of loneliness with which it is oppressed? Such are my feelings to night Hattie; the fire blazes cheerfully, my law-books are on the mantel looking reproachfully down upon me for this days neglect, and every thing tells me I should [go] to work and make up for the loss of today, but "the heart, the breast, is lonely still" and I can do nothing but wish, and wish, and wish again that you was this night by my side to make the demon of loneliness vanish from my presence. But as this cannot be, I quit every thing to commune with you in the only manner possible, and pour my overflowing soul into your sympathetic ear. Tis always sweet to talk with one who values what we say, and of course I prefer talking to you even tho' it be in this unsatisfactory manner, being so vain as to think that you will regard my letters as I do yours.

You say you fear I have been disappointed for several mails in not receiving a letter from you. Indeed my dear Harriet I was. In justice to one whom I know to be faithful and devoted I *should* not say that I was somewhat alarmed as well as disappointed at your silence, but I must if I would speak truth say that such was the case. I really was thinking that something was going amiss. This is foolish perhaps, nay I *know* it to be extremely so, but the recollection that I have enemies of so much influence with your relations keeps me in constant dread, and when your letters fail to reach me at the accustomed time I am soon plunged into an agony which is increased with each successive mail that brings me nothing. I really suffered, to some extent from last sunday evening untill yesterdays mail brought me your welcome, yes thrice welcome letter. I beg of you my Dearest Harriet not to think from this that I am doubting *you*, or treating you with the least shadow of injustice for I know that you will believe me sincere when I say that after what has passed between us, if you be not constant and sincere, there is no constancy or sincerity left upon this earth. But I am happy again and I will promise you not to disturb you with my unhappy moments soon again. Indeed it is wrong I believe to do it now, and I wish that I had not—so I beg your forgiveness. I was extremely sorry that I could not be present at the many scenes of pleasure lately exhibited in your village. I am however happy in thinking that you have been participating in those pleasures; you have such charming society to mingle with that I do not wonder at your unwillingness to leave Burke. Our own village is still quite dull as regards pleasure; but we are expecting some three or four weddings before long. There will probably be no stir however at either of them. The weddings I allude to will be those of Miss Cordelia Gilliland to a Mr. Aston[9] of Tennessee, thought be on hand directly, Miss Mary Shuford and a Mr Graves[10] of Caswell county, only rumored, Jesse Smith & Miss Magie Graves[11] &c, &c. The latter is only rumored also. Miss Gilliland by the by, is an old flame of mine, and Miss Graves is the young lady with whom I told you I flirted in retaliation you know. I

9. After his marriage to Cordelia Gilliland, daughter of the late Lewellyn Gilliland of Buncombe County, Edward J. Aston, a native of Rogersville, Tennessee, moved to Asheville where he became a leading citizen. John Preston Arthur, *Western North Carolina: A History (From 1730 to 1913)* (Asheville, N.C.: The Edward Buncombe Chapter of the Daughters of the American Revolution of Asheville, N.C., 1914), p. 396; Buncombe County Inventories, Accounts and Doweries, 1845-1860, State Department of Archives and History, Raleigh, N.C., p. 184.

10. On August 30, 1853, Mary E. Shuford, who had lived in the household of James M. Smith at the Buck Hotel, married William B. Graves, a merchant of Yanceyville. *Census* of Buncombe County, 1850; *Census* of Caswell County, 1850; Buncombe County Marriage Register, Buncombe County Courthouse, Asheville, N.C.

11. Jesse Siler Smith clerked in the store of his father, James M. Smith. Miss M. F. Graves, twenty, of Yanceyville, probably "Miss Magie Graves," was a sister of William B. Graves. *Census* of Buncombe County, 1850; *Census* of Caswell County, 1850.

have not spoken with Dr Lester only for a moment since his return and cant say when *it* will come off; if I find out I will write you. You have heard before this I suppose of the death of Lenoir Avery,[12] I was pained to hear it, and also the ill health of Sam McDowell. What suffering they undergo for gold! I shall close this by hoping that it may reach you in happiness and health. I shall lay my head upon my pillow to night with sincere and heartfelt petitions for you and thanking God that you have been the means of my forsaking a great sin. I am fulfilling my promise nobly, far beyond my utmost expectations. I have no objections to your going to Salisbury and do not fear that you will flirt with any one. Goodnight my dearest Hattie,

Good night: Zebulon

Morganton Nov 30th 1852

My beloved Zebulon;

Notwithstanding I have a very sore eye, I must write you (at least) a short letter by this Mail—I have suffered considerably with my eye for several days past & it is so unusual for me, that I have been somewhat uneasy, but my fears are this morning all removed, as my eye is so much better. I was frequently troubled with sore eyes while going to school,[13] but since I left school they have never been the least weak & I think now I am only suffering from reading & writing too much by candle-lighting as I did a great deal of it after I found that my eye was weak. I intend now being very careful until it is entirely well, so dont allow yourself to be the least uneasy.

I wrote to you by last Mail, but neglected having my letter mailed—I wrote the letter principally to assure you that I would certainly excuse you from visiting me just now, under the circumstances—you know, dearest, I am not unreasonable & am fully convinced that you will come as often as possible, for it affords you I

---

12. Thomas Lenoir Avery, son of Isaac T. Avery of Swan Ponds, died in Marysville, California, of Asiatic cholera September 23, 1852. Edward W. Phifer, "Saga of a Burke County Family (The Sons)," *North Carolina Historical Review* 39 (Summer, 1962): 324.

13. In 1847 HNE was a pupil of Miss R. Gould, a Yankee spinster. Miss Gould's school was in the house of James McKesson in Morganton. Whether Harriett subsequently attended a school elsewhere is not known. Information transmitted by Dr. Edward W. Phifer of Morganton, N.C., from the reminiscences of Mr. Nelson Powell, who was living in Morganton in 1847.

have, no doubt, equally as much happiness to be with me as it does me to have you visit me; the *long* visit that you promised me before long I hope will more than compensate for your necessary delay. I am anticipating much pleasure at that time with many of our friends but my greatest enjoyment will be with my own dear one. Miss Ann is looking very happy indeed & I suppose of course the Dr is—I was at Dr Happoldts this morning & judge from Ann's conversation that the wedding will certainly come off soon, though she did not say any thing to me upon the subject of being Bridesmaid.

I have abandoned the idea of going to Salisbury entirely & think now I shall remain at my much valued home all the winter & dearest you must visit me often—Your esteemed friend Mrs Chunn has been endeavoring to persuaid me to return home with her, but I have not the most distant idea of doing so—She is indeed a charming woman—& one to whom I have always been much attached & I can but love her now more than ever—as I think she is such a warm friend of my much loved Zebulon—she has been speaking very highly of you since she came over.

When do you leave for Cherokee? What a disagreeable time I fear you will have—I will be so anxious about you until I hear you have returned safely home but you must write as often as possible while you are on your circuit—I suppose though it will be useless for me to write to you until I learn you are at home as you would probably not receive my letters for a great while.

How sad is the death of Mr Lenoir Avery—I do most sincerely sympathise with his deeply distressed friends,—just think it is just now a year since they were so much distressed at the murder Mr W. W. Avery commited & now they are again called to pass through the furnace of affliction. Hearing such melancholy news from California causes those of us who still have friends there suffer great anxiety about them; We heard only a few days ago from Brother Sam—his health has been very bad, but he is now quite recovered. Our other friends there, I believe, are quite well. I must close in great haste as we have company—Do write soon & as often as possible.
My love to your Mother, Sisters & Aunt—God bless you dearest. In haste.

Your devoted Harriett.

Decr 3d 1852

My Own dear Harriet,

    I was made happy as usual by the reception of your letter last night and sit down this evening to answer it, full of pleasing and buoyant hope. I can scarcely ever feel any other way but happy, no matter what befalls me, when I receive again and again letters from you, still breathing affection and still uttering nothing but the language of love! It is impossible for me to tire of them, or even feel *patient* when looking for one and I am now when at home always at the office waiting for the mail to come with an impatience as great and as feverish as that which consumed me when waiting for the first letter I ever recd from you. They are truly a source of infinite enjoyment to me during the weary months of banishment from your presence that I have to endure. I was sorry tho' to learn by your last that you had been suffering from sore eyes, but I hope as you say that you are recovering and that your recovery will be permanent. I wish I could suffer for you Harriet and prevent you from ever feeling the pangs of pain—But this is a foolish and puerile wish—there are sufferings of the mind and wounds of the heart which I *can* prevent and I should be careful to see that I perform things within my power without grieving at my inability to do other things. I shall do well Harriet if I attend to those things, as it is my duty to do—and I trust in God that my conduct toward you shall ever be such as that no pang you ever suffer may be attributable to him in whom you have reposed so much. I did not go to Cherokee as I expected. It was so far and no one was going from here at all, and having some business in Madison County I went there. I will start to Macon next week. I am promising myself a long visit to you when the courts are over and hope at that time to repay you as well as myself for the great privation we will have undergone in not seeing each other sooner. Dr Lester says that he will not get married untill february; consequently I will not wait for him—

    Miss Cordelia Gilliland was married on Tuesday night in the Methodist Church—a manuvre rather new in this town. They have gone to Tennessee. Miss Clara Patton is at home I learn; I think I will go out and call upon her tomorrow, as I would like to have a talk with her—she has lately been with *you* and may probably have a great many pleasant things to say to me. This is one of the greatest inducements I have to visit Miss Clara, independent of her many other charming qualities: she is almost all the time teasing me about you. We heard a few days ago that Dr Neilson was still in very bad health and had lost one of his negro boys— We hope however that it is not the case and the report was not well authenticated. Mrs W—— has gone to Raleigh I suppose and you have declined going to S—— with her. I would have been pleased at your going if it would have given you pleasure—and if you would have been back at home when I go to Burke. But you love *home* and I am pleased to see it, the woman who loves home will strive to make home agreeable. I augur much from that fact. If you will write again, I will get it before I start to Macon by next Wednesdays mail. I will write often during my absence. May God protect you Hattie is my earnest prayer. Your own true Zebulon.

Quaker Meadows Dec 7th 1852

My beloved Zebulon;

Accept my many thanks for your kind letter, that gave me so much pleasure last evening & as you may not hear from me for several weeks, in consequence of your being absent attending the courts, I must, at least, write you a short letter by this Mail. I hope however, I will not be deprived of the pleasure of hearing from you every week—you dont know how much oblidge to you, I am, for writing me so regularly—I believe you have not allowed longer than one week to elaps without writing since your visit to me at Rutherfordton—do dearest, continue to write weekly & I will continue to bear patiently the *great* privation of not seeing you oftener. I am delighted that you did not go to Cherokee—I suppose you will have company out to Macon & I hope you will also have pleasant weather.

I was quite surprised to hear that Dr Lester & Ann would not be married until february—I presume he does not fear Mr Murphy[14] now & is willing that the wedding should be postponed —their approaching nuptials is one of the principal "on dits" of our Village—I guess persons generally will be quite disappointed to hear that it will not take place for so long.

I was pleased to hear by a letter from our friend Clara that Cordelia Gilliland had married such a promising young man; she is an old school mate of mine & of course I feel interested in

---

14. John Hugh Murphy, of Burke County, son of John and Margaret Stringer Avery Murphy. Elroy McKendree Avery and Catherine Hitchcock (Tilden Avery), *The Groton Avery Clan, 1616-1912*, 2 vols. (Cleveland, Ohio: n.p., 1912), 1: 652.

her—by the way—I think you wrote me she was an old flame of yours & most assuredly it was gratifying to you, to see her marrying so well—I very much approve her notion, of marrying in the Church, though I would prefer meeting at my home, a number of friends after leaving the Church. How numerous weddings have been during this year! I fear after Leap Year is over they will not be as general, but I hope they will not entirely cease—there will certainly be one (that is so much talked of now) that will not come off until next year & I guess our happiness will not be compleat, till that time arrives—Matrimony is generally productive of such happiness & I can but hope that our union will equal, if not surpass the happiness of many. You are not mistaken in supposing I *love* home & I will ever strive to make our home agreeable. How could I do otherwise when the companion, that will share the pleasures of this anticipated home, is so dear to me & so much loved by me & one that I am assured loves me with equal ardor? I was anxious to accompany Cousin Eliza as far as Salisbury but disliked to leave Aunty & Uncle alone. Brother James went down with her & I think intended going all the way—from Mr Sawyer's account I suppose Raleigh is at present a great place for those who are in pursuit of pleasure only—he spent this night week with us & appeared quite in the notion of going there are near there, to live—I imagin this would be agreeable news to many of the Asheville people. I received a very long & very intersting epistle last evening from My dear friend Clara—she always says something nice about you in her letters to me. I hope you have called to see her before this—she said in her letter she was expecting you soon—I would like to know what she has done with Mr Murphy—he & William Gaither[15] left Morganton a few days after she & Muff & have not returned yet—I suppose he [Mr. Murphy] did not go on home with Clara as she would have written me.

I was sorry to hear of Dr Neilson's misfortune, and that his own health continues bad—I hope he can very soon return to Carolina—We rec'd a letter from Brother Samuel yesterday—he is now quite well, though he has been an invalid much of the time since he left home—I should not be atall surprised to see him at home next Spring—I would say to all of our friends—Come home. I will certainly expect you over immediately after

---

15. Son of Burgess Sidney Gaither and Elizabeth Sharpe Erwin Gaither of Burke County. John McHugh McDowell, *The McDowells, Erwins, Irwins and Connections* (Memphis, Tenn.: C. B. Johnson & Co., 1918), p. 212.

your Courts are over. I hope the time will appear as short to you as it will to me & that you will spend it as pleasantly as I hope to—My sheet is almost filled & I have not said half that I wanted to, but I will reserve the rest to talk about when we meet or to write about if I should write again before you come over— Write me when you will return to Asheville & I will endeavor to have a letter there for you upon your arrival. My love to your Mother, Sisters & Aunt Mary. Need I urge you, My own one to think often of her who loves you with all the ardor of an affectionate heart while you are off on your circuit exposed to so many temptations—I flatter my self that a thought of me may frequently prevent you from engaging in those things that you know are wrong—but dearest remember that you are not accountable to me— Though I am pleased to have you consult my happiness & your happiness is mine, still I dont want you to strive alone for temporal happiness but above all things seek to please our Alwise Father. I suppose I need scarcely to remind you of your promis with regard to the third commandment—I feel assured that for my sake (if you are prompted by no higher motive) will induce you to keep your resolution most nobly. My eye is almost entirely well—I trust I shall not again be troubled with sore eyes —it was my own imprudence that caused me such suffering & I certainly deserved it. I really must close—May the choicest blessing be showered upon you My dearly loved Zebulon is the continued prayer of her whose love strengthens dayly for you—I am truly sorry that you cannot hear from me for so long, as you say my letters afford you such infinite enjoyment. Do write to me again before you leave home. How are you & Cousin John Woodfin getting on? I have heard nothing from him for a long time. My own one farewell. Your truly devoted Harriett.

Asheville, Dec 8. 1852

My Dearest Hattie,

    This is another wet gloomy day, and so unpleasant that I have concluded not to go up to town this evening, but spend it in writing to you and reading some law. As usual however I must write to you *first* and let "Chitty on Contracts" take his chances afterward; thats my way of doing business, the most important things first you know, and the minor things such as reading law shall be attended to if *possible*. Writing letters to you is becoming a habit with me and has so grown upon me that I can not be easy or contented untill I sit down to write. I console myself on this point however, by saying that this is at any rate not a bad habit and therefore I am not at all alarmed at its taking such a hold upon me; indeed on the contrary I think I rather encourage it and cherish its growth! Yesterday was the very antipode of this, I never saw a more beautiful day than it was. I had to ride some twelve miles into the country and starting quite early I was almost dazzled by the glittering rays of the bright morning sun. The earth was covered with an intense hoar frost and the sunbeams piercing the small transparent fog caused by the melting of the frost made every bush appear loaded down with crystal tears and even the dew-laden air was glittering with silver! The time honored mountains in the distance whose dark bases were upon the earth reared their summits to the skies glittering with new fallen snow upon which the morning sunbeams flashed intensely bright and seemed as if dancing with joy in honor of the young day! I thought those mountains Harriet, a fit emblem of the good and the just, whose brows are covered with the white garb of purity as they approach unto Heaven although this course on earth may appear dark and gloomy! Dont you think there is an aptness in the figure? O, it was a most glorious scene! and I envied myself the pleasure of beholding it unaccompanied; that always detracts from my pleasure on such occasions; now who do you suppose I wanted with me that morning? Cant you guess? I was bouyed and made light of heart by the glory of the scene and invigorated by the sharp morning air, so I galloped along, happy *almost* happy, and thought of—who? Well, I'll tell you who when we meet if you will ask me, and I know you will have so much curiosity that you won't forget it. Will you?

Well I reckon this is the last letter you will get from me in some time as I start to Macon on friday and it will be uncertain about my writing untill I come back. I will write however if I can, be assured of that. As to business I am really somewhat encouraged; I shall go to Macon with smart hopes of doing something, and at home I am getting on "right down sharp" as the yankees would say. I am going to make big speeches from one end of the circuit to the other and push myself along as much as the nature of the case and my native and *proverbial modesty* will permit. Time and perseverance can work wonders, and its my candid opinion that *you and I* will make some noise in the world yet!

Well I havent yet been to see Miss Clara, owing to a great many things; but I am invited out there tomorrow night to a party and I intend going there by all means. Cousin Clara Erwin[16] is out there I suppose—If any others are there I am not aware of it. Miss Lou and Cousin C—— called here yesterday in my absence *quensecontly* I didnt get to see them. A'int you somewhat surprised that I dont visit the Ladies more than I do? I am really surprised at myself, for I am so fond of them that it would seem as if I should always be with them and especially with those ladies out there in whom I recognize so many noble qualities—But the fact is Harriet, you rob the young ladies of my admiration for a thousand fine qualities, by presenting them all for my admiration in yourself and that too in such a superior light, that I have scarcely anything left for others. I aint flattering you, you know that my days of flattery are all past and gone. I hope you have written by the evening mail as in that case I will get it before I leave. I recd. some interesting letters from C. Hill not long since and learned that one of my favorite young ladies there, Miss Morrow[17] is going to be married. Ah, me!

My sheet is nearly run out and so I will only add a superfluity, viz: That I am now, have been for a long while and shall be untill death lays me low your sincere and truly devoted Zebulon.

Asheville Dec 10. '52

My dear Hattie

I had been intending to write to you all day but really could not get time. I have spent a very busy day indeed in doing some business that was needful to be done before I left home which kept me in town untill nine O'clk to night. I then came home packed up for an early start in the morning and having waited until nearly 11 O'clk for a visitor to leave who seemed determined never to go (as is generally the case), at his departure I sit down to say a few words to you before I go, as I can not suffer the opportunity to pass of writing again before being necessarily

16. Seventeen-year-old daughter of William C. Erwin of Burke County and his late wife Matilda Walton Erwin. Ibid., p. 222; *Census* of Burke County, 1850.

17. Mary Jane Morrow married Joseph Thompson in June, 1853. Orange County, N.C., *Marriage Bonds*, State Department of Archives and History, Raleigh, N.C.

silent for some weeks. I wish to indemnify you as much as possible, by writing thus often, and hope that you may feel somewhat compensated by getting two letters this week for not getting one next week. I shall probably be at home in ten days or two weeks at farthest. It is useless to say that I would be exceedingly gratified to find a *long* and affectionate letter waiting for me on my return; affectionate I *know* it will be and long I hope it may be. At the same time I would remind you as I have often done, that I am quite thankful and content to receive either long or short, and thats *the long and the short* of it.

Well, what news have I got for you? I thought when I began to write I was in too much of a hurry to speak of news, and Pope in one of his letters to Mrs Martha Blount says that it is not much sign of *lovers* being together when they begin to ask each other what the world is doing! But when have I written you a short letter? and when have I written one but what was full enough (in all conscience) of love? I will therefore tell you that Miss Clara gave a party on Wednesday evening last which I attended of course—It was quite a pleasant one indeed and I had a most glorious private chat with Miss Clara about you, which I enjoyed even more than the party. She told me as I expected, a great many fine things about you and I listened with such delight and earnestness that I think she was more than once quite amused at my eagerness to hear you praised—I called again yesterday and made most outrageous long stay for a mere call, a custom I have, you know. I know of but one man who can beat me at that, and he is Mr Victor Barringer. We have some pretty fine ladies over here after all beside those at Pleasant Retreat, and I am really beginning to think that the unsociable character of our village (I mean amongst the young people) is altogether owing to the gentlemen. In fact such is the really true case. But why have I digressed in this way when I should be telling you how much I am going to think of you while I am riding through the mountains and how the thought of you will often cause me to turn away from evil and make me a good boy? Indeed Hattie I will—think of you all the time—and you will most assuredly have a great influence over me for the better. You know at any rate that I shall endeavor to do right and shall combat evil habits as much as one can who is so much under their control as I am.

I really thank you much for the letter by last mail—it was a charming as well as gratifying one to me. I do want to see you so bad that I am truly distressed at the thought of being away from you so long as I will have to be. As you say, I enjoy each succeeding visit more than its predecessor! When I think of meeting you again and seating myself by your side for a "war-talk", I get so nervous that I feel as if I could'nt behave myself. My visits are really becoming dangerous, for I dont think I can make many more of them without begging you to precipitate our marriage. But of that hereafter. Adieu, my dear, sweet Hattie, a thousand adieus of a warm fond heart. May God bless you, and may his guardian angels watch over you with a constancy only equalled by the love of your Devoted Zebulon.

Asheville Dec 24. [1852]

My Dear Harriet,

I got back home from Haywood Court on last wednesday night and was somewhat disappointed in not finding a letter waiting for me. I bore it patiently however, thinking that you might have not expected me at home untill the last of the week. I am therefore looking anxiously for a letter by sunday evenings mail. I had a most disagreeable spell of weather indeed to go to the courts in. The earth was glittering with snow the morning I left home; a large amount of it having fallen the night before, and the air was so very cold that I had almost declined going. But I struck boldly off in Company with Esqr Williams[18] and P. W. Roberts, and as is generally the case found the reality not so bad as my imagination had pictured it, for I suffered very little really from the cold, although it was very unpleasant traveling— Alternate rain, snow & sleet characterised the weather during my absence, whilst the mud and bad roads will not admit of a description. In consequence, the courts were rather poorly attended and very little business done. I made a "tall" speech in Franklin and marked my name to three or four cases on the docket. I have a great many amusing things to tell you when we meet in relation to my peregrinations out there. In Haywood I did not do so well as the weather was worse if anything than the week before and almost every case on the civil docket was continued; besides it was my first attendance there. I left there as early as possible,

---

18. William Williams of Buncombe County went from the mercantile business into the law, at which he was not very successful. Arthur, *Western North Carolina*, p. 391.

which was on Wednesday morning and ploughed my way home through the mud.

I was very much tempted yesterday morning to leave my business and run over to Morganton as I had an invitation from my friend Mr Brown[19] to go over with him—But if he had gone, he said he could not have staid but two or three days, and my own business being rather pressing during this time and my approaching Court (on Monday week) I thought I would decidedly prefer waiting until after Court at which time I hope to have leisure for quite a long and pleasant visit. Besides I must own that I prefer, much prefer, visiting you at a time when everything is quiet at Morganton, as parties which I would be compelled to attend would really be an annoyance, when your private company was to be had *solus cum sola*. Miss Clara has again gone over to Burke and I suppose will see you before her return—Her going was the inducement to Mr Brown to go, and as he would not go without me, I was sorry to disappoint him.

I am almost distracted to see you again! Some little circumstances are transpiring that make me exceedingly anxious to have a long talk with you—About what? Our union? Certainly, about that very thing. You may say truly Harriet that you occupied my almost every thought during my absence, for beside the constant and unwavering inclination of my heart towards you at all times and under all circumstances, the frankness of Capt McDowell put it in the power of the good folks out west to remind me of you frequently. My good Landlady at Franklin told me that she knew all about it, teasing me not a little. Indeed where ever I was known, the fact of our engagement seemed almost equally as well known. This was not in the least degree annoying however as I have almost ceased to become annoyed by peoples' teasing me, and had the good effect of keeping my mind the more constantly fixed upon your injunction, to think of you and refrain from anything evil. I did so, and am gratified to report my progress in the reformation which I promised you. Indeed my *beloved One,* you have a most unlimited influence over me! You may judge something of it when you consider with what strength and tenacity evil habits fasten upon the moral constitution of

19. William Caleb Brown was a son of John and Ann Evans Brown of Lewiston, Pennsylvania. In 1843 John Brown, a lawyer, moved his family to Buncombe County because of his interest in large tracts of land in western counties. The Vance and Brown families became close friends. In 1858 William Caleb Brown and ZBV formed a law partnership in Asheville. Johnston, *Papers of ZBV,* 1: 54, n. 106, n. 108.

man, and see that I am fast conquering a most dangerous and tenacious one for your sake!

Where and how will you spend your Christmas? Do write me all about it; I hope to hear that you have spent it happily. I have no particular pleasure in view. A caged fox was to have been turned loose tonight to have a race. I went up into town to join it, but it began to rain pretty hard and poor Reynard who has already run one hard race is reprieved untill tomorrow, when he will have to run another. Rather unrefined sport, but beside that and the popping of a few crackers in the streets by little boys our village evidences not the least excitement. It is quite late and my sheet is filled so that I shall only add my usual protestations of undying devotion, and pray you to accept a fervent and earnest blessing warm from the heart of your own Zebulon.

Quaker Meadows Dec 25th 1852

My beloved Zebulon—

After wishing you a happy Christmas, I must express to you the pleasure it affords me to withdraw myself from the family for a short time to commune with my own loved one, knowing that the trifling offering of a short letter will be an acceptable Christmas present to you. Greatly would I prefer enjoying a "tête-à-tête" with you this morning—but being debarred that pleasure, I must resort to the means which the God of benevolence has placed in my power.

I was just thinking this morning that this would *perhaps* be the last Christmas that we would spend in a state of "single blessedness" & the thought made me both sad & joyful—Sad— when I think of biding farewell to the home of my childhood— how tenderly remembered & how strongly affection clings to the sunny & endeared spots around the home of childhood—no matter with what feelings we bid an adieu—whether with bright prospects—or in adversity; in either case, the mind ever turns with pleasing recolections to the spot where every object, tree, flower, rock & shrub is associated with our earliest, & must I say happiest days! I can but hope that many more happy days are in store for you & me & this hope makes me happy now—yes dearest no matter, how far I may be removed from other friends—the one that I will love above all others, I trust will ever be near me, & this will *more* than compensate for the absence of those whom it has heretofore given me so much pleasure to be with. What ere our fate in this life may be, I ask, that we may share it togather—for I am persuaided that if we will both act well our parts we will be contented in each others society & contentment is happiness,—I could continue this strain for some length, but I must be brief this morning.

I hope by this time you have returned however; what disagreeable weather you have had; I have thought much about your being exposed; I looked a little for a letter from you by last mail informing me of your arrival at home, but come to the conclusion (when they returned from the office without one) that you were still absent; I expect to hear by next mail from you & will be a little disappointed if I do not, but my own one, I will not censure you, for I am confident you write when it is possible—two week appears a long time to pass, without my hearing from you & I believe it has been that long since I received your last, & it is also two weeks nearer the time of your long visit—how many more weeks will elaps before that time arrives? Cousin Wister Tate told me a few days since, that you were coming over with him from Yancy Court—& I will certainly look for you then & I suppose not very long after that visit, you will accompany Dr Lester over to the celebration of his & Miss Ann's nuptials, so I am hoping to see much of you during the remainder of the winter—I have seen Ann frequently since I wrote you last—she told me all about her's & the Drs arrangements &c. as she knew the Dr had told you.—

I was glad to learn by your last letter that you had a pleasant evening at Mr Pattons, & I was particularly pleased, that you enjoyed so much the society of my dear friend Clara—She was expected in Morganton last evening & I regret that it is raining to day so it will prevent me from seeing her—I hope she has not been disappointed in her visit—Dont you think Clara Erwin a lovely girl? I love her very much—she & your particular friend Miss Lue are both great favorit's of mine.

I saw Mollie Jo a few days ago—she desired much love & a kiss to her dear cousin Zeb.— & now, my own love, after assuring you of my so often expressed attachment—I must close my brief epistle.

This is really a gloomy Christmas day, but I have spent the short time I have been writing to you, most delightfully; I am generally happy when engaged in anything that will afford you pleasure, that is, as far as it is pleasing in the sight of our hevenly Father—may our efforts to make each other happy meet with His approbation is my sincere prayer—May heaven protect you My dearest & may I soon have the pleasure of seeing you in fine health & spirits—I hope you will continue the habbit of writing to me weekly.—I have much more to say but have neither time nor space so I must bid you adieu with the promis to write again.—My kind regards to your Mother, Aunt Mary & Sisters. In love yours *Harriett.*

ZBV visited HNE the latter part of December, 1852, and left Morganton on January 1, 1853.

Asheville
Jan 7. 1853

My Dear Harriet

I have just returned from the court house this (friday) afternoon, where I have been engaged all the week, and take advantage of this my first leisure to write you a short letter. I was sorry I could not write by Thursdays mail, but it was really out of the question for me to do it. The weather was so severe that there was litte business done on monday and tuesday, so that wednesday was my busiest day during the week—Tomorrow after dinner I start for Madison, thence to Yancey so that this is my only chance of writing—

Well, well, we had fine weather after all to go home in. We got to Carsons early on Saturday evening and got home on Sunday evening about 6 O'clk. As I expected it turned out my business suffered some little by my being absent the preceeding week of Court, and I was unsuccessful in a few cases where attention might have saved me. But I dont regret it: it only proves the necessity of my getting married the sooner. I was not quite so fortunate in all respects this court as I was at last court, but I think I did pretty well notwithstanding. Mr Woodfin arrived last night. I suppose you saw him as he passed through your village—

What speed did you have in getting up a grand rally of the reading society? I hope you were successful in getting the thing under way again. I understood that Mr McKesson was to give a party this week, when I was in Morganton—Did you attend? and have a pleasant time? Our Buncombe Ladies I suppose will remain with you untill after the wedding—That reminds me of my friend Mr Brown—poor fellow; I am extremely sorry for him. As we came home, it seemed to almost kill him to see me so happy and reveling in the glories of the future, when he could see nothing but darkness and despair. He will start to California[20] soon, & I have been persuading him to make a declaration—at all hazards, but he cant sum up the courage requisite to so dreadful a thing as that. I think it likely he will go over with us to the wedding if not gone by that time, in order to take one more long-lingering glance at Miss Clara [Patton]! What a silly youth! Several young gentlemen are speaking of going over with the Dr on the 27,"—among them are Dr Hilliard[21] (the good looking gentleman whom you prefered to an intelligent one", dont you recollect?) D Rankin,[22] Mr Pink Deaver[23] Jesse Smith and—I forget the remainder. We are anticipating quite a jolly time and hope to enjoy ourselves extremely.

Well, I have filled these pages with little or nothing of interest to you, what shall I say for the ballance? My Mother & Sister are all quite well and beg me in return for the kind messages which you so frequently send them, to mention them to you sincerely—Aunt Mary is already from the representations I make to her (of course they are quite glowing) your warmest friend and is constantly wanting to visit Burke on purpose to see you. Indeed my friends here are almost quite as anxious for me to bring you to Buncombe as I am myself. You need not write before the last of next week as I will not be at home to get it probably before the week after next as I expect if it be good weather to

20. He was going to join his brother, John Evans Brown, who had been prospecting in California since 1849. A fascinating account of John Evans Brown's cross-country journey from Asheville to California is found in his "Memoirs of an American Gold Seeker," *Journal of American History* 2, no. 2 (1908): 129-54.
21. Dr. William Lewis Hilliard began his medical practice in Asheville with Dr. Thomas C. Lester. Gaillard S. Tennent, "Medicine in Buncombe County Down to 1885," reprinted from the *Charlotte Medical Journal* (May, 1906), pp. 14, 15.
22. David Rankin, a close friend of ZBV's. His father, William David Rankin, ran a large Asheville mercantile establishment in partnership with R. W. Pulliam. Johnston, *Papers of ZBV*, 1: 20, 21, 96 n.
23. Pinckney Deaver, son of Colonel Reuben Deaver, who operated a summer hotel at Deaver's Springs, five miles west of Asheville. *Census* of Buncombe County, 1850; Minutes of the Buncombe County Court of Pleas and Quarter Sessions, Minute Docket, October 8, 1852, State Department of Archives and History, Raleigh, N.C., Book C, p. 658; Arthur, *Western North Carolina*, p. 502.

go up into Watauga County before I return. Wont you write by Mr [James] McKesson to me at Yancey Court? do if you please, if he be not gone when you get this.

Adieu for some time my Dearest One & believe no one more faithful and devoted than your constant Zebulon.

Asheville Jan 16. [1853]

My Dear Harriet,

I got back home from the courts sooner than I expected in consequence of the disagreeable state of the weather. I had intended as I wrote you to go up into Watauga County which would have detained me a week longer but the rain continuing to fall in such quantities rendered the roads almost utterly impassible so I gave it up and came home from Yancey on friday evening. It was well for me that I did, for immediately on my arrival I was seized with a violent tooth-ache which has not left me yet, although it is so much better this morning that I am able to write; I brought this on me I suppose from exposure in attending court in such dreadful weather as we have had; I never saw worse, and I am resolved not to attend any more courts this winter. After my approaching trip to Morganton is over I shall be compelled to settle down and do some reading or I will positively not be able to get license in August, which I extremely anxious to do.

I was sorry I told you not to write me untill this late, for I was sorry I could not find a letter from you in the office when I got back. It was my own fault however, and I promise not to do so again—Mr Merrimon got back from Raleigh last week, having obtained his [superior court] license.

I expect Dr Lester will be accompanied next week by some of our Buncombe ladies—I hear several speaking of going—Miss Harriet Osborne,[24] Miss Ada Morrison[25] Miss Mary Gilliland[26] &c, &c—

24. Harriet Osborne lived in Asheville in the home of the Albert T. Summeys. She was probably a relative of Joseph R. Osborne of Asheville, who was one of the "securities" of Albert T. Summey when he became guardian of Ada Morrison and her brother. *Census* of Buncombe County, 1850; Minutes, Buncombe County Court, July 2, 1851, p. 610.

25. Julia Adelaide Morrison was the daughter of the late Washington Morrison and Mrs. Albert T. (S. Rose Morrison) Summey, who owned much property in Asheville. *Census* of Buncombe County, 1850; *Asheville Messenger*, August 15, 1850; Minutes, Buncombe County Court, July 2, 1851.

26. Mary Gilliland was a daughter of the late Lewellyn Gilliland of Bun-

I have been trying my best to write you a letter this morning, but find it almost impossible—my tooth now & then gives some pangs which almost throw me out of my chair, and so distracts my ideas that I cant think of what I am saying. Please Harriet accept this short letter in the spirit in which it is intended and excuse its being so short; you know I dont often write you short letters—I can not add anything more except the usual assurances of my devoted and unfailing love, and the hope that if this evenings mail does not bring me a letter that the next mail at least will bring one from Harriet to her own faithful and

       Constantly devoted Zebulon—

       Quaker Meadows January 17th [1853]
My beloved Zebulon—

I fear you were somewhat disappointed that you did not receive a letter from me, by last Mail & I would have written, had you not said in your letter to me, that you would probably go from Yancy to Watauga & be absent until sometime this week; I hope however you have returned by this.—I was delighted to receive your last epistle informing me of your safe arrival.

I hope the bright anticipations that you, together with your other young friends have, with regard to your approaching visit to our Village, will all be realized.—they are making great preperations at the Drs & I think, are expecting quite a large company from Asheville—I understood that Mr Wash Hardy[27] had brought intelligence that Mr Deaver & Mr Smyth [Smith] had declined officiating as attendents—Ann says if it so she has not heard it, so I cant believe that it is the case. Dr Happoldt intends having a large party—every person in Morganton are invited & I think he has sent to other places 80 invitations—We are all looking forward to it, with great delight—& I am confident we will have a merry time. Mollie Jo requests me to remind you of your promis to take her over with you so you must come prepared to take her—

  Would you not like to have me accompany you also? If

---

combe County. *Census* of Buncombe County, 1850; Buncombe County Inventories, Accounts and Doweries, 1845-1860, State Department of Archives and History, Raleigh, N.C., p. 184.

 27. Washington Morrison Hardy, a son of Dr. James F. E. Hardy. Johnston, *Papers of ZBV*, 1: 43, 168 n.

Dr Lester intended returning immediately to Asheville, I think it more than probable that I would go over, but as they do not intend doing that, I dont care particularly about going—dont infer from this that it would not afford me pleasure to be over there with you—indeed nothing would be more agreeable to me than to be where I could see you oftener—you know, for my own dearest one I am never more happy than when in your company—& when you are absent from me I am happy in the remembrance of you—Cousin Woodfin & Cousin Eliza insisted that I should visit them after the Drs wedding—they were under the impression that Ann & the Dr would go over from here—I suppose you have seen them since their return home—Cousin Woodfin was teasing me a great deal & insisted that I should send you a kiss by him—how he intended delivering I know not unless through one of his little daughters; Has it been delivered yet?

I heard from you at Yancy through old Mr McKesson, upon whom you made quite a favorable impression—I think, he told me it was his first acquaintance with you & he then commenced speaking in the highest praise of your character—You know it pleased me of course.

Well, dearest, I suppose I may look for you in Morganton on Wednesday evening—I will probably be in the Village, & if so, will expect you over at Sisters immediately after tea; if I should not be there I hope you will come to the Quaker Meadows early Thursday morning—I think though, I shall be in the Village—I hope you dont expect to wait with me at the wedding, if so, I am sorry to disappoint you, but I dont think I ought to stand up with you; Miss Maltby says she intends that pleasure for herself—I suppose you knew she was one of the attendents; She is a friend of mine & I hope you will be pleased with her.

My sheet is almost filled so I must close—You will not hear from me again before you come over, but I will look certainly for one more letter (at least) from you—My affectionate regards to your Mother, Sister, & Aunt Mary—I hope the latter will ever be as warm a friend of mine as you write she now is—I trust you found your sister at Yancy, quite well.—& Now My own one I beg you to write soon & may you, in the hour of temptation continue to think of the requests of her, whose constant prayer is that the one whom she so ardently loves, may resist evil. You will perceive by letter has been briefly written. Oh! I had almost forgotten to mention your friend Mr Brown—poor fellow—I am truly sorry I can offer him no other consolation than that he will be rejected in the kindest & most lady like manner—I hope he will be over at the wedding.—Adieu dearest one Your own Hattie

---

Saturday Jan 22, 1853

My Dearest Harriet,

Just cast your recollection backward if you please, and see how long it has been since you have written me one word! Dont you really feel a little ashamed at the thought of letting me go unwritten for nearly a month? Well, now I thought so, and since you acknowledge that you do, I forgive you. You've been fixing for the wedding? well, havent I been doing that too, and a great deal else? and havent I written to you every week since I left you? I really intend to have a scolding prepared for you by the 27th, and before we make friends I shall most certainly exact an extra quantity of K——s—you know what, for your treatment of me. I'll have vengeance, depend upon it, for your keeping me in waiting so long for a letter. Really Harriet, jesting aside, I have felt a little uneasy, lest you might be sick or something that way, and for some days past I have been trying to find out by other means whether or not you were well. I hope however that my fears are groundless, and that I will find you quite hearty when I go over. Doubtless also you will have the best kind of excuses for not writing, so I forgive you most fully in advance.

I have been very unwell for some time past. I was suffering with the toothache when I last wrote, and business which I could not defer or get around compelled me to ride into the country on tuesday & wednesday in consequence of which I took severe cold. I have been out very little since, and have had such a cough that I began to think of declining the Drs party. I am now a great deal better and hope to be entirely free of any cold or cough by the time I meet you. We start from Asheville on tuesday morning, and according to the Drs arrangements will not be at Morganton untill Thursday some time during the day. I was much in hopes that we could have got to M—— on Wednesday; in that event, I intended spending the day following with you, if you could have permitted it. We will remain in your town untill Monday and I hope to spend most of the time with you. Three or four ladies will accompany us. I have the honor of escorting Miss *Harriet* Osborne; in making my selection as to which one of the ladies I would take I chose her, for various reasons, the most obvious and sensible of which is perhaps on account of *the name*. Shakespeare says there's nothing in a name, but to my notion old Shake told a "whopper" when he said that, and another great poet backs me in the assertion, for [Thomas] Campbell very pertinently puts the question,

"Who hath not owned with rapture smitten frame
The power of grace, the *magic of a name*"

There is indeed "magic in a name" and I'l have the name when there is nothing better to be had. Do you suppose the young Lady would feel complimented if she were to hear this? You feel flattered I know, dont you? Tell Cousin Mary Jo that I have an arrangement for her to come home with me, and she must be ready, as she promised me faithfully she would come home with me from the wedding.

We have had Haywood Gaither[28] with us for some time, came with us from Yancey and has been very attentive to Miss Morehead. He left yesterday morning I believe.

I have nothing more of news to add that would enlist your attention and besides I feel that I prefer saving what else I have to say untill I meet you and then I hope to say a great deal. I really almost dislike to visit you on occasions of this kind where I shall be so much with you and have so little chance of talking to you, but its better after all than not seeing you at all. God bless you, my own sweet Harriet, & grant that I may meet you in health & Happiness. Yours in devoted love, Zebulon.

ZBV was in Morganton the latter part of January for the wedding of Ann Judson Happoldt and Dr. Thomas C. Lester.

Quaker Meadows Jan 31st 1853

My beloved Zebulon—

I need not ask you to excuse a short letter this morning as you must know that I am not well enough to write much,

28. Alfred Haywood Gaither, lawyer of Burke County, son of Burgess Sidney Gaither and of Elizabeth Sharpe Erwin Gaither. McDowell, *McDowells, Erwins, Irwins*, p. 212; Augustus Summerfield Merrimon's Diary, vol. 2, December 5, 1850, to August 5, 1851, Augustus Summerfield Merrimon Collection, Southern Historical Collection, The University of North Carolina at Chapel Hill, Chapel Hill, N.C.

although I am greatly better than I was the day you left—I passed a very disagreeable day, notwithstanding, I was surrounded with charming company, but besides not being well, I had just bidden you farewell & you know that was enough of itself to mar my happiness—I remained in the Village until yesterday afternoon—went out to Church in the morning—heard a most excellent sermon & came out home in the afternoon quite a sufferer, but am glad to inform you that this morning finds me greatly improved—I can speak so as to be heard this morning, for the first time since Saturday morning & hope by tomorrow to be able to converse as usual so you must not be uneasy about me—I intend taking *good* care of myself for your sake, at least. Did you remain at Col Carsons until today or go on yesterday? I heard after you left, that some of the company were determined to go on immediately to Asheville.—Dr Lester & lady will not leave Morganton before tomorrow. Dr Happoldt & Miss Dorcus are thinking of accompanying them to the Drs Fathers—how very quiet our Village will be—so many persons are leaving—I dislike to give up my friend Annie so much but I console myself with the thought that ere long we will both belong to the same circul again—My friend Clara also leaves in the morning—that is a departure that I regret very much indeed & Brother James—I dont know what I shall do without him. I think though that he is leaving with the determination to apply himself to his books & for this reason I can most willingly give him up—I hope that he as well as yourself will be well prepared for Licences in August—I believe it is his intention to apply at that time.

Mollie Jo came out home with me yesterday—she desires much love to you. If I am well enough I intend going up to McDowell [*County*] next week, in company with my friends, Miss Maltby & Miss Gaither[29]—I hope I shall be well enough for I want to go very much.—

How is Miss Harriett Osbourn's health since her return home? I hope she has entirely recovered & that you all arrived without any accident—You dont know how I have grieved over saying to you what I did the night before you left—I am shure I was wrong—I would not have had you to propose to Miss Harriett to go home with anyone else for any thing—you must both

29. Julia M. Gaither, of Morganton, daughter of Alfred Gaither and Catherine Reese Erwin Gaither. *Census* of Burke County, 1850; Alphonso C. Avery, *History of the Presbyterian Churches at Quaker Meadows and Morganton from the Year 1780 to 1913* (Raleigh, N.C.: Edwards and Broughton Printing Co., 1913), p. 97.

forgive & forget the remark, it was so unkind in me. Brother James is preparing to leave, so I must close my very short note—I could & would write much more but have not time—I must say again, dont be uneasy—Remember me most affectionately to your Mother, Sister & Aunt—I will write you very soon again & you must also write—I will expect a letter by thursdays mail—Do excuse great haste—God bless you dearest—Good bye—Your own Harriett—

Asheville Feb 2d 1853

My Dearest Harriet,

    I set down this evening in rather low spirits to write you a letter in accordance with my duty and my inclination. I am quite unwell with another attack of the tooth-ache. I went to the dentist this morning to have something done with it as I have been suffering long enough; he declined pulling it as it is a front tooth and is very little decayed. He says it was shattered in pluging and that it will get well *probably* in a year or two! Poor comfort indeed, is'nt it?

    We had beautiful weather to come home in. We spent Sabbath at Mr Carsons and got home on Monday evening about 7 O'clk. I regretted so much that I could not stay longer with you, but Harriet I really could not without treating Miss Osborne impolitely. The only gentleman in our company who proffered to take my place with her was one with whom she would have been quite unwilling to have traveled. Indeed my situation was rather a delicate one with her anyhow, as she was under the constant impression that I was unsatisfied with having her to take care of, and no attention or assurances to the contrary on my part could remove it. So you see that I was uncomfortably situated, and I felt it my duty to use every exertion to make her feel at ease; something I did not feel myself.

In addition to the unpleasant regrets connected with that matter and my being quite unwell, I have also been suffering acutely on account of your health. I left you with a very severe cold which had taken effect upon your lungs and knowing the danger of such an attack upon such a constitution as yours I was really much alarmed, & have been ever since I left you. I hope you called in Dr Tate and took medicine as you said you would, and that tonights mail will bring me intelligence of your recovery. I hope you will inform me truly as to the state of your health and if you have really a bad attack I assure you I will be with you as soon as I can possibly get there after hearing the news. And here permit me to say Harriet, that I hope you will take warning in your future attendance upon parties, and do not jeopardise your own health and my happiness by adhering to the foolish fashions of society. But enough of this: I hope my fears are all groundless and that you are by this quite well. I trust you will excuse me, my own Dear Harriet, for dwelling upon this subject so much; you can scarcely concieve my anxiety under existing circumstances, but if our positions were reversed you might then think me excusable. If I were to say Hattie, that you were my only earthly treasure and the only object on this earth for which I care to live, I would not perhaps say the truth, for I have a mother and brothers & Sisters and God forbid I should overlook them in any event. But if I were to say that you are the *first* and chiefest object of my earthly existence, the being before *all* others for whom my heart gives it noblest throbs and my soul its holiest aspirations, I would say truly—*most truly*, and I believe Hattie you will acknowledge it. You will see then my anxiety is most natural, and if I should now & then weary you on the subject of your health, as perhaps I often do, my hope is that you will forgive me. I found my Mother and all my folks quite well when I got home. Mother & Sister return the kind messages you sent them with usury and are quite anxious to hear by the mail this evening of your recovery. My business has suffered somewhat by my absence and so soon as I get well enough I propose being quite busy for some weeks. I am more & more gratified with the treatment I receive from your relations in Burke and hope earnestly that they may never have cause to change the opinion they seem to have formed of me. Do remember me to my sweet and artless Cousin Mollie Jo; I wanted her to come home with me so bad. And Miss Maltby—will you mention me respectfully to her? Please say at any rate, that I was sorry she was so much out of the way that I could not see her before leaving—The Dr & Mrs Lester are gone I suppose: we are preparing to give them a reception when they get home. Make Cousin Mary Jo write to me, she owes me a letter any how for one I wrote long, long, ago. May God bless you Hattie and restore you to health, so that you may live long and happily to bless and cheer your own devoted

Zebulon.

Quaker Meadows Feb 8th 1853

My beloved Zebulon,

 Knowing your great anxiety to hear from me & especially at this time, as I was so unwell when I last wrote I sit down this morning to inform you of my entire restoration to health—I know dearest nothing I could say would cause you more happiness—I wrote you just a week ago by Brother, that I was much better & I hope since the reception of that letter you have not allowed yourself to be so uneasy as I know you were before—In that letter I also assured you that I intended to take better care of my health in the future—& I am fully of that determination, for I am confident that continued imprudence would soon destroy my health entirely—you beg me not to jeopardise my health by adhering to the foolish fashions of society—Many thanks dearest for the advice & believe me I intend following it—it will afford me pleasure to be careful of my health, as the happiness, of one who is as dear to me as my own soul, is conserned, as well as my own, for without health there is little happiness—yes My own one, even were it a sacrafice I would most willingly make it for your sake—How sorry I was to learn by your last letter that you were so unwell with another attack of tooth-ache & I was provoked with the dentist that he gave you such poor comfort—did he believe what he said? If so I sincerely hope he is mistaken—Whenever I hear of you being the least unwell, I am anxious that the time should come when I can be constantly with you, & I almost reproach myself for not concenting to be married when ever you say—indeed, I have made up my mind to leave it entirely with you to appoint the time when our nuptials shall be celebrated, provided you dont say before May.

 I regretted to hear that Miss Osborne was under the impression while in our Village, that you were unsatisfied with having her under your care—I hope you have succeeded in removing the impression—I have often reproached myself for insisting upon your remaining with me. I believe though, I alluded to that in my short letter by Bro James so I will not dwell upon the subject now, as it is by no means a pleasant one to me—I hope Miss Osborne has entirely recovered & that when your Asheville ladies again visit Morganton, their stay will be longer & more agreeable—I fear they were not very favorably impressed with our Villagers any way & that they will not repeat their visit—I dont think they ought to form an opinion, as their sojourn among us was so short that they did not give us an opportunity of showing them any kindness—Were they really dissatisfied with their visit here?—I was glad to hear that you spent the Sabbath after you left M—at Col Carsons—I suppose of course you spent the day profitably as you had such fine company to spend it with—You found Mrs Carson[30] very agreeable & intelligent, did you not? You have the Misses Patton in Buncombe again—have you seen them since their return? I guess my Brother will spend much of his time in their company.

 I have not delivered your messages to Mollie Jo & Miss Maltby, but will the first opportunity—I wrote you that Miss Maltby & I were going to McDowell on a visit & that we would go up yesterday, but as Cousin Mira Woodfin is over & will be going up on Thursday on her way home we concluded to wait & go up in company with her—If the weather is good we will certainly go up then so you will probably not receive another letter from me for two weeks as I think of being absent at least ten days—you must not let this prevent you from writing though, as I can get your letters when I return home if not during my absence—I am certainly expecting a letter by Thursdays mail & I hope it will bring me intelligence that you are entirely free from tooth-ache & in the enjoyment of your usual health.—I suppose my dear one you are quite determined to settle in Asheville, if you were not I would insist upon your coming to Marion—I dont know any village that I would prefer living in & I think it a fine place for a lawyer—There was a house & lot with every convenience sold there the other day for $1400.00 & I really felt very much tempted to get Uncle to purchese it for me—it is such a nice place. I dont wish to persuaid you to do any thing against your wish & I do hope that if you think in justice to yourself & your Mother, you ought to remain in Asheville you will not be influenced in the least by what I say—My friends have all been telling me that if it suited your business, I had best live in Marion as the climate would suit me better than Buncombe but they dont wish to persuaid me to do any thing against your interest— Uncle could still purchase that property for very little over what it sold for—Do dearest dont think from what I have said that I wount be satisfied to live in Asheville—I can be contented any where in this world with you & if you have decided to live in Asheville I know you think it best that you should & I will not mention going any where else again—If you think it wrong in me to

---

30. Mrs. Jonathan Logan Carson was the former Mary Sturdivant Presnell. Moffett Sinclair Henderson. *The Flags of Destiny* (n.p., n.d.), p. 60.

say what I have I hope you will forgive me—Write me upon the subject in your next—My much love to your Mother—sister & Aunt.—I hope you will excuse me for crossing my letter—I thought I would close without mention to living in Marion—but Sister came just as I was about closing & insisted that I should ask you what you thought of it—she requests me to say to you for her that she would be delighted to have us live there—she also desires to be kindly remembered to you & now dearest I must close—May the merciful kindness of our heavenly Father follow you through your journy—& when life's toils are over, may you with all our friends form one unbroken family in our heavenly Father's house, not made with hands eternal in the heavens—This letter you will see is written in great haste & finished with a pencil—I did not have time before I left home to finish it & just brought it in with me unfinished & I cant find a pen to write with so you must excuse me for writing with pencil—My coming to the Village was very unexpected. Brother & Sister went out to stay a few minuts & would have me to come on—Farewell My own one—write soon to your own Hattie—P.S. Please dont think anything of what I wrote about going to Marion—I did it at the request of Sister—I hope you will say nothing about it at-any-rate, as I fear your friend[s] might think that I was not willing to live at Asheville—

Tuesday evening Feb 8. '53

My Dearest Harriet,

You can well imagine the pleasure I felt on the reception and perusal of yours by James McDowell. I had expected most confidantly, a letter by the mail on Wednesday night, and when I failed to get it I can assure you that I felt exceedingly uneasy. Next morning however I learned that James was in town and the thought at once struck me that he had a letter for me, & so it turned out. So "alls well that ends well." I was indeed gratified to learn that you were better and in a fair way to recover; but I was chiefly rejoiced at the promise your letter contained in regard to taking better care of yourself at parties of that kind in future. The manner in which you expressed it too was indeed pleasing to me—"*for your sake at least*", you say you will be more careful. Indeed Harriet, *my* Harriet (since you acknowledge my claim upon you) I thank you for the sweet promise, and hope in regard to that matter, you may think of me when tempted to break it and refrain. This is but fair since you conjure me to think of you when tempted to break the promise I have made you—

How are you spending your time now? As I told you before when with you, you must really calculate on a long time intervening before I see you again. I am sorry to say this but am compelled to do it. My time My Dearest One, is getting to be of greater value to me than formerly, and it stands me in hand to improve it, tho' alas! I do not do it. For though my business be neither very pressing nor important yet I am never away from home two days at a time but some serious call for my presence is made. Under these circumstances you will see the necessity of my self denial and I hope you will imitate. This is particularly unpleasant to me at this time as I enjoyed so little of your company when last over, and you were so much vexed at my leaving when I did. Nevertheless I shall go to see you at all hazards about the middle of march, and of course if an opportunity should present itself sooner I will not fail to improve it. Meanwhile I shall of course write regularly once a week as heretofore.

Jim McD—— has gone to hard study I believe as I can see nothing of him in the streets, day or night. Indeed I am a *little* fearful (? how much?) he will study himself blind—but I hope for the best—I have not seen the Burke—Buncombe Ladies since they got home which was on Wednesday night, last. I hear that Miss Lou is unwell but I hope nothing serious. Last evening I spent in paying a visit to the Ladies at Rose Hill. Miss Harriet (a-hem!) and Miss Ada are quite well and seem to me extremely pleasant notwithstanding you think them stiff. Have you received the Feb. No. of the University Magazine? I think it extremely poor except one article. That I wrote myself and of course I dont think it poor: I mean "Calico—Its wonders & misteries." Read it to oblige me so that I may know it has had one fair reader. Tomorrow I start down into Madison County and shall be absent two or three days—We have heard nothing from Dr Lester since he left your village—He is happy however, where-ever he may be, and that I'll ensure. Write again soon, and believe me my Dearest Hattie to be now as ever, your very sincere and devoted—

Zebulon

Saturday. 12 Feb. [1853]

My Own beloved Harriet,

 Although I suppose it will be several days before you get this letter, as you say you are going to visit McDowell, yet as I have to leave town on Monday morning to be absent some three or four days, I can not do otherwise than sit down to answer your last interesting favour. It was indeed full of interest to me, since it prefered a claim upon me in more than one respect. You say My dear One, that you have made up your mind to leave me at liberty to appoint the happy day which shall unite our hands as firmly as our hearts have long been, provided I do not appoint a time before May. I am scarcely competent to the task of expressing my sincere thanks for this, but suffer me to assure you that I am truly gratified. Not alone because it gives me the power to hasten my own, & I hope also your happiness, but because it gives me still another assurance, and an unmistakeable one too, of your love. Indeed Harriet, I become daily more and more convinced, not only that you love me, but that you love me truly, *sincerely and devotedly*. Who can fathom my unuterable feelings when I think of such a thing? Indeed sometimes I become almost wild with Joy at the thought and my heart almost bursts from my breast! And this feeling still seems as fresh and vivid as when I first heard you say that your own heart appreciated and sympathised with, the tumultuous heavings of mine. It seems a joy that I can never get used to, and to which time can never render me callous or indifferent. I feel Harriet, that I can never repay your love sufficiently. My sensibilities are too narrow and contracted to love you as you should be loved, and it would require a being of superior existence to do you justice. I have often wished that I could expand my soul by some undefined process untill it could find room for the emotions which I feel, and those which I know I ought to feel if I could. Dont think me crazy Harriet; I am sound & sane, neither am I loving you more than I ought as you sometimes seem to think I do. I am tonight in a very enthusiastic mood, thinking of you and wishing for you by my side, thats all. When those paroxisms seize me, the only remedy I have is to catch up a pen and go to writing to you. I have been attacked with quite a violent one ever since I got your letter which was on Thursday morning, and this letter is the finish of it. I shall get better soon. Since you leave the matter all to me, I think when I next see you I shall take an almanac with me and we will appoint *the day*. My friends are quite willing for *it* to come off soon, and I think my friends are quite right of course.

I am fearful Harriet that it will not be consistent with *our interest* (for of course we have but one interest in common) for me to comply with the preference which you and your Burke friends express in regard to my leaving Asheville—at least for the present. As I have told you before however, I fully recognise your right to be heard upon such a subject and I am very far indeed from thinking you did wrong in saying what you did in your last as you seemed to fear. It is most undoubtedly as much my duty to consult your wishes & pay a due regard to your preferences in all things, as it is yours to submit to mine, and I trust you will ever find me acting up to this in practice. I want to have a talk with you upon this subject, as my reasons are too numerous and lengthy to put down on paper. Indeed I could not well enumerate my reasons for wishing to remain here, in a letter, & moreover I wish to talk with your friends upon the matter as it is my wish to consult your friends as well as yourself before I take any final step. I have not yet bought property in Asheville nor will I untill we determine on the matter and I hope you will do the same thing, at least untill I see you again. Do write as soon as you get home. I shall be quite anxious for a letter if you stay away as long as you contemplate. My love to Mollie Jo and best regards to Mrs. McKesson—I am Harriet, your own true and very devoted Zebulon—

Asheville. Feb 19. 1853.

My Dearest Harriet,

I am again at home after a weeks riding in the country and sit down in haste to get a letter in tonights mail for you.

I left home on monday morning to go with the commissioners who were to locate the town of Marshall in Madison County and was quite busy with them untill Thursday evening when I got back home with them. On Friday I went back again & just got home this evening amid a very wet and disagreeable snow storm. I am in consequence, hourly expecting another attack of my old adversary—the tooth ache; indeed I am surprised that it has forborne so long already. I am so nervous that I can scarcely write; I dont know wether you will recognise my hand. The commissioners located the town of Marshall upon my Mothers lands[31] on the River, so you may expect to see, the next time you pass that place, a flourishing & romantic little village; that is if you dont pass there too soon. Gen. Avery,[32] your good democratic friend, was one of the gentlemen with us, and I became quite attached to him. I was with him a great part of the time and think him quite a gentleman, besides being a clever fellow. I missed my usual letter from you this week in consequence of your absence from home, but I hope you will have had many pleasures from your trip by the time you get home. That will more than compensate me for the privation I suffer in not getting a letter. I am always gratified in hearing of your happiness. I suppose you have many pleasant places to visit in McDowell?

On Thursday evening while at home I went with Jas McDowell to spend the evening with Miss Harriet & Miss Ada. They are quite well, and Miss Harriet modestly enquired after your health by asking rather significantly if *her* friends in Burke were all well. She knew that you was sick when we left Morganton and expressed a great anxiety to learn if you had recovered. I have never been to see the Ladies at Pleasant Retreat since they got home, but Jim has and he reports them well.

We are anticipating a gay time when Dr Lester and Lady get home, as there will doubtless be several parties given him. I hear that Mrs Jas. W. Patton, Mr Jas. M. Smith & Mr T. T. Patton intend giving him parties. The young gentlemen of the village will also give him one, so you see our usually dull town will be astir for a week or two at any rate.

Well Hattie, I have given you all the news I can think of likely to interest you, what shall I say next to fill out my letter? Shall I tell you that I have a notion of appointing an early day in May for the consumation of our happiness? No; I wont say anything

---

31. Madison County had been created from a part of Buncombe in 1851. The county seat of Madison was to be named for John Marshall. Dr. Frontis Johnston states that "about fifty acres of land at Lapland were given by Zebulon B. Vance to Madison County by deed of April 20, 1853, 'for the purpose of locating thereon the town of Marshall.'" It was to Lapland on the French Broad River that David Vance had moved his family before 1836. He had acquired about 1,500 acres of land there. David Leroy Corbett, *The Formation of the North Carolina Counties, 1663-1943* (Raleigh, N.C.: State Department of Archives and History, 1950), p. 144; Johnston, *Papers of ZBV,* 1: 1, n. 2, n. 3.

32. Clark Moulton Avery, son of Isaac T. Avery of Swan Ponds, was a militia general. Information furnished by Dr. Edward W. Phifer, Morganton, N.C.

about that; I want to *talk* that all over with you face to face. I am so exceedingly anxious to see you again since you wrote me last that I fear I shall not have courage to stay away from you as long as I have threatened—I can think of nothing else since the subject has been broached, but my happiness on that eventful day! I muse upon it day and night, morning noon & evening, and really, sometimes I almost wonder how I will live with so much happiness in my embrace! Its almost enough to run me crazy—I am so much moved by the extremes of either grief or joy. Write me another long letter when you get home and tell me of your trip to McDowell—I hope you have delivered my messages by this time to the Ladies—Miss Maltby & Mollie Jo. My good Mother rejoices in the prospect of seeing you *soon*, and desires me to mention her to you kindly—Adieu, my Own Sweet Harriet, May God protect you with His omnipotent arm & suffer me soon to become the humble instrument for your protection & comfort while on earth is the prayer of your ever devoted Zebulon.

Quaker Meadows Feb—1853

My beloved Zebulon,

I know it seems a long time to you, as well as my self, since you had a letter from me & it is a much longer time than I had any idea would elaps, when I last wrote, though I believe I mentioned to you, that I would be absent probably two weeks, on a visit to my friends in McDowell, or at least, that two weeks would intervene, before you would again hear from me:—that length of time I think has already passed; I hope though you have not allowed yourself to be uneasy, but have attributed my silence to the proper cause.—My visit was longer than I anticipated—I was to have returned home on Saturday last, but it being such a disagreeable day, we were detained, until Monday, so I did not arrive at home until Tuesday morning & it was then too late to write & send the letter to the Village that evening to be mailed by six o'clock.—I was truly delighted to find upon my arrival at home a number of letters for me, among the number, two from my beloved one that were prized far above all the others—it had been more than two weeks since I had received a letter from you, & I flatter myself that you can well imagin the joy of my heart, at even the sight of a letter from you, dearest, & my pleasure was much greater when I read & found that you were quite well, & I judge from the tone of your letter, in fine spirits;—it is so unusual for so long as two weeks to elaps without my receiving some intelligence relative to my own one that it seemed to me really a great privation.

I was pleased to find that you did not think I had done wrong in mentioning to you, in my letter, my preference for McDowell as a home;—I regretted, no little after I had sent the letter that I had done so—we should never be persuaided to do, what we do not think we ought to do—I felt very much inclined, at the time that I wrote, to wait until I saw you to mention the subject & had I acted in accordance with my own feelings I would certainly have waited—however, it doesent matter now, as you beloved one, did not reproach me in the least for it—& why did I fear that you would? as you have never censured me, not even when I did wrong—accepting when I objected to your returning to Asheville with Miss Harriett—& then I was so much in error, that I will, it appears, never get done apologizing for my great injustice to one who I am persuaided would be constantly in the society of his sincerely attached Harriett, if it could be so.

I have already filled two pages & a half of my sheet & have said nothing of my charming trip to McDowell. Miss Maltby, Julia Gaither & myself were the company. We went up on horseback & alone—I enjoyed the ride much I assure you, & our friends gave us such a cordial reception & did so much to make us happy, that we could not fail to enjoy ourselves—I will relate to you many of the amusing occurances of the trip when we meet—which I know will not be a great while—My visit was principally to an Aunt & Uncle, with whom I used to reside—Mr & Mrs Ephraim Greenlee[33]—I believe I have never spoken of them, to you before—I will also tell you something more about their very great kindness to me when I see you again—it is quite strange to me, that I have not, long ere this, mentioned them to you—if you did not know me well, dearest, I should almost fear you would think me ungrateful—but I know, you know me too well to charge me with any such thing—I have sins enough without it. You have not written recently, how well you are living up to your promis, in

---

33. Ephraim M. Greenlee, sixty-nine, farmer of McDowell County, was a first cousin of HNE's grandmother, Mary Bowman Tate, hence HNE's cousin, not uncle. Greenlee's wife was the former Sarah Hollingsworth Brown. When HNE lived with them is not known. Ralph Stebbins Greenlee and Robert Lemuel Greenlee, *Genealogy of the Greenlee Families in America, Scotland and England* (Chicago: privately printed, 1908), p. 235.

regard to profanity—may I hope that you do not violate it? Oh! that I may have a reply to this, in the affirmative—I sincerely trust my own beloved, that you will forsake all other sins, as well as that one—Do dearest dont trust alone to my prayers—they will avail not, unless accompanied by yours.—I suppose you saw Mr George Erwin[34] & his family as they passed through your Village on their way to Irwin—I was truly sorry to have them leave here & I know they regretted leaving.—It is so very late that I must lay aside my letter until morning—I intended when I began my letter to close it to night but it is too cold, as I have allowed my fire to go almost out—so I must retire—May our heavenly Father watch over us during the night & through our entire lives, is the sincere prayer of her who loves you—Good night.

  I have only time to add a few lines to my letter this morning—I hope to hear from you today, as last evening was the time for the mail & more than a week has passed since the arrival of your last letter.—Have you seen Clara & Lou since their return to Buncombe?—Why do you call them the Burke-Buncombe ladies? because they are more agreeable than most of your other ladies, I suppose—though I must admit, you have some charming girls belonging to your society—You write to me as though you thought I considered, Miss Addy Morison & Miss Harriett Osborne stiff—I do not think Harriett so but Addy certainly is very reserved—however I like her very much & hope you will no longer think I do not.—I have not yet written to my sweet friend Clara, but I fully intend doing so by this or the next mail. How comes on my studious brother? I am truly delighted to hear that he is such a student.

  You ask if I have received the Feb. number of the University Magazine—I have & had read the article—"Calico—Its wonders & misteries," before you requested me to read it—I will not tell you, my remarks about it after I had finished it, though— Harpers Magazine continues to be very interesting to me—I have not been reading a great deal of late—but now that I have gotten settled down at home again, I hope to be able to read some at-any-rate—

And you have not heard from our friends, the Dr & Mrs Lester since their marriage—their friends here have heard frequently—

---

34. George Washington Phifer Erwin was a son of James and Margaret Phifer Erwin of Bellevue in Burke County. Before his departure for Tennessee he had operated the family plantation. McDowell, *McDowells, Erwins, Irwins*, p. 227; *Census* of Burke County, 1850.

they were quite well, & of course, very happy—I suppose you will have them with you, before long—I am very anxious to see Annie & hope she will come over immediately after her arrival in Asheville.

I really must close my letter; I have now written much more than I had any idea I would, this morning.—My love to your Mother, Sister, & Aunt.—I hope to see you soon dearest, at least by the middle of next month.—I think we will have a great many things to talk about then—if you do not forget them when we meet.—Sister desires to be remembered to you. I can say but little about Mollie Jo—as I have not seen her since my return & for some time before—I hope though she is quite well—Hoping to hear from you very soon & intending you shall also hear again from me before long, I must bid you Adieu.—May God keep you from all temptation.—Your own Harriett

———•———

Asheville 28 Feb '53

My Dear Sweet Harriet, how much I rejoiced in the reception of your affectionate letter last night! I was indeed thinking it a long while since I had heard from my own dear Hattie, although I was not uneasy and had, as you hoped, attributed your silence to the proper cause, your absence. I knew you was in McDowell, for I heard from you there. Mr M Erwin said he met you in the road and that he supposed you were well. But still, tho' I knew why you did not write & had heard you were well, I was not satisfied—I wanted to see a letter from you, and the one I got last night made me really quite happy. I went by the Post office on my way to church but when I got your letter I had to go into my room and strike a light to read it, and became so much occupied with reading and thinking of you that I forgot church untill the service must have been half over and then I am ashamed to confess that I came home without going in atall.

Harriet, it is almost impossible for me, much less you, to form an adequate idea of the intensity of my love! I become astonished at myself sometimes, when I see how severely I am agitated by such an almost every day event, as the reception of a letter from you. I believe I felt more joy last night on reading your affectionate and devoted assurances, than I felt at the reception of a letter in the young days of our courtship, if possible! Oh, how can we be otherwise than happy most happy, my beloved Harriet, when united forever, if we use properly the blessings which the goodness of God has showered around us! Misfortune can not harm us in the least, if our hearts remain thus united—I defy and laugh at her most deadly shafts, so long as you can say with truth and sincerity, "My beloved Zebulon". I am almost crazy Hattie, and have been for some two or three weeks past, ain't you beginning to think so? I am now trying to study, but it really is almost impossible. Indeed I have began entertaining serious doubts whether I shall ever get Superior Co License at all; because it seems I cant study of anything but you untill I get married, and after our marriage I am thinking it will be more difficult than ever. So what *shall* I do? Marry and risk it; is'nt that your advice? Thank you, it shall be followed most religiously.

But I am running on most unusually and not answering your letter at all. Dr Lester got home on Saturday evening in good health, both he & Mrs Lester. We are going to give them some parties this week and the anticipation that I shall be busy with them, makes me write this far ahead of the mail in order that you may not be disappointed in getting your weekly letter from your very devoted Zebulon. I called on them directly after their arrival and found Mrs Lester quite delighted with her trip to Charleston. She will return to Morganton in a few days. She says she is in a great hurry for you to come to Asheville, and in fact so am I! Now isn't that a singular coincidence!

My dear Harriet, I was called off up street this morning when I had written to the above stopping point and was detained there all day, & I now take up my pen to finish this letter. Its about 12 O'clk and I have just returned from a party given this evening by Mr Smith to Dr Lester. Owing to the rain which has been falling all evening and is still pouring down, there was a very slim turn out. Indeed to tell the truth it was quite a poor showing and I begged Mrs Lester (confidentially) not to think it was the best we could do. Every thing was most exceedingly dull. I made several unsuccessful attempts to get up a little fun, by letting off some of my comicalities, but it would not do, and so we all left as soon as possible. The young gentlemens party

[*remainder of letter missing*]

8th March '53 [1853]

My Dear Harriet,

    I thought that I would almost be compelled to let this mail depart without a letter for you, but fearing you would be uneasy I have stolen the time to write you a note. I have been very much confined for three or four days past with attending to various things—Last friday morning my Mother got a severe fall upon the frozen ground and dislocated her shoulder and she has been suffering intensely ever since, requiring me to be almost constantly with her. She is getting better now, but very slowly—During a portion of the day I am compelled to go up into the village, and sitting with her the ballance of the time has prevented me from writing untill this time.

    I suppose you have heard that Cousin George's youngest child died a few days ago. I recd a letter from him last week saying it died near Newport Tenn. on the 27 ulto. Poor Cousin George! He appeared to be much distressed about it. We gave quite a nice party to Dr Lester at Dr Boyds [the Eagle Hotel] last wednesday evening. I enjoyed myself very much as we had a dance—The Dr & Lady have been going to dinings, parties, tea-parties, &c, untill they are quite tired of them, they say. You may look for them in Morganton soon, next week I believe.

My old *friend* Mr Sawyers has been with you lately I believe. He has been teasing me considerably since he came home, and seems to be making extremely free with all the information he acquired there relative to you and me. He is such a contemptable character that I will not suffer him to annoy me with his gossip if I can help myself. Cousins John McD—[35] & William Erwin[36] spent a day in Asheville as they went on to Cherokee, and I promised to go home with them as they return. You need not look for me much however, as it will be uncertain whether I go or not. I will not leave Mother untill she gets better than she is now. I do hope to see you before long however; I have so much to say and I am really getting *very* bad off to see you. It seems

---

    35. Dr. John Calhoun McDowell, nephew of Mrs. Charles McDowell, was a practicing physician and a farmer in Burke County. Dr. McDowell was married to William C. Erwin's sister Sarah. McDowell, *McDowells, Erwins, Irwins*, pp. 210-11, 262; Edward W. Phifer, "Certain Aspects of Medical Practice in Ante-Bellum Burke County, N.C.," *North Carolina Historical Review* 36 (January, 1959): 40.

    36. William Crawford Erwin, son of James and Margaret Phifer Erwin of Bellevue in Burke County, was a merchant in Morganton and a widower with five daughters. McDowell, *McDowells, Erwins, Irwins*, p. 222; *Census* of Burke County, 1850.

already six months since I left you. My good friend Mr Brown left us last week for California and I was truly grieved to see him leave. He is a noble, warm hearted fellow, and sincerely devoted to his friends, among whom I think I stand high. The tears were standing rather blindingly in his eyes as he shook my hand, perhaps for the last time, and if it had not been that I reserve all my tears for my seperations from you I would have given a few to him. His fate is the more melancholly on account of his being so deeply in love with Clara Patton and having to leave her without seeking a knowledge of his fate there and every prospect of her being anothers before he comes back. Desperate, suicidal condition, isn't it? Oh, how thankful and grateful to you ought I to feel, for being so happy in a reciprocal love! Mr B—— goes through Morganton & will remain there a day or two; I told him to call on you, has he done it? I have seen our lady friends Miss Lou & Clara—they are both well. I dont get much time to visit them and dont expect they think me polite, but cant help it.

It is very late, and having been interrupted several times since I began to write, I hope you will excuse both the brevity & imperfections of this. I hope to hear from you very soon, I am anxious to hear again from you. You feel so near and dear to me that my heart is very lonely when I dont hear from you often. Indeed its lonely all the time when absent from you, but in all its sadness it doesnot forget that wise men of old looked to the east, and it imitates. God bless you, my dear loved One and keep you safe from harm is the unceasing prayer of the fond longing heart of your Zebulon.

March 13th 1853

My Dear Harriet,

I can not refrain from availing myself of this quiet Sabbath evening to write you a letter although I know it can not leave before Wednesday. When-ever I get into one of those contemplative moods, and begin to look upon the past and the future seriously, my thoughts of course are cheifly engrossed with your image and I am not content untill I am sitting down writing to you. I am thinking tonight about our approaching union and my reflections are full of anxiety as well as joy and happiness—

Doubtless Harriet, you can easily conceive whence arises my anxiety, as I have often spoken with you upon the subject before, and as you have as often begged me not to suffer such reflections to distress me more, I will not dwell upon my anxieties in your presence any farther, but only endeavor to look at the glowing side of the picture. The bright side, is indeed my dearly loved Harriet, glorious enough to dispel any amount of gloom which other circumstances might throw around us. A mind less provident than mine, might go entirely crazed in view of such exalted happiness; and as you can testify from some of my letters I am not far from that point. Indeed, I have rhapsodised so much that any one else would have been completely disgusted with my ravings and I have sometimes been a little fearful that even your love could not much longer prevent your good sense from informing you that you were tired of it. But bear with me a little while longer, and then I will place you in such a situation that you will have perfect liberty to make me hush when you want me to.

I have been thinking to night how much better I could spend the Sabbath evenings in your company, than in this way! If I take up that holy volume which you presented me, after reading a few chapters I become wearied; then what—? its too bad to read law isn't it? Its still worse to read politics, and novels on Sunday are really out of the question ain't they? Well, I seize my pen and write to you, go down stairs and talk to Mother a while, come back and yawn a time or two and bed time arrives, and so passes my Sunday evening. Now Hattie, if you were by my side, I could do better than that I know. I could read good books more, and when not reading, I could talk with you, and trust to your piety to lead my conversation in the proper channel. I could never weary of hearing religious truths fall from your lips, and I could be more than content to spend the day at home, as it should be spent abstaining from all every day considerations—. Not only in this respect, but in a thousand others, could I be bettered by having the advantage of your society, and I am fully determined that we shall marry as soon as possible—I sent word to you by Cousin John that I would be over by the last of the present week, and I think I will, but please do not look upon it as certain, for I cant say with certainty untill the time arrives whether I can go or not. Mother is doing very well, and I hope by that time she may be well enough for me to leave her. I am crazy to see you again.

Dr. Lester & Lady go over some time this week I think. You

were right in supposing our villagers pleased with Mrs Lester. I think all who have made her acquaintance are delighted with her—Did you see Mr Brown as he passed thro' your village? I hope you did. Our ladies and gentlemen are expecting another gay time when Mr Jesse Smith gets home with his bride—another addition to our Society—If our young gentlemen hold on in the course they have taken, our town will soon be filled up with strange ladies.

Please Hattie, remember me respectfully to Mrs McKesson—I am extremely grateful for the many civilities I have received from her. And now as it is quite late, I must bid you good night, hoping that your slumbers may be sound and refreshing, and that God may protect you in all the hours of the day, as well as through all the dark watches of the night. Your Sincerely devoted Zebulon.

Quaker Meadows March 14th 1853

My beloved Zebulon,

 I imagin you were a little disappointed that you did not receive a letter from me by last mail—I wrote to Brother asking him to say to you that I would write by this mail, giving you a good excuse for not writing then.—Dont you remember in your last letter but one, you wrote me that you received my last letter while on your way to church & that you became so much interested in it, that you returned home without attending church at all? Now my love, this is my reason for not writing by last mail, fearing that you would make it convenient to go again by the Post Office, & be prevented from attending church—I dont think I shall ever write to you again by the Saturday evening's mail, if this is the effect my letter's have; I will send my letters hereafter by wednesday's mail, so I will not again be the cause of your neglecting so important a duty as going to hear the word of God preached.

 How truly sorry I was to hear of the suffering of your good Mother—I hope she continues to improve & will very soon, be entirely restored—you know I most sincerely desire you to give her your constant attention & would not have you, under any circumstances, leave her while she is atall unwell & will not expect you over until I hear that she is greatly improved. If my love for you, dearest, could be increased it would be, when I see you manifest devotion to your Mother—to me this is one of the most commendable traits in your character—it argues much in your favor—I observed it in you, before I ever thought of loving you; Please present me most affectionately to your Mother & if possible write me every mail concearning her—I shall be anxious to hear. I have been quite unwell myself, for several days but have been pretty well to day or at least better than I was yesterday.

I do most sincerely sympathise with Mr & Mrs George Erwin in their bereavement—I suppose they had arrived at their place of destination when Mr Erwin wrote you.

You ask me, if your friend Mr Brown called to see me while in our village—he did—& I liked him more than ever—I think as you do, of him, that he is a noble fellow—I really felt sad to bid him farewell—I hope however to see him again as he told me he thought probably he would return next fall—I consider him a warm friend of yours & for this reason, think much more hightly of him than I otherwise would;—I was in the Village at the time he was there, he called at sisters to see me on tuesday morning & told me you would be there that evening—you must know I was quite delighted to receive such pleasing intelligence & was most cruelly disappointed that you did not come, although I thought he must be mistaken as you had mentioned nothing of it in your letter that I received a day or two before—he told me you were to bring Mrs Lester over in company with Mr Smyth's [Jesse Smith's] wedding party—did you have any idea of coming over at that time, or did Mr B only tell me so, thinking it would be agreeable to me? Mollie Jo told me that he seemed quite disappointed himself that you did not come; he visited her several times during his short sojourn in our Village & I thought was quite smitten.

We are daily expecting Annie Lester over & I am becoming quite impatient to see her—I was really pleased to hear that she had made such a favorable impression upon the people of your village—I think her every way worthy of their admiration & esteem, as regards both appearance & character—you know I am a great admirer of her's, & hope to see her very soon,—What havock matrimony is making of our happy circul, it really makes me sad to think of it—there are now four weddings in agitation & it is probable they will all come off this summer. In your last letter, speaking of my friend Clara & Mr Brown you said you thought there was every prospect of Clara's being anothers before Mr B's return—do you think Mr Murphy will be the favored suitor?

My Brother Jimmy, I guess, for all accounts, is a frequent visitor at Pleasant Retreat; I wish you would write me in your next, if you think he has an idea of addressing either of the ladies there & which of them you think he admires most—dont let him know that I have asked you these questions.

My sheet is almost filled, so I must close—have you heard recently from Dr Neilson? My love to your sister & Aunt. It appears a long, long time since I saw you, but I hope it will not be a great while, before I shall have that pleasure—as soon as your Mother is well enough I know you will come over. God bless you my own loved one & keep you safe from harm is the uncesing prayer of your own *Harriett*.

Tuesday morning.—I am much better to day than I was yesterday—indeed I am almost entirely well—though I was quite sick for a day or two—Yours H——

Part IV

March 23, 1853, to July 26, 1853

In March, 1853, ZBV visited HNE.

Asheville, Mar. 23rd 1853

My Own Dear Harriet,

According to the promise I made you, to write by the next mail after reaching home, I have seated myself this evening to fulfill your expectations in that respect. I was so late in getting off from the Quaker Meadows on monday morning that as I expected, when I got to Col. Avery's[1] I found Dr Hardy gone. I however pushed ahead in a gallop and over-hauled him at the junction of the two roads, at a place bearing the poetic name of "Turkey Tail".[2] Dr Lester came up with us shortly after, and we joged on without any rain untill late in the evening. Just before we got to Gen Burgins it began to rain on us pretty smartly. From there we came home to dinner without accident or adventure. I found my Mother so far improved as to be able to walk about the house; she will certainly be entirely well in a few days if she does not get a fresh hurt in some way. Our other friends here are all quite well.

I learned on coming home the distressing news of another great fire at the Warm-Springs, which consumed a very large stable and twenty fine horses and mules, all belonging to Mr Jno E Patton. This gentleman has been singularly unfortunate from the effects of fire, having had his splendid dwelling house, and a large stable burned before this. Only a few months ago he had a lot of horses and mules burnt in a livery stable in Alabama. Our whole community sympathise most sincerely with him. Report says that the scene was a most awful one; the poor beasts chained in the midst of the flames and unable to escape made noises the most piteous and dreadful. I have not heard all the particulars, but suppose a great many other valuable things were consumed. What a consolation it is to me to know when I lay

---

1. Isaac Thomas Avery, only son of Waightstill Avery, a native of Connecticut, from whom he inherited his large plantation in Burke County. In addition to being a planter Isaac Avery was a banker and a leading Democratic politician. Edward J. Phifer, "Saga of a Burke County Family (The Parents)," *North Carolina Historical Review* 39 (Spring, 1962): 140-47.

2. Turkey Tail, a town in southwest Burke County, so-called because of an old root that resembled a turkey's tail. The name was later changed to Glen Alpine. William S. Powell, *The North Carolina Gazeteer* (Chapel Hill, N.C.: The University of North Carolina Press, 1968), p. 192.

down to rest at night, that I am not going to wake in the morning to behold a fine stable and twenty horses & mules burnt to ashes! Blessed are they that have nothing, for they shall not lose it by fire or water, neither can the sherriff execute it. Oh enviable position of a poor man! Riches *really,* exist in the mind, and I feel confident that in my imagination I am a much happier and richer man than Mr Patton can be for the next twelve months in even his happiest mood.

On my return I found a long letter from my friend Mr James A Patton, to whom you reccollect I told you I had written in relation to his being present at our wedding. He enjoys himself at my expense considerably and then goes on to say that it will be almost impossible for him to be present if we marry in May, as he will very busy untill June, when after getting his license he wishes to go North—He says however that rather than disappoint me he will if possible reverse his arrangements and come *any how.* I will inform him after another mail, of the change in my happy prospects and thank him sincerely for his evident anxiety to accommodate me. His letter is a very interesting one and I wish you could see it, but its confidential. Poor fellow, he is repenting in sack cloth and ashes for youthful errors, and Mentor-like, I must give him about eight pages of wholesome consolation. Jesse Smith will be at home on Monday next, according to a letter received from him this morning—at which time there will be quite a large party at his Fathers.

I will for three or four days to come be quite busy in preparing a speech for the Yanceyites, which I will deliver on Friday 1st of April, to a *doubtless,* large *and admiring audience!* Now aint you beginning to get quite proud of the fame I am acquiring in this mountain world? I declare its truly amazing, isnt it? I think we will have to go to Yancey, where my talents alone can be appreciated. But enough of folly—.

I have been struggling manfully to get reconciled to the great disappointment I met with in the delaying of our nuptials, and I think I will get so after a while. I do not of course attach any blame to you for my disappointment, and I hope you will not suspect that I do; for I have no doubt but that you would have acceded to my wishes, if I had urged it so strongly as my feelings prompted me to do. But I felt that I would be wrong in urging you to a step that all your friends were opposed to. What *all* say is the right way, *is* perhaps the right way, and I will try to teach myself ever to disregard my own preferences when your good, or peace of mind is at stake, and Mrs McD. said she believed both were, in this case. I will do my best to act with patience, and I beg you Harriet, not to reproach yourself with my disappointment or anything of the kind—I am going to work again with my studies, and if you could only see with what a determined, devouring countenance I look at my law-books on the mantel you would believe I was in earnest! Already Old Chitty begins to tremble in his shoes, and Stephen cries out, "Is that you Col Crockett? if it is, dont shoot, I'll come down".

In the meantime I will write to you often as usual and visit you seldom, I think it makes me worse to see you often. I have not given out the idea however, of spending a month or two in Morganton reading law if I possibly can—My Mother sends her kindest regards to you & Mrs McDowell. I have not heard from Sister lately, but will bring her home in a week or two. I know she would be delighted to receive a letter from you. I have not seen James McD, since I got home, but expect to this evening. God bless you my dearest sweetest Hattie. I hope you will write soon and let me hear of your health and happiness—two things most precious to your

      Devoted Zebulon.

      Quaker Meadows March 28th 1853

My beloved Zebulon,

  I take my pen this after-noon to commune with you as both my duty & feelings urge me to do. It is just one week since you left me. I have been enjoying myself finely, visiting; I hope the time has passed as pleasantly to you dearest & much more profitably—I thought much about you the day you left & also the day after—it was such disagreeable weather for traveling—I judge from your letter tho' that you did not suffer so much as I feared you would—Accept my own one, many thanks, for informing me, so soon, of your safe arrival.—I was truly delighted to hear of your Mother's improvement; return to her the kind regards of Aunt & myself—

  I suppose you did not expect to hear from me by last mail—Did you attend church? If not, you cant say that the reception of a letter from me prevented you, nor will you ever have that as an excuse again. I trust you will spend your future Sabbath's better than those that have passed, if you really did spend them as you told me you did when you were over—however my writing to you upon the subject will do but little good, if what I said to you does not have the desired effect—so I will say no more, but hope that a higher power will influence you to keep holy the Sabbath day. I feel confident dearest that when we can be together on that day, that you will, for my sake (if prompted by no better motive) engage in nothing that will cause me unhappiness.

You say you hope I will not reflect upon myself for your great disappointment in the delaying of our nuptials—but I do reproach myself—I should not have written that I would accede to your wishes, & you would then never have urged me to do so. I certainly feel that it is much the best for us to wait, now, & have no doubt but that you do. If the weeks of the next four month's fly as rapidly as the past week, I fear our nuptial day will be here, before I am ready for it—is this not the case with my beloved one? I guess Mr James Patton will be pleased to hear of the change in your arrangements as he evinced such great anxiety to accommodate you—you say you received a long & interesting letter from him—it would afford me great pleasure to read it, as you seem willing that I should, notwithstanding its being confidential.

I suppose you have Messrs [John] Murphy & [William] Gaither in your Village. They left Morganton on Saturday morning—I think their lady love's ought to teach them better, than to travel to see them on the Sabbath—I guess Miss Muff [McEntire] is on a visit to the ladies at Pleasant Retreat or Mr Gaither would not have accompanied Mr Murphy; however it may be that they have gone via Rutherfordton & will not be in Asheville before the last of the week. I presume there is do doubt about Mr Murphys success—I dont think he would visit a lady on uncertainty.

Cousin Kame Henson has at last returned; he arrived in Morganton on Saturday evening—I saw him at church yesterday—he is looking so handsome—I hope to enjoy a "tête-à-tête" with him before long.

I have seen Annie Lester several times since your departure—I was at her Father's on Saturday—she was quite well & still my beautiful & lovely friend—I think her prettyer than ever—Dorcus has been very ill ever since she came over so she has not yet been out to visit me—Dorcus is much better & I think they will certainly be out this week—I hope the Dr does not think of taking her home for several weeks yet—Do You think you would allow me to remain so long from you?

I suppose Mr Jesse Smyth [Smith] has arrived with his bride—this, I believe, is the evening of the party at his Father's— Is not she (Mrs Smyth) an old flame of yours? It is quite late & I expect to go to Sallie's tomorrow so I must close my letter this evening, notwithstanding its being the day before the mail leaves. I hope you will not be too busy preparing your speech to write me by next mail; I will be disappointed if I do not receive a letter—but dearest, will not reproach you in the least. I always feel that you will write if possible & havent for a long while attributed it to neglect when I dident receive my weekly letter which is very seldom the case. I have been quite well & in fine spirits for the week past, indeed I have felt better than I have for a good while. Really I must beg your pardon for the sadness I endulged in when you were to see me—I hope you dont think of my many careless words. You know my beloved one, I love you too much to live without you; even the thought makes me sad; I trust dearest to be the means of making you happy—it was only my unfitness for the duties of a wife that ever made me think for one moment of never becoming one—but I feel assured that you will over look all my frailties or at least take a charitable view of them—yes I know we love—truly & devotedly & where there is such love there will be happiness.

You must remember me kindly to your Sister Ann & write me when you get home with her. I think I shall write to her very soon after her arrival—I hope she & I will live as sisters.—

I have seen but little of Mollie Jo since you were over, but know she would send her love & a kiss if she were present— I hope she & Kame are very happy.—I had almost forgotten to thank you for the present you sent by Cousin William Erwin—I think [it] very handsome. I really felt provoked with myself that I did not thank you for it before while you were here. My love to Brother Jimmy—I hope to get a letter from him soon—May the choicest blessing of Our heavenly Father attend my own loved one. I have omitted several things that I intended to write—but it is now too late. I will write next week. In haste

Your own   Harriett

Tuesday 28th Mar.

My Own dearest Harriet,

I set down this morning to write you a letter, feeling very dull in spirit and slightly unwell. I hope however most earnestly, that this bright and glorious mornings sun may on the contrary, find you radiant with health and happiness and that you may be able to enjoy to the utmost the glories of this lovely spring sunshine. My own ill health consists only in slight heaviness in my head and a little sore throat, caused from being up very late last night at a party given to Jesse Smith & Lady at his Fathers. My depression of spirit comes from a most distressing occurrence which happened there—truly distressing and awful in its effect. Jesse Smith got home yesterday and his Father had invited every one almost in the village. At an early hour the house was crowded to overflowing, the young and the old great & small; I never saw a larger or happier crowd in Asheville. In the midst of all the gaiety & flow of spirit consequent upon such an occasion, *death,* the grim King of Terrors entered into the room and claimed his victim! Mrs Israel,[3] (probably you know her, or at least, have heard of her) the unfortunate Lady, about 10 o'clk was sitting close by a group of Ladies with whom I was talking, when feeling somewhat unwell, as I afterwards heard, retired to another room; in a few moments Dr Lester was called out to see her, and he reported that she was very ill in consequence of having eaten something which did not agree with her. Still no serious alarm was felt, but judge of my concern & surprise when I learned this morning on getting up, that she had died in an hour or two after the party broke up! 'Twas really fearful wasnt it? Death in such a scene as that! Drs Hardy, Lester, Hilliard & all of them did their utmost to save her, but of no avail. She was seized with a severe stiffening, kind of nervous cholic, which in a few moments gave her all the horrors of death long before the breath left her. Oh, that we could study well these unmistakable lessons of the great Teacher! Oh, that man would list to the voice which says "be ye also ready", and strive to prevent the frail bark which bears his soul from being hurled over the great Niagara of eternity unprepared!

I feel most exceedingly gloomy this morning and shall all day.

3. Probably Claudia Blackstock Israel, wife of Jeptha M. Israel, of Asheville, an old friend of ZBV's. Claudia was a daughter of Nehemiah Blackstock. *Census* of Buncombe County, 1850; Marriage Register, Buncombe County, September 16, 1851, Buncombe County Courthouse, Asheville, N.C.

I am glad such feelings can take hold upon me now and then; I feel that they are purifying and refining to my spirit, and will not endeavor to shake them off but rather they should stay as long as possible—Also, they visit me too seldom and depart too soon anyhow! Oh, how naturally my thoughts revert to you when these feelings are upon me! How incessantly I have thought of you this day and wished for you by my side!

I do not feel like writing of anything else, scarcely, today—altho' I could otherwise have said a great many things to you. I have been reading very well since I got home, much better than I expected I should do—in fact I congratulate myself on a speedy return to studiousness. I am getting to love my room again and avoid going into the village only when I have business. I have just finished preparing my speech for the Yanceyites, and have to start then to deliver it and bring Sister A home day after tomorrow. After my return from that place I intend to shut myself up and *study, study, study,* without any interruption save a week or two at the Courts. I look for a letter from you tomorrow night, and hope I may not be disappointed. Please my Dearest One, write to me as often as you can: its my greatest comfort, getting letters from you. Short ones will do me if you cant write long ones. I most solemnly promise never to let a letter from you prevent me from going to church again, and I hope you will not make me go a week without a letter if you should happen to miss wednesday's mail, as you threatened me. Now will you? God bless you my dearest Harriet and keep you in health and happiness—I will write you a long, *long* letter when I get back from Yancey & tell you a great many things which I can not speak of now. Farewell My Noblest of women and believe me as ever your own devoted Zebulon.

Quaker Meadows April 4th 1853

My beloved Zebulon,

I received your letter by Thursdays mail giving an account of that most distressing death which happened in your village & amidst such a gay assemblage of persons, as the one you described—'Twas really fearful. Death in such a scene. We should constantly bear in mind, that we know not the day nor the hour that we are to be summoned, to quit this vail of tears & join the disembodied spirits—it may be at as unexpected time as the present—Death has no set time or place, but claims his victims at all times & seasons—

"Thou has all seasons for thine, Oh death."[4]

Mrs Israel, I presume was a pious lady, so her surviving friends can indulge the consoling hope that their "loss has been her gain." but even with this pleasing hope, what an affiction it must be. Death might have claimed as his victim, that evening my beloved—one of a different class—one who was an enemy to the truth & had spent their whole life perhaps in rejecting the offers of salvation—but no—He chose to spare those that they might not be hurled into eternity unprepared—& will they still perish in their wickedness & fail to profit by such a lesson? I trust not. It is a melancholy admonishon to us all, to "be also ready," & to strive to prevent *Death* from finding us unprepared. I was pleased to see the effect this distressing occurrence had upon you, my own one. I understood the young gentlemen of Asheville were still anxious, after the death of Mrs Israel, to give Mr Smith a party & I was gratified to hope, from the tone of your letter that you were not among the number who would endeavor to chase away the gloom that such an occurrence ought to bring upon a community, by plunging in the gayeties of the dancing room—It really gave me pleasure to read in your letter that you would not shake off such feeling's but rather that they should remain with you longer—tho' the cause of them was truly painful. I do sincerely trust dearest that they will prove profitable to you, as you say they are. I feel, this afternoon very much as you did, when writing your last letter to me—that I can write of scarsely anything else but what I have already filled two pages with. In your last letter you did not mention how your mother was—I hope however she is by this time entirely restored—my much love to her. I suppose you have returned from Yancy where where you wrote me you were to deliver an address the 1st of April—Your sister Ann has also returned I imagin—I guess you are all happy in having her again in the home circle—please present me affectionately to her. I hope dearest to hear by Thursday evenings mail of your restoration to health—you wrote me last week that you were unwell & I have been anxious to hear from you.—I have been so well & happy since you were over—the glories of the charming spring weather that we have had I have enjoyed to the utmost—I have been riding, walking, visiting about with my many lovely female

4. Felicia D. Hemans, "The Hour of Death."

companions—it would really be sinful in me if I were not happy & contented under such circumstances indeed we should strive to be content even when surround[ed] with trials.—

How often, have I, when feeling quite unwell appeared unhappy—this shall not be so in future. I went last week on a visit to Gen'l Averys, in company with Maggie McDowell, Miss Mary Martha & Miss Tene Avery, we had really a pleasant time visiting there & at Ephraim Greenlee's—At this time I am at home alone—Aunty is at Cousin John McDowell's, will be absent several days—I look for Mollie Jo & Kame out tomorrow—they appear quite happy & I suppose will marry notwithstanding the opposition of her friends.

We are delighted to have Annie Lester still with us—I spent a pleasant evening with her & some other friends at sisters on Saturday—I remained with them until about 8 o'clock & then came out home—I had a very pleasant ride indeed—James McKesson accompanied me. I hope Dr Lester will not come for Annie soon—she has visited but little since she came over on account of Dorcus—who has been very ill & is now but little better. I hope however, she will recover soon. I don't think Annie ought to think of leaving while Dorcus is sick; so I hope the Dr will consider this & not come for her, for some time yet.—I hope certainly to receive a letter from you on Thursday night informing me of both your health & happiness—I will endeavor to write you by every Wednesday's mail—but you must not ask me to write by Sabbath mail as I have said I would not do it—Farewell my much loved one. God bless you & keep you out of all temptation & believe me as ever

Your own
Harriett.

Asheville, April 5th '53

My Dear Hattie,

Another week has past and its revolving hours have again brought me to the time for writing to my own sweet One; the pleasant task is again mine and with cheerfulness and pleasure I enter upon it. I recd yours last week, and I can assure you that it quadrupled the joy I usually feel in reading a letter from you to learn by this one that you were in such fine health and spirits.

It seems that the wish I expressed in my last as to your enjoying the delightful spring sun was actually fulfilling at the time I wrote—I was really glad to hear that—Oh, that your days may be always bright and peaceful! On the morning after the reception of your letter I left for Burnsville and got there early on friday morning. I delivered my address at 12 O'clk to quite a large audience. I recd a great many compliments (?) after its delivery from the appreciative citizens of Yancey, and have since recd. a written request from a committee on behalf of the school, for a copy of the MSS. for publication—This request was seconded by the principal himself in person who strongly urged me to comply, not merely (as he said) because he wished to compliment me but because it would most probably be of some service to his school by giving it notoriety in the neighboring counties and showing the people that he was at work up there in the mountains. With my *proverbial* modesty, (which I believe my most prominent feature) I have been trying to decline but have not yet determined as they seem so urgent. I would infinitely prefer not having anything published with my name to it; for I assure you I am not ambitious of having a common place speech of mine to go forth upon the community the subject of a thousand criticisms and unkind remarks among the sneering, both as to the speech and my motives in publishing it. And yet if I could really think it would be of the least service to that school (or any other) I would readily consent to brave all this and allow them to publish it— But enough of this; you will I fear, think me too full of my own importance.

    I got back home on Saturday night and brought Sister with me. She has been sitting with me since I began to write, and says she would be much pleased indeed to receive a letter from you, and would reply promptly—She desires me to give her love to you. She will remain with us only a few days as she is under obligation to teach in Burnsville another session. I regret this very much, as I am quite unwilling for her to stay any longer where they have so little society, and beside this, she is not at all stout, and has been studying pretty severely for a long time.

    We had a pretty smart snow-storm last night; the hills were quite white this morning, but it is again getting pleasant and spring-like, at the expense of the peaches however. What a very changeable climate we have! The young gentlemen gave Mr Jesse Smith a very large party at Dr. Boyds on friday night last, and I hear quite an agreeable one too—As I was not present, I cant say farther of it. Yesterday evening I visited Cousin Harriet Erwin & Miss Kate McD——[5] at Dr Hardy's—Spent the time very pleasantly—Cousin H—— was teasing me a great deal about settling in McDowell, saying a gentleman had offered you a tract of land there if you would marry and settle on it &c. What gentleman was it: Mr Erwin[6] I suppose—he teases me a "dreadful chance"— We speak of having a pic-nic on friday, out on the banks of the Swannanoa, but I dont know that I can attend as I must make up the time I have lost by going to Yancey, in my reading. I am still doing pretty well in that regard, and I have made it a custom to read some law every day when at home, no matter what I may have to do, or how little it may be. In pursuing this plan I frequently find myself astonished at the quantity of reading I can do in a week when perhaps I have been busily employed at something else almost all the time. We really have time to do almost any and everything we wish Harriet, if we would only work. Oh what a sense of shame and regret seizes me when I reflect upon my mispent time! And *can* I, O, *can* I, have manliness enough about me to improve well that which is yet to come: In this my beloved One, I look to you to help me; I shall expect you my dearest Hattie, to spur up my energies when they may incline to falter, and ever urge me forward in the path of duty and usefulness, and it may be—renown. I often reproach myself bitterly for not having been more active and busy since I came home from school, but I beg you not to think I am going to continue so, for when the cause of my present restlessness is removed, or rather when *it is brought nearer to me*, my soul is full of noble resolve to conquer or perish, in my profession.

I hope to see Mrs Wm McK. here next week, and yet I dont see how I am to enjoy her company much as she will be at Mr W——s all the time I imagine.

God bless you my dear Hattie; I earnestly hope that kind Heaven

5. Harriet Erwin of McDowell County and Katherine McDowell of Burke County were nieces of Mrs. J. F. E. Hardy of Asheville. Harriet was a daughter of Adolphus Lorenzo Erwin and Mary Gertrude Simianer Erwin. Katherine was a daughter of Mrs. Charles McDowell's brother James McDowell and Margaret Erwin McDowell. After the death of her mother Katherine was brought up at Belvidere by her grandmother and her maiden aunts. John McHugh McDowell, *The McDowells, Erwins, Irwins and Connections* (Memphis, Tenn.: C. B. Johnson & Co., 1918), pp. 204, 211, 261, 262.

6. Adolphus L. Erwin, who had left his law practice in Morganton and moved to a large farm at Pleasant Gardens in McDowell County. Alphonso C. Avery, *History of the Presbyterian Churches at Quaker Meadows and Morganton from the Year 1780 to 1913* (Raleigh, N.C.: Edwards and Broughton Printing Co., 1913), p. 79.

may continue its blessings of health and spirits upon you and that your next letter may assure me such is ever the case, and rest assured that there is nothing on this earth capable of rendering so truly happy your devoted and affectionate betrothed Zebulon.

———•———

Quaker Meadows April 12th 1853

My beloved Zebulon,

Again it is my pleasant duty to write you & inform you of my continued good health & spirits. I recd your last epistle by Thursdays mail, & I can assure you the perusal of it afforded the usual joy I feel in reading your letters—Can there be a greater pleasure than receiving letter from an absent one who is so near & dear? to me, there is not. A letter from an absent friend always finds a welcome in my heart but yours dearest, are prized far above all others, you know, & it is an agreeable task for me to reply to them because you say *your* greatest happiness consists in getting letters from me; this, my love, is my principal reason for writing to you every week; I sincerely wish that I could be with you more & not have to write so much but as this cant be (I know that it cant) I content myself with the great privilege Providence has blessed us with, that of writing & receiving letters.—I think tho' I perhaps write you oftener than is necessary—dont you? however if it is a source of comfort to you I will most willingly continue to write as often as ever. Have you abandoned the idea of coming over here to spend a month reading law before you apply for licenses? You wrote not long ago that you had not—if it is not entirely convenient for you to do so, my dear & if it is not consistant with your business, dont come only because you can be more with me. You are well aware that it would be very agreeable to me to see you often, but not at the expense of your interest & well-doing. I was pleased to learn that you had returned to studiousness so much better than you had expected—I hope you will continue to love your room, & avoid habits that a young man in villages are very apt to indulge in—And you have delivered your address at Yancy? I read many compliments— I dont doubt, atall, but that they were all deserved; you know dearest I of course, have a high opinion of your talents & think they will vie with any young man's in the state. If I thought telling you so would excite your vanity, I would most assuredly not speak to you in this way—I dont believe I ever expressed myself thus to you before & you must pardon me for it this time—have you made up your mind to have it published? It might probably be of service to the school as the principal says—& you ought, most willingly [to] submit to the multitude of unkind remarks that it will no doubt meet, from many of the community.

You write your sister intends teaching another session at Burnsville—& that she would only be at home a few days—thinking she might perhaps have left before this letter gets to you, I concluded not to write her until I should receive an answer to this—my kind love to her, also your mother.

You have Annie Lester in your midst again, do you see much of her? I suppose she has gone to housekeeping. When have you seen my friend Clara? I had a long letter from her a few days ago—I have answered it by this mail—You wrote me you had been to see Harriett Erwin & she was telling you I had had the offer of a tract of land if I would live in McDowell. Well so I had—I fully intended telling you of it when you were over but I forgot it. Uncle Ephraim Greenlee was the person that made the offer not Mr Erwin—the proposition was this, that if I would live in Marion he would make me a title to seventy five acres of wood-land—if in the country more—it was tempting was it not? Ephraim was in earnest too—But enough of this.

Did you attend the pic-nic you wrote me was in contemplation? You dont know how much gratified I was to know that you were absent when the party given to Mr Smith came off—I think it was perfectly outrageous to give the party under such circumstances—would you have attended if you had been at home? I hope not—I was really astonished to hear, so many of the ladies were out—You could'ent make me believe the Morganton society would have acted so, as fond of dancing & gayety as the majority of them are—but I will not say more upon the subject as I can not look upon it with the least degree of allowance. It is very much condemned by our whole community. I hope you have seen Uncle as he is now in your Village—I wish you could come over with him; by the way is'ent almost time for me to expect another visit? but I believe I have promised not to insist upon your visiting me more frequently.—How comes on my dear Brother Jimmy? We hope to have him with us in a few weeks—Sister Maggie was disappointed in getting over this week—hearing of the snow over there put her out of the notion of going, & besides she was not very well—She desires her regards to you; Mollie also desires her love—she says she has the blues badly—I will tell you the cause in my next if she will permit me. How is your friend Miss Harriett Osborne? I must close my letter in haste—I hope to hear from you by Thursdays mail. God guard & keep you, my dearest much loved Zebulon, from all temptations. Do come see me when ever you can conveniently & believe as ever

>Your own devoted
>Harriett.

>April 12. '53

My Dear Harriet,

This is tuesday night of our court, and having been all day tramping through the streets in clouds of dust almost equal to an African simoon, which a brisk March wind stirs up, and having been pulled and hauled about by annoying men, iether drunk or fools, untill I am nearly tired to death, I can assure you it is with the greatest imaginable pleasure that I sit down in my room tonight to commune with One whom I so much love. How refreshing it is to sit down thus, and think for a while of nothing else but you, and dwell in the bright dream land of our future! How delightful to turn my disgusted senses from the many corruptions and wickednesses always to be seen about a court, and let them feast for a while uninterrupted, on the good, the pure and the lovely! It is really refining and elevating to an indescribable degree! and I often think that the man who possesses a refined nature and has not such a mental retreat as this is a wretch most miserable indeed! I often think too, that from mingling with this impure world and contacting with its blackness I would become a perfect barbarian, if I did not have such a limpid fountain of purity to resort to and cleanse the muddy stream of my own thoughts.

Well, but I am to write you a letter, not to branch out into rhapsodical lunacies as I usually do. I was quite happy in the reception of yours on the same evening that my last started to you. You are still in health and happiness, and I am still happier in the knowledge of that fact. May yours which I expect tomorrow bring me the same heart-gladdening intelligence. On last Thursday night, the young ladies of the school gave a very neat party to Mr [Erastus] Rowley; I was there, and enjoyed it. On friday we had a most delightful pic-nic, out on the banks of the Swannanoa. I attended that also, and had the pleasure of being a great deal with our friends the Misses Patton, and others. So you may see that I too have been enjoying life for a week or so past. Among all the pleasant times I have had I enjoyed none so much as when with my recently discovered Cousin *Harriet* Erwin, (bless the name!) of whom I have written you before. She is indeed a most lovely young lady; dont you think so? I am taken with her very much, and altho' I cant say she captured my heart for of course I have none to be captured, having deposited it with you long since, yet I believe I can say that she captured the place where my heart used to be. At any rate my breast feels as empty as the head of a young lawyer, and that being the case *you know* I have nothing left.

Mrs McKesson is with us; I have not seen her yet, but want to very much and dont know how I can. I will see her tho' at any rate before she leaves us. Capt. McDowell is also here; I have seen him of course. He enjoyed the discussion to day between Messrs Clingman & Gaither[7] very much. It was a pretty warm one, and I believe that Col Gaither obtained a slight advantage over Mr Clingman—Tho' the fact is quite undeniable that Gaither is an inferior man by the side of Clingman, and but a poor match for him politically. I am trying my utmost to keep from getting excited, but find it mighty hard to be prudent.

I must really close, there is a gentleman with me to night, but I gave him the papers and told him to read untill I could write a letter, and he is getting to look like he thought there were as polite men in the world as me. I forgot to mention Mother before—she is almost entirely well—Sisters and all. Dr and Mrs Lester are keeping house. I am going to visit them soon.

Write soon, my dearest One—I need not repeat how anxious I look for your letters. Love to Cousin Kame & Mollie Jo. Miss

---

7. Congressional elections at this time were held in August of the odd-numbered years. Burgess Sidney Gaither, Whig, of Morganton was attempting to deprive Thomas L. Clingman, Democrat, of Asheville of his seat. He failed. In 1858 when Clingman was appointed to the United States Senate, ZBV defeated William Waightstill Avery in a special election held to fill the vacated congressional spot. Samuel A. Ashe, Stephen B. Weeks, and Charles L. Van Noppen, eds., *Biographical History of North Carolina from Colonial Times to the Present*, 8 vols. (Greensboro, N.C.: Charles L. Van Noppen, 1905-17), 2: 96, 97; Frontis W. Johnston, ed., *The Papers of Zebulon Baird Vance, 1843-62* (Raleigh, N.C.: State Department of Archives and History, 1963), 1: xxxiii, xxxv, 5, n. 20.

Remine, our Teacheress, will get married in the morning before breakfast to a Mr Crawford[8] of Tenn. &c.

Good night Hattie—excuse this hasty and imperfect letter—it is the best I can do under the circumstances—Of course I will do better next time, the promise of all malefactors.

Goodnight once again—
Zeb.

Saturday 16th April [1853]

My dear Harriet,

As I have to go to Madison Court in the morning and will not be at home again in time to write you by Wednesdays mail I sit down this evening to write, in order that you may not go without a letter beyond your usual time.
Our Court has just adjourned after a pretty hard weeks business. As I have no Superior Court license, I of course had nothing to do, but still I have been quite busy in attending to other business of a harassing and annoying kind, and am as glad as any one to see the end of the week. I did pretty well in the way of getting business, and if I had Superior Co License, would have done a great deal more. I still feel in the finest spirits with regard to my future in the profession, and can see no earthly reason to be discouraged. In Madison and Yancey my prospects are fine and I have there already my name on the Sup Co. docket, hoping to have license before the October Term. But enough of this—I really think I talk too much of myself *even to you*, and it is [a] fault I should dislike to fall into.

You speak of the great impropriety our people committed in attending the party given Mr & Mrs Smith at Dr Boyds, so soon after the sudden death of Mrs Israel. I do think indeed it was very wrong, and I am glad I was not there. You ask me if I would have gone to it, if at home. I dont think that a fair question, scarcely, as to confess the truth I fear I would have been tempted to go, and that avowal I know in your eyes, robs me of all merit in the matter. I did tho' use my influence with all parties to have it postponed indefinitely, and when they asked me to become a manager, I refused, and notwithstanding, during

---

8. Miss L. L. Remine ("Rennie") married Robert A. Crawford. Buncombe County Marriage Register. Buncombe County Courthouse, Asheville, N.C.

my absence they put my name on the tickets. Well I didn't go, anyhow, so I am not so guilty as if I had gone. There was a small party out at Pleasant Retreat on last wednesday evening, to which I did not go for the best of reasons, viz; a want of an invitation. I had a strong suspicion some time since, tho' I never mentioned it to you or any one else, that those ladies were getting up a kind of coolness toward me which I could not account for; and this confirms me in my opinion. I am so perfectly unconscious of ever having given either of them cause of offence in the slightest degree, that I can not have the remotest conception of what they are offended at if such *is* the case. Of course, I shall sure attempt to find out.

I am sorry that I will have to travel on the Sabbath, as besides being wrong, I know it gives you pain to know of my doing so. But really, a lawyer is almost obliged to do it, and I hope by refraining from it whenever it is possible, I shall be held somewhat excused for it when actually necessary.

Sister returned yesterday to Burnsville, and left with a great deal of regret. We were all oposed to her going back to that lonely place, but having promised some time ago that she would teach another session there, and Mr Adams[9] having made his arrangements to that effect said he would be without a teacher for the next five months if she did not go. The people there are very much attached to her and exceedingly kind, but nevertheless [it is a] rather rough place for a young lady to spend her time in. But she is very studious and reads with great avidity and industry, and I have been lecturing her on the importance of improving her mind whilst she is there cut off from the enjoyments of good society—She is studying a pretty solid course of mathematics, and endeavoring to prepare herself for an instructress in some school of more importance.

My Mother is quite in health, tho I very much fear she will not have the use of her arm perfectly again; it is not right some how. Sister L—— [Laura Neilson] is quite well also. We hear frequently of late from Dr Neilson and that for some time past he has been doing a very good business—better than we had reason to hope.

I am going as soon as I finish this, to see Mrs Lester at

9. The Reverend Stephen B. Adams of the Methodist Church established the Burnsville Academy in 1851 and taught there for several years. John Preston Arthur, *Western North Carolina: A History (From 1730 to 1913)* (Asheville, N.C.: The Edward Buncombe Chapter of the Daughters of the American Revolution of Asheville, N.C., 1914), p. 428.

her house—I have not called since they went to housekeeping. I will also see Mrs Jesse Smith—And now my own dear, beloved Harriet, what can I add to the many heartfelt assurances of undying love I have so often given you! How can I make you conscious of the undiminished love that still rages with increasing strength in my boosom! Concieve all that I could say, my dearest, and then know you have fallen far short of the reality—I hope you will write next week, for I shall be back here before I go to Yancey—Adieu Harriet, and receive and accept the blessings of your sincere and ever affectionate Zebulon.

Quaker Meadows April 18th 1853

My beloved Zebulon,

It is quite late at night, so dearest, you must excuse a short letter. I received yours by Thursdays mail &, as usual, was delighted to get it—however I had one objection to it, & I will leave you to guess what it was.—I have been most of the time entirely alone. How much I have thought about my dear absent one & the happy future that I hope to pass with him. What joy is like the joy of anticipation? What pleasures like those we look forward to, & "dwell upon as some bright land that we shall inhabit when the *present* shall have become the *past*"? I dont think, as some, that it is foolish to anticipate—if it were not meant for a solace, would it have been so strongly implanted in our hearts as an alleviation of the sorrows of life? I do think tho', that in our most sanguine hopes of the future we should remember that we may meet with many disappointments & indeed, it is for our good, that we should meet with them. But I was to write you only a short letter as it is after 10 o'clock—so I must be brief—

I was pleased to learn from your last that you liked Harriett Erwin, so much—I think her a very lovely girl—What a fancy you seem to have for the Harrietts: why is it? I am glad you have been enjoying this fine Spring weather—I think pic-nics are so pleasant at this season—Your Village has of late been very gay—unusually so for the winter—We have been very quiet ever since Dr Lesters wedding, but notwithstanding we have had a vast deal of enjoyment & of the most pleasant kind, to me. Dr

McRee[10] gives quite a large party on Thursday evening & I suppose it will be the first of a number as repoart says Cousin William Erwin[11] will be married the 19th of May & William Gaither[12] the 20th—there is, I imagin, no doubt but that these weddings will come off at the appointed times.

You write me you are endeavoring to act prudent with regard to the congressional election, do dearest persevere in it—I do sincerely desire that you will not get excited—I am becoming more & more anxious every day—that you will let politics alone but I very much fear you will not—After reading your last letter I felt very much inclined to sit immediately down & write you a long letter beging you to say nothing that you could avoid; cocearning the election, but upon reflection I remembered you had told me you did not intend to take an active part & then felt satisfied that you would not—When you see what confidence I place in you, how can you do what you tell me you will endeavor not to do—but perhaps it is not becoming in me to write you in this manner so I will change the theme—

Is James McKesson in your Village? he left Morganton in the stage on Saturday night, very much intoxicated—his friends were very much opposed to his going, but he would go—is he still drinking? poor fellow, I fear he is gone; there is very little hope for such a disobedient son. Please write me concearning him.

We are expecting Cousins from your Village, this week, & it is probable you will not hear from me again for two weeks; if I can tho' I will write next week—I mention this, that you may not be disappointed, if you should not get a letter. You saw Uncle when he was over: you were mistaken in supposing Sister had gone over—she was quite disappointed in her trip. We have such a lovely young lady now on a visit to Burke—Miss Sallie

10. In 1841 Dr. William Lucius McRee began the practice of medicine in Morganton. When ZBV was a boy Dr. McRee treated him for the white swelling and also for a rupture caused by falling from a tree. Edward W. Phifer, "Certain Aspects of Medical Practice in Ante-Bellum Burke County, N.C.," *North Carolina Historical Review* 36 (January, 1959): 34; Clement Dowd, *Life of Zebulon B. Vance* (Charlotte, N.C.: Observer Printing and Publishing House, 1897), p. 12.

11. William C. Erwin was engaged to marry a widow, Mrs. Alexander Francis Gaston, the former Lauretta Murphy, daughter of John and Margaret Stringer Avery Murphy of Burke County. Elroy McKendree Avery and Catherine Hitchcock (Tilden Avery), *The Groton Avery Clan, 1616-1912*, 2 vols. (Cleveland, Ohio: n.p., 1912), 1: 652.

12. William E. Gaither's financée was Martha A. ("Muff") McEntire of Rutherfordton. Rutherford County Marriage Bonds, State Department of Archives and History, Raleigh, N.C.

Grier—she is an old school mate of mine—I know you will be pleased with her; she will spend the summer with us. Has your sister returned to Burnesville? if not, when does she go? My much love to her, also your good mother—I had quite a pleasant dream about her last night—How comes on your Aunt Mary? you have not mentioned her for several letters—my love to her.

  I have recd. the April numbers of Harpers & the University Magazine—I find Harpers quite entertaining—there are two books that the literary part of our Community are very much pleased with, or at least the ladies are; the gentlemen dont often fancy, I believe books of their caracter that are written by ladies. "Queechy, & The Wide, Wide World"[13] are the books to which I alude—have you seen them? I have not yet, but hope to soon.—Miss Maltby says she wants me to read *Queechy* it is a story of Yankee life —her urging me to read it is my principal reason for so doing— If you have seen the books, write me what you think of them.

  Mollie Jo desires much love to you—I have not seen Kame since the reception of your letter—he is now in Charlotte.—I must close—I will write when ever I can—Come to see me as soon as possible—you dont think of applying for licenses in June, do you? I really feel ashamed of this & the last letter I wrote you—If they had been written to strangers or one who I thought would look upon them with a cold & critical eye I certainly should not have sent them—but no, they are to one that will ever look upon all my imperfections, charitably, be them what they may—God bless you, my own dearest one & may you resort to the *true fountain* of purity to cleanse the impurity of your heart—& do dont ever allude to me again as a limped fountain of purity. I am as ever.

Your own
Harriett

Asheville, April 22d. [1853]

My Dear Harriet,
  I am again at home and having recd your letter and being especially delighted by the perusal of it, I can not but feel in haste to reply to it. Tomorrow (Saturday) I expect to be busy the

---

 13. By the popular American author Susan Warner (1819-85), pseudonym, Elizabeth Wetherell. *The Wide, Wide World* was published in 1851 and *Queechy* in 1852, both in New York by George P. Putnam.

greater part of the day in making a settlement of some business between two gentlemen who have a law-suit on hand, and fearing I might not be able to write to you by Sundays mail, I sit down to perform that, to me sacred task, this evening.

I was at Madison Court this week, and I declare really, my fondest expectations were more than realized. I got five or six suits in the Superior Court, altho' I didn't have license, trusting to have them by October Court at least—I think I shall get a fine practice in that County. The most of the Citizens are anxious for me to settle there, but I have no idea of doing so. Fearing that my numerous clients would be disappointed if I did not get license in August, I have determined to attend no more courts this spring but to stay at home and read. I will therefore not go to Yancey as I expected. I intend from this untill August to read with all the industry I can command, and will only leave home when unavoidably called away. Will my visits to you be of that nature? Unavoidable, think you? You have mentioned the subject of my making you another visit, in two of your late letters and I have not yet told you when I could see you again. The truth is, I have been a little afraid to mention the subject, as from the course of reading I have before me, I have thought it scarcely possible for me to visit you more than once between this and August, and I feared you would not like to hear me say so. Its only three months now, untill the Supreme Court meets in Morganton, and I can truthfully assure you, I have full six months hard reading before me. You dont wish me rejected I am certain, and therefore you will readily acknowledge that it is best for me to sit right down to work and *stay* at it. You will I am sure, my Dear Harriet, make such a sacrifice for my good, and I hope it will be of assistance to you to know, that I suffer as much or even more, by the seperation than you do. Consider again that a few months (I cant say *short* ones) only will bring us together as I hope forever—But I feel confident Harriet that you need none of all this persuasion to induce you to do that which your good sense will teach you is best. I have such confidence in you Harriet, that I would not be afraid to call upon you to make any sacrafice whatever, if I could but once get you to believe it *right* that you should do so. To set a time then, when I could certainly go to see you I am at present unable, but I will venture to promise myself that pleasure on or about the first of June—somewhere about five weeks from the present.

The books you mentioned I had never seen, tho' having

heard of them often I had wished for them frequently. This morning I saw Miss Kate McDowell & Harriet Erwin in Mr Edneys new store, and while looking with them, over his books, came across a copy of the "Wide Wide World". I bought it with the intention of sending it to you, but Miss Kate expressing a great desire to read it, I loaned it to her. I will send it to you when she reads it, which I hope will be shortly. I will send to Raleigh for the other Book "Queechy" and get it for you soon.

I am going to follow your advice about the Cong'l Election as closely as it is possible for a man of my excitable nature to do. I assure you however, that there is nothing more capable of exciting me in spite of myself, than an election in which I feel interested, and your confidence in what I say about keeping cool, more likely to be misplaced in this, than in any other respect. I should like very much to be at some of those wedding parties to come off shortly in your town if it were possible. I hope my dearest, you will enjoy yourself at all of them—Tell Cousin Kame when you see him, to come over to Buncombe. I am sorry there is a prospect of your being prevented from writing to me, by having Company; but I can submit, knowing you will write when ever you can. Mother, Sister & Aunt Mary Baird are all quite well. Mother sends her love to you. Sister is out somewhere visiting— I have found out how I came to suppose Mrs McKesson was in our town. I would like to see her here yet. Jim McD—— I believe is going to Burke in the morning. I have not seen James McKesson—I dont know whether he is here or not—I have enquired for him but cant hear. If here he does not go out from Mr [Alfred B.] Chunns—I will conclude this letter by begging you My beloved Hattie, to believe me with the same devotion and warmth of heart as ever, to be your affectionate Zebulon

---

Friday April 28. '53

My Own dearest Harriet,

I hope you were not disappointed in not getting a letter from me by last thursdays mail. Notwithstanding I wrote by Jas McD. a day or two before, I fully intended writing to you again by last mail, but was prevented, by having Company with me just at the time I ought to have been writing. I was very sorry you could not write to me, but I knew it was not practicable for you to do, or you most certainly would have given me a short letter. And now I will have to wait untill next wednesday before I can hear from you, since you wont write by Sundays mail. Now aint that a *'leetle'* cruel in you! But you requested me not to insist on this point, and thats enough for me to know—so I say nothing more. I hope you got my letter by Mr Jim McDowell. I hope also, you may get some books, "The Wide, Wide World" &c which I started to you this morning by Cousin Lucius Tate.[14] He and Mr Murphy have been in our town since monday (I think). Mr Murphy, has *certainly* done or said something to the point this time, as he has been unremitting in his attentions. He is on the road, coming and going out there nearly all the time, and spent a night or two there besides. I have been unable to tell from his great, beefy countenance, what his luck is, but appearances are decidedly in his favour. Miss Clara has been a little unwell ever since he has been here I learn, but nothing serious. Well my dear Love, I hope you have been well and happy since I last heard from you, and have enjoyed the presence of your Cousins. I believe you have not seen them in a long while. I hope your enjoyment will not be chilled, by any thought of the unpleasant circumstances that have existed between them and myself. Banish all such thoughts, my dear Harriet, if you can without being deceitful, and be happy. I have been enjoying myself too, this week, for my conscience approves me in regard to study. I have read hard and faithfully for several days, and have kept to my room closely. The truth is I got myself scared about getting license & that spurred me up to work, and I think if I can keep myself scarred from this untill August I will get through without any trouble. I would feel dreadfully mortified at receiving a rejection right under your eyes, but never fear; I'll *work* from this [time] on. As an earnest of my reform, I rose this morning with the sun and did a considerable chance of reading before breakfast: something I have'nt done since I left College. So you see there is hope. I have been to call on Mrs Lester a time or two lately, and found her too unwell to see company each time: she was a little better yesterday evening. I am invited to come down and make myself at home with them some evening when she gets well. Their nice little

14. William Lucius Tate, third son of Dr. Samuel Tate of Burke County, was at this time practicing law in Morganton. Soon afterward he established himself in Haywood County. William S. Stoney, *Historical Sketch of Grace Church, Morganton, N.C.* (n.p., 1935), p. 49; *Asheville News*, July 28, 1853; Sam J. Ervin, "The Tates of Burke County, N.C.," unpublished manuscript supplied by Samuel McDowell Tate of Morganton, N.C.

house looks exceedingly neat and comfortable and tho' it is small the great magician, Love has waved his magic wand there, and no doubt to them it seems a fairly-like palace. Oh but it filled my bosom with glowing anticipations and made my heart throb wildly as I began to picture our own hopes in a similar condition! I sighed too, you may depend, a deep—long sigh, the overflowing of a full and fond hearts impatience, as I thought of the distance and the difficulty, but good hard sense came rustling up like a tyranical pedagogue to a snub-nosed urchin, and sternly said, "shut up your whiffling, and mind your books". Well thats good advice and I'm going to follow it, simply because I cant help myself, and not because I believe so much in its soundness. I am exceedingly distressed about not being able to go to see you sooner and oftener, but that cant be helped either. I expatiated on this head sufficiently in my last, I believe, and can add nothing to what I have said, only that I feel a stronger conviction of the necessity of staying at home, than ever, and also an increasing sense of the unhappiness it will cause me.

Oh, has'nt the weather been delightful? Especially the moonlight nights just past! The world seems full of beauty and loveliness—and nothing but the awful terrors of the Supreme Court has kept me from committing—poetry. I feel terribly like rhyming and dont think I can stand the temptation much longer. Heart, hope, heaven Harriet, love, twinkling stars, silver moon, opening flowers, murmuring brooks, forest melodies, cottage home, trailing vines, &c are strangely mixed up with assumpsit, debt covenant, trespass, on the case demurrer, oyes, gen'l issue, *nil dibet, non est factum, hoc paratus est verificare* &c, as I sit by the window alternately reading and looking out upon the sky. Hope I'll survive tho'. Mother, Sister and Aunt Mary are all quite well—the two former send their love and the latter would if she was here, so accept it anyhow. You will certainly write by next weeks mail to your own truly devoted and ever affectionate Zebulon
Adieu Dearest Hattie.

Quaker Meadows May 2nd 1853—

My beloved Zebulon,

Two weeks have elapsed since I last wrote you & it does really seem too long a time to allow pass without writing you at least a few lines, but for this time, I must be excused.—I received your letter by Brother Jimmy & also one this morning—of course they made me extremely happy, & this lovely evening I seat my self to reply to them, feeling assured that my reply will meet with quite as warm a welcome. The lovely month of May is again with us decked in all its beauties.—how I do enjoy this season—when I am surrounded with every thing to make me cheerful & happy, would it not be the vilest ingratitude in me not to be? & besides all these enjoyments I have the great pleasure of receiving weekly assurances of the sincere devotion of my own one—how very dear these messanger's of love are to me! & while they are granted me I will most willingly forego the pleasure of having you visit me & I dont at all doubt but that it is right for you not to come sooner or oftener.

You speak of the charming weather we are having & the beautiful moonlight nights—indeed they are delightful—they are well calculated to inspire the poet; I often wish I was a poetis—but it has not pleased an allwise Providence to grant me the gift, therefore I am content.

I am truly glad to have brother James at home now—& I enjoy his company so much—I guess he will not remain with us much longer, as he is one of Mr Gaither's attendants. Cousin William Erwins & Mr Gaither's approaching nuptials create quite an excitement in our midst—they are much talked of just now—I suppose you have heard the 19th of this month is Cousin William's wedding day—these weddings, I imagin, will cause much gayety; I hear of several parties—I dont expect to attend many of them as I am anxious to spend the month of June at the Springs with several other lady friends—I dont know, certainly, that I will—but my anxiety to do so is very great—so dont be surprised if when you come over in June, you have to extend your visit over there—

I enjoyed Cousin Elizia's hurried visit very much—she was over but a very short time—her little daughter Anna & myself had many delightful rides on horse-back—how charming it is to ride or walk through the beautiful wood's! I am such a lover of nature that I cant resist being out in the open air these lovely mornings & evenings—I can scarcely sit still long enough to write a letter.— Cousin Mira did not accompany cousin E—— [Eliza] over, we are looking for she & cousin John at our Court.—I fear my enjoyment during that time, will be considerably chilled but I will endeavor to over come all such feelings & act kindly towards Cousin John if he will allow me, but not with duplicity—that I can not do, nor ought not—however we must forgive as well as forget past injustice & by our uprightness, over come the unpleasant circumstances that have existed between those relations of mine & yourself [and] have some times made me very unhappy, but I endeavor to banish all such thoughts & hope for better things—But enough of this.

I had a long letter yesterday from my friend Clara—I will tell you some of the contents when we meet—You are entirely mistaken, I think, in supposing she feels coolly towards you—I hope so at-any-rate—as Clara is such a friend of mine—I dont only hear this from herself, but others.

I am delighted to learn my friend Annie Lester is so nicely situated & so happy & contented—she is most certainly deserving of her happy lot—I hope she has entirely recovered. I recd a letter from her not long ago & intend writing to her soon,—I also had a letter from my friend Mary Henson[15] last week—she desired to be kindly remembered to you—Mary is not yet married, has postponed her marriage until fall—Cousin Kame I believe is on a visit to your Village—poor fellow I feel truly sorry for him & vexed at him also as I hear he has been drinking—do dont let him know tho' that I have heard it. I am so much oblidged to you for the books you sent me by Cousin Lucius Tate—I have been reading them & am much pleased with them—I have been reading a good deal lately—What a student you have become & I am really pleased to know it—may I hope dearest you have improved as much in over coming that evil habit, that we have so often spoken about? I hope to have a reply in the affirmative to this question.—

Mrs Chunn is over now—what a lovely woman she is: & Julia[16] is also such a sweet girl—I think her quite a pious girl & you know with me that is a *great thing*—Sister Mag—speaks of going over with Mrs Chunn & I suppose will.—& Aunt goes over to Rutherfordton on Saturday—so I will be at home alone, for two weeks—I will take great pleasure in writing to you while alone—& dearest you must write me often—My much love to your Mother, sister, & Aunt Mary.—I regretted your sister Ann had to return to Burnesville—I am going to write to her before long—And now my sheet is filled so I must close—Mollie Jo desires her love—her situation, at present is by no means an agreeable one—I suppose you know the cause—as there are always many so ready to carry bad

---

15. Mary M. Henson married a Dr. Lee of Mississippi. McDowell, *McDowells, Erwins, Irwins*, p. 195.

16. Julia Chunn, oldest child of the A. B. Chunns. *Census* of Buncombe County, 1850.

news—I could write much more but have neither time nor space. God bless you my own dearest one.—I will write next week.—Your own Harriett

———•—•———

Asheville, May 6, 1853

My Dear Harriet,

Circumstances compelled me to go to the country yesterday, and being absent all day I did not have the chance of writing you a letter by the last mail. I regret this of course, and if I had known that I would be absent, I would have written the day before, as I dislike very much to disappoint you *even for one* mail, and never do it when I can possibly avoid it. I know the feelings of disappointment well, *very* well, for indeed I have drunk of that bitter and heart-freezing cup full often, and to tell you truth Harriet, I was made quite unhappy last evening on the non-reception of a letter from you. Your last letter bears date April 18—and up to this time is nearly three weeks since I have heard anything from you. I am not disposed to complain in the least, nor do I wish you my dear Harriet to think this letter as any way written in that spirit, for I am sure you will have sufficient reasons for your silence when you do write. But notwithstanding all the thousand excuses which I imagine for you, and the reasoning I made use of to calm my anxiety, I was greatly dejected last night at not getting a letter. I hope you are not unwell—I should have heard of it if such had been the case, as Dr Henson has been with me and would have known it if you had been unwell. Mrs Woodfin too, has been at home almost a week, on whose account you said you would be unable to write—while she was with you. All these things fill me with anxiety, an anxiety too, that nothing but a letter from you can dispel. I do hope earnestly, that you will forgive my weakness in this respect, which has so often before, been annoying to you: I can not control my feelings. True love is always jealous and impatient, and I have frequently thought mine more unreasonable and foolish than that of any one else. Hoping then that you will forgive me freely, for troubling you with the relation of my unhappiness and ascribe it all to its proper and only cause, the sincerity and devotedness of my love for you, I will close this unpleasant portion of my letter, and speak of something else, if my feelings will permit me.

Cousin Kame & Mr Corpening were with us from last friday untill monday morning. I had quite a pleasant time with my good friend Kame, in discussing the scenes of the past, and depicting those of the future. He and I prepared to make a visit to Pleasant Retreat, but when it came to starting, he backed out and we took another direction. I saw Miss C[lara] & L[ou] in town on tuesday last. They were both quite well. I guess from Kames conversation that he & Cousin Mollie are no longer engaged, if they ever were. What do you think of it? or do you dare say to any one what you know? Kame is a noble fellow, and I hope he will marry somebody, and do well.

Our female School has begun again with about 50 pupils under the Charge of Mr Carlyle,[17] and there is a prospect for its doing better. What is more interesting to me, is that Miss Margarett Love[18] has taken charge of the music department and is now at her post. She is said to be the best performer in the western part of the State, and tho' I dont believe that yet she is certainly first rate. I heard from Kame, that there is a Miss Bingham in Burke at Col Avery's. She was an acquaintance of mine in Chapel Hill and I should be delighted if I could get to see her. There are three sisters[19] of them and in Orange County [they] are celebrated for beauty and intelligence. This one is Miss Robena, I believe. Have you met her? and how do you like her? How long will she stay in Burke? My acquaintance with her was only slight. My dear Harriet, I hardly know what else to write—I feel very little like writing on general topics, and it is with difficulty I have written this much. I could write much more of the same nature with that on the first page, but forbear. My Mother and Sisters are quite well. How is James McD—— and when will he return to Buncombe?

Hoping to hear of your health and happiness soon, I will assure you of my truth and sincerity when I say that I remain as ever your devoted and affectionate, Zebulon.

17. The Reverend John M. Carlisle of Pendleton, South Carolina, was the newly elected president of Holston Conference Female College. *Asheville News*, July 28, 1853.

18. Daughter of Colonel James Robert Love of Waynesville, who represented Haywood County in the House of Commons in 1821-27, 1829, and 1830. W. C. Allen, *The Annals of Haywood County, N.C.* (n.p.: 1935), pp. 122-23.

19. Anna J., Robena, and Eliza were daughters of William J. Bingham, second headmaster of the Bingham School, and Eliza Alves Norwood Bingham. They lived at Oaks in Orange County. *Census* of Orange County, 1850; Ashe, *Biographical History*, 6: 74.

Quaker Meadows May 10th 1853

My beloved One,

Imagin my extreme disappointment when they returned from the Post Office yesterday morning without a letter from you to me— I can but believe there is one, so I will send again this evening, & if again disappointed I will rest contented until Thursday's mail, feeling confident that you would have written if possible—I am at home with no one but Uncle for company, but have some such charming book's that I am not atall lonesome. I would be quite happy, if I could only have my beloved Zebulon with me & dearest the time is not far off, when I will have this pleasure—how rapidly & I fear improfitably will the weeks pass ere that happy period arrives! indeed I sometimes fear it will come before I am ready for it— Is it so with you? Aunt left on Saturday for Rutherfordton, brother James accompanied her—I look for him at home this evening or tomorrow & I will then not be so much alone—I dont know when he intends returning to your Village, but, I presume, not until after Cousin William Erwin's wedding which comes off Thursday week—

I have been enjoying myself finely since I last wrote—I have had such a pleasant visit in company with some others, to Belvidere—indeed we had quite an adventure getting there—We have a Creek to cross & it was so much up, the gentlemen got their feet very wet—although there was danger we all enjoyed it very much & got to Belvidere without any accident—We remained there until the next evening when several other gentlemen came out from the Village & the evening was so delightful. We enjoyed the ride home very much—Cousin Kame accompanied me home & spent the evening with me—I enjoyed his conversation I do assure you—he talked a great deal about you, & told me several things, that pleased me, relative to you—he also amused me by telling me you manifested a great desire to talk about me all the time—Kame told me all about his love affair that evening—his & Mollie Joe's engagement is all over with—I think she is very unhappy—& that is the cause— however, I hope she will forget it soon—tho she says she cannot nor never will love another.[20] I tell her, it is all nonsense—I must say dearest that I dont regret it is broken off—not that I dont love both of them as much as ever—but I do not think it a suitable match by any means—I told Kame so, & he agreed with me—he is about to renew an engagement with a very lovely girl, & I hope he will suc-

20. In 1855 Mary Joe Tate married Lawrence Augustus Adams of Augusta, Georgia. Stoney, *Grace Church*, pp. 12, 20, 21.

ceed—she is just the kind of girl to suit him,—he told me he would visit her this week—More of this when we meet—I am still very anxious to go up to Piedmont Springs[21] but fear I will be disappointed; at least I dont think I will go so soon as the 1st of June—I expect to go tho', sometime during the summer—I hope I shall not be disappointed in your expected visit—I believe it is only three weeks until the time you have appointed to come—I sincerely trust you can come at that time—I know you will if possible—it seems a long, long while, since you visited me last—do stay as long as convenient, to compensate for your absence.—

I had a letter from June Tate yesterday, also one from Mollie Wilson; they both desired their regards to you—June says nothing about when he will come home—I judge from the way he writes it will be a good while before we welcome him back—do you know we are looking for Brother Sam this month? he wrote he would probably leave for home in April or May—I do hope he will come; tho' I think it doubtful—

I write by this mail, to my friend Annie Lester—I hear she speaks of coming over, Court week; I hope she will—My much love to your Mother, Sister & Aunt.—Do please, excuse this short letter, I will write again next week—May the blessing's of God be with you —And now my dear love farewell.

Your own Harriett.

P. S. Have you heard from your friend Mr [William Caleb] Brown? You know I feel quite interested in him.

Asheville May 13—'53

My dearly beloved Harriet,

By last mail I was rendered supremely happy in the reception of two letters from you informing me of your health and happiness. Last weeks mail did not get through on account of the high waters and so it happened that I got both of your letters at the same time. Your last one contained your expressions of disappointment at not getting my weekly letter; I hope you will perceive from the date of it that it too was detained by the failure of

---

21. Piedmont Springs, a resort fifteen miles west of Morganton. Henry E. Colton, *The Scenery of the Mountains of Western North Carolina and Northwestern South Carolina* (Raleigh, N.C.: W. L. Pomeroy, 1850), p. 49.

the mail. I would have written immediately on the reception of yours, but the office is closed so soon after the mail gets here, that there is scarcely time to write by the return mail: so I hope you will forgive me. I would have written tho' by the return stage, at least a short line, but I was out of town and didnot get in untill after dark. I was so sorry I wrote such a letter as my last, full of anxiety and impatience at your long silence, which is now so easily accounted for. I did not much look for a letter during the two weeks as you told me you would not write in that time, but after the time was out I became very unhappy indeed, untill the day before yesterday when I rec'd your kind and affectionate letters. I will tell you all about it when we meet, meanwhile I am again perfectly happy and satisfied, and hope you are also.

Well Hattie, this is my birth day! To day I am just twenty three years old. Dear me how time has flown! It seems but yesterday when I was a prattling, mischievious school urchin, without any serious thought or anything else to indicate the man that was to be—, celebrated only for wickedness and wildness! And now I am in my twenty fourth year, at mature manhood, on the eve of matrimony and the duties and cares of life crowding upon me and driving sleep from my pillow! And what have I done in all this time to make myself admired or respected! Alas, little, *very little*. But I will do better in future, I am determined on that; with the help of the Almighty, and you my Dearest will I press forward with renewed energy. And how have I celebrated this all important day? By reading law in the morning untill 10.Oclk, then going up into the village on some business which detained me untill dinner, and since dinner by sitting down to commune with you. Thats a very good and innocent celebration, isnt it? The next one, my 24th—,I intend spending with you in proper person, if we should both live untill then.

Well Kame laughed at me for talking so much about you, did he? The impudent puppy! Well I know I must tire my friends sometimes when talking about my dear Hattie, not thinking but they feel as warmly interested as I do. I have often been severely bored by my friends talking to me in the same manner, and I should recollect that, and not bore my friends to death in that style. And you laughed too did you? Of course you did, and doubtless amused yourself very much at the expense of your poor, half crazy lover. Kame is a friend of mine tho', and I forgive him; and by a still stronger feeling existing between you and I, you are also forgiven. I am truly sorry for Cousin Mollie Jo! Oh! how I could sympathise with her if I were there! You say you told her "that it was all nonsense" to say she could never love any one else. I didnt think you so stoical and hard-hearted Hattie, and that was such poor consolation to a heart smarting under such a severe shock. I suppose if I were to say that I never could, and *never would* love any one but you, you would tell me, "Oh, that's all nonsense"! No, I dont think you would say that to me, either, for I know you believe I love stronger than falls to the lot of most young men to do. I was not aware that there was any impropriety in the match, as you think, only Kame's disposition to spree occasionally, which I think matrimony would soon wear off him. I shall perhaps you say, find you at the Springs when I go over in June—very well, I will follow up of course but on account of the company likely to be there *in our way*, I should prefer meeting you at home. That need not prevent you from going tho' whenever you get ready, for I will follow you with pleasure. I have spent several evenings this week with the Ladies—one with Miss Love, and with Miss Clara & Lou, and last evening with Miss Harriet & Miss Ady [Ada Morrison]—Miss Clara was extremely *polite*. I think I was right in my conjecture, and believe the cause to be, that she has heard of something I have said of Mr Murphy. You know I have a poor opinion of him, and have expressed myself often to that effect—during my visit there she was pretty severe on some gentlemen who had made similar remarks. Well, I dont mind it anyway. They are in Rutherfordton now I suppose. Mrs Lester is nearly well—Her and I speak of going over together, if she doesnt go too soon.

Well, I am almost through my sheet—there are some other things too, to write of yet, but I'll put them by for next time. Give my abundance of love and sympathy to Cousin Mollie Jo, and "all others in Authority." Mother & Sisters are both well & desire to be mentioned to you. I am still quite studious and begin to feel confidant of success. And now my dearest Love, accept all the blessings my fond heart can utter upon you, and believe me your ever devoted, & ever affectionate Zebulon.

May 17.—'53

My Dear Harriet,

 As you said in your last that you expected to be alone for a week or two, and would find my letters a great pleasure to you during that time, I sit down this evening to write you another for tomorrow's mail. I would have been very happy indeed, if I could have passed a portion of the time with you, and would have done all in my power to prevent your getting lonely; but cruel circumstances deprive me of that happiness. I am however getting so impatient to be with you again, that I dont believe I shall be able to stay away as long as I had intended. I must request you not to look for me before June, but you need not be surprised if you see me before that time. It would greatly disarrange my business to go before then, but my impatience has more than once before outran my better judgement, and may do so again. I should dislike to visit you untill after the weddings &c are all over, since besides having no invitation to either of them and not wishing to put myself in the way of one, I never enjoy a visit to you on an occasion of that kind as I have frequently told you.

I wish I had something like news to tell you of, but such an article is most extremely scarce in Buncombe. It seems that all the stir and gaiety is to be in Burke, and we are to have none of it. However, I look for better times. Cousin Harriet Erwin left for home last Saturday at which I grieved exceedingly. Indeed I have a *most* decided *penchant* for the *Harriets*, and know of but few young ladies of that name but are favourites of mine. *One* there is, in particular, that I fancy very much indeed. Probably you could guess who she is.

I rec'd two letters from Chapel Hill a day or two ago, giving me a summary of College gossip and items concerning my ladyfriends there. Miss Morrow[22]—the young lady who used to be so anxious for me to get letters—is engaged—and stands a good chance of coming to the mountains at which I should be delighted. I must not tell you who it is, tho, as secrecy is enjoined on me. It surprised me very much. My Chum Johnson writes me that [it] is currently reported there I am married, and he can scarcely convince them of the contrary. They are anticipating quite a brilliant commencement, and insist on my attending. When you write to Cousin Mary Henson, please remember me to her most affectionately, as also to Cousin Mary Lizie—I believe you said she mentioned me in a late letter to you.

I see Mrs Lester almost daily—she is quite well again and looking so lovely that I really think the Dr is to be envied—tho not by me

22. Mary Jane Morrow married Joseph Thompson in June 1853. Orange County Marriage Bonds, State Department of Archives and History, Raleigh, N.C.

of course for in a few months I hope to be able to compare wives with any man in the State.

I am still studying pretty hard, and staying in my room closely. A portion of this evening I amused myself exceedingly, by looking over a huge pile of old letters which have been accumulating for five or six years past. Some of them were exceedingly funny, and the thought struck me that some of them had best be destroyed before they came to your sight, as they related to my old love adventures—of which I am now very much ashamed.

I hope to get a letter from you tomorrow evening My dear One, informing me of your continued health and affection for your absent lover. May all the blessings of heaven rest and abide with you my darling Harriet, is the prayer of your ever devoted and affectionate Zebulon.

Morganton May 24th [1853]

My beloved Zebulon,

I have only time to say a few words this evening—I have been in the Village since early this morning surrounded with company & this afternoon I feel truly sad—We have just heard Brother Samuel is at this time very ill[23] in Raleigh We heard from him at New York—he was detained there several days with sickness—but wrote us he thought he would be able to get home by this afternoon or some time this week. Poor fellow—how truly melancholy it makes us all feel to know he is so near home & there is a very strong probability he will never get here. We never knew how very ill he has been & is still until this afternoon—Brother James left early yesterday morning hoping to meet him certainly at Salisbury—but alas—[the] poor fellow is now very low—without any of his friends from home—Aunty, Uncle, Sister & Cousin Mira will all leave very soon in the morning for Raleigh—where he is sick—How lonely & sad I will be, but I will endeavor to look to that sorce from whence cometh all comfort—How I wish I could have you with me, but it is so late I cant write much more for fear the mail will close—I will write you a long letter perhaps by next mail—or cer-

---

23. Sam McDowell was ill with what was probably Asiastic cholera contracted in California. He died October 1, 1853. Augustus Summerfield Merrimon's Diary, vol. 2, December 5, 1850, to August 5, 1851, Augustus Summerfield Merrimon Collection, Southern Historical Collection, The University of North Carolina at Chapel Hill, Chapel Hill, N.C.

tainly by the next.—I will be in the Village most of the time that Aunt & Uncle are absent—You I know will write to me by every mail & come to see me while they are all away from me, if you can—I rec'd your letter by last mail & as usual it gave me great pleasure—Cousin John & Cousin M—— [Mira] are remarkably kind to me—My love to your Mother & Sister. I was sorry to hear your sister was unwell—hope however she will soon be well—And now my one beloved one I must close. I wish I could write more—my thoughts are constantly of you & how extremely anxious I am becoming to see you—I can wait patiently till the time comes tho' if it is not too long—I feel so much anxiety concearning Brother that I can scarcely write atall, but can not let the mail go without at least a few lines to my dearly loved one—You see you are ever remembered by me.—May the blessing of God rest upon you is ever the prayer of her who loves you devotedly—Do excuse great haste—I have a great deal to say but have not time—Farewell Dearest—Your own Harriett.

ZBV arrived in Morganton Monday, May 30th. He evidently attended the wedding of William C. Erwin and Mrs. Lauretta Murphy Gaston while he was there.

Asheville, June 4. 1853

My Dear Harriet,

I got home to day for dinner, after quite a pleasand ride, and have only time to write you a line this evening as I believe I promised I would—I found my friends all well, and not expecting me untill tomorrow. You may rest assured that the friends of Sam McDowell were rejoiced at the news I brought of his health being so much better than they had reason to expect from the reports prevalent here.

I distributed the *mail* as soon as I got in according to request, so that those wishing to hear of Sam could do so immediately.

I have pretty well goten over the severe disappointments I met with in regard to being with you, while in Morganton, and feel now somewhat ashamed that I suffered myself to act so much like a spoiled boy, and get so vexed at what was unavoidable. Dont you think I was smartly childish? Of course you will forgive me though, since I suffered and acted for you.

I am going to work on Monday morning, bright and early, upon my law books and dont intend losing any time that can be saved, between this and August. I am compelled necessarily to attend some of the Courts in July, but intend reading at them industriously— Mr Murphy has gone out to see Miss Clara this evening, and is I suppose, as happy at this moment, as I was on Monday night when I first met you: No, he isnt, either, I wont allow any one to be so happy as I was then. He is doubtless as happy as it is possible for *him* to be, however and thats enough.

    I have no news, nor time to write it if I had, this evening. I am anxiously waiting to hear from you as to your health; you were unwell when I left; do write immediately; a note you know will do, if you cant write lengthily. I will write again on Wednesday—

    In haste, your devoted Zebulon.

                              Quaker Meadows June 7th [1853]

My beloved Zebulon,

    This is the first quiet day I have had since you left—I have been in a constant scene of excitement & am truly glad to spend a short time in quietude—I fear you were disappointed in not receiving at least a few lines from me by last mail, but really I could not conveniently write—we had visitors all the time.—I remained in the Village until Saturday morning—attended the party at Cousin Williams, very much against my will as I thought it, exposing my health too much but I had to go on Miss Sara McD's account.— The wedding party are all still in Morganton spending the time just about as you left them. I dont know how long they will remain. I suppose tho' until the parties are all over & they I guess, will not all be over with before next week—Mr Thomas Walton[24] gave one last evening—I did not go out—Miss Julia Gaither gives one tonight—I will probably attend it, & it is the only one I will

---

24. There was a dual reason for Colonel Thomas George Walton to entertain for the Erwin-Gaston wedding party. Walton's wife, Eliza Murphy Walton, was a sister of the bride, and his own sister Matilda had been the first Mrs. William C. Erwin. Colonel Walton, a gentleman farmer, had represented Burke County in the House of Commons in 1850. Colonel Thomas George Walton, *Sketches of Burke Co.* (n.p., n.d.), p. 3; Stoney, *Grace Church*, p. 14.

attend this week as we have a meeting in our church, commencing on Thursday evening, that I expect to enjoy much more—I believe there is to be a party every evening during the week & several next week—but enough of this.—

I was truly glad to receive your letter by last mail & regret that you could not be made happy by the reception of one from your truly affectionate Hattie, at the same time.—I am happy to write that I am much improved since you left—I have been adhering to the Dr proscription strictly & intend doing so.—I hope to be in good health by the time you come over again—I am going to be very prudent & take care of myself for your sake dearest, if nothing else—

I think Brother Samuel has improved considerably since his arrival—how delighted I am to have him, with us once more—I hope he will continue to improve, & soon be entirely restored;—he—will go over to Asheville about next month I suppose—

I enjoyed your visit so much my Dear one—I hope you can come over again between this & August.—Remember me very affectionately to your mother Sister & Aunt—I hope to see them before long—Have you seen Annie Lester since your return? How is she? I will write to her soon—please present my much love to her. I must draw my short note to a close with the hope you will excuse its brevity—I will write next week again & will endeavor to have my epistle more interesting than this—They have just called me to dinner & I must say farewell—God bless you—my own one— In haste—

         Your own Harriett

         Asheville, June 7. 1853

My Dear Harriet,

I sit down to write to you this evening, to say that I expect to be absent from home for about ten days, and within that time you need not expect a letter from me. I have been prevailed on almost in spite of myself to go to a Rail Road Convention at Cumberland Gap, Tennessee on the 11th inst. I was appointed one of the delegates from this County some two weeks since, but had not the least idea of going, and fear now that I shall repent of it.
Most all of the delegates are prevented going, on one account or another, and it being considered by our people absolutely of the

greatest importance that we should be represented there, I have been importuned by many, untill I have consented to go, with three or four others. That convention will take measures for determining at what point the contemplated Charleston and Cincinattie Rail Road shall cross the Blue Ridge. Buncombe is one of the Routes[25] in contemplation, and hence the importance of our people being represented in that meeting. We start in the morning. Mr Woodfin who goes with us has promised to give me law-lectures all the way there and back, so I am in hopes to lose no time in studying, by going—

I will not be here to get your letter tomorrow evening, which I regret exceedingly, as I am so anxious to hear from you, and also Sam McDowell. I have heard nothing from you yet, since I left. I think you ought to have written me by Mrs Woodfin, but supposed you did not think so. I have barely time to write a line this evening as I have a great chance of business to do before I leave home, which will keep my busy untill I start. Please therefore accept and excuse this short letter from your devoted lover. You know that I am not in the habit of writing short letters to you, and I hope you will on that account the more readily excuse me. Believe me my dearest love, to be as usual your own truly affectionate and devoted

Zebulon.

Asheville, June 15th 1853.

My dear Harriet,

I got home yesterday evening from the Convention, and hasten to get a letter in the mail for you this evening. I beleive you have not been without a letter from me so long for some time, and you would have had one last mail of course if I had been at home. I found yours waiting for me when I returned, and tho' it bore date June 7, yet I was very glad indeed to get it, as it gave me the welcome intelligence of your much improved health, as also Sam McDowell's. I was really quite uneasy, during the greater part of my absence, about you, as you know I left you quite unwell and had heard nothing of you whatever when I left for Cumberland Gap.

25. As early as 1835 a railroad was advocated that would connect Charleston and Cincinnati via Asheville, the French Broad River Valley, and Cumberland Gap. Such a route did not become a reality until 1885, however. Sadie S. Patton, article in the *Asheville Citizen*, December 11, 1949.

Contrary to my expectations, last wednesday morning ten other gentlemen beside myself started for the Convention. When I found so many going, I tried to get off, as I knew I would be running a considerable risk by leaving my studies at this time, but they really almost forced me off, and I may say that I was *compelled* to go. We had quite a disagreeable ride through the dust, which in consequence of extreme dry weather is very great, and under a broiling sun. We arrived at the foot of the mountain on friday evening. On Saturday morning, we arrived at the top of the mountain where the convention was to be holden. About two thousand people were there assembled, consisting of delegates from the states of Tennessee; Kentucky, Virginia and N Carolina, and floods of people from the three former states who were not delegates. The proceedings of the meeting will be published at large in most of the state papers where you can read them if you feel a sufficient interest in the matter. The greatest enthusiasm prevailed and spirited resolutions were adopted in favour of a route from Charleston to Cincinatti. A great many speeches were made, among which those made by James M Edney were the most remarkable and entertaining—*of course*. Being placed upon the Committee which had all the work to do, I had no chance to make a speech if I had been so inclined, and in such a crowd I had no great inclination. We left the Gap late in the evening, and came down to the village of Tazwell [Tenn.] where we staid all night. In the morning, I am sorry to say I could not get the gentleman with whom I was traveling, Mr Johnston, to lay by and I had to travel all day on Sunday. I really did want to remain there that day both in order to observe the Sabbath, and to be with some relations of my Fathers living there, whom I had never seen before or scarcely heard of. Among them a very pretty and agreeable young Lady, that I met with there, and with whom I was much pleased as a relation. Without incident or adventure we all got home safely last night. I am going to double my dilligence at study to make up my time lost in going there. I know that it was wrong for me to leave my books at this stage of the game, but still I dont feel that I am in any danger of a rejection, tho' I have had so little examination I cant well say how I am prepared.

I am in hopes to get another letter from you this evening and think I shall not close this untill I see whether you have written or not, I hope you have.

I thought it doubtful whether I could see you again before August when I was with you last, and I reckon my trip to Kentucky has caused me to lose so much time that it will be hardly possible for me to visit you again before that time. If I can by industry so redeem my lost time as to make a visit to you *safely*, I will certainly do so.

I have just returned from the Office and am greatly disappointed at not receiving a letter from you. I fear you are again unwell, and what increases my concern is the fact that I must wait one week longer before I get an answer to this. I hope however that you are not unwell, and that the cause of your silence is from my telling you in my last that I should be absent for about ten days, and therefore you supposed me not at home. Please my dearest one, dont disappoint me next week. Really I do pray for August to come round—I am so full of feverish anxieties on your account that I am seldom at my ease. I am literally crazy with the desire of being with you constantly, to watch over you and cheer you when lonely, and share your joy when you are gay. Above all my Noble Harriet I am most desirous of being with you when you are sick— love can almost conquer disease, and frequently supercedes the necessity of a physician! But you know all this, and doubtless fear sometimes that my devotion is too fluently expressed to be as deep and vast as it should be. I am anxious to give you the final and conclusive proofs of it, and I thank Heaven the day is not far distant when I can begin to supercede my words by actions. Goodby Hattie my Dearest Love—may Heaven protect you—Zeb.

P.S. our family are quite well. Please remember me to Sam, and give me an acount of his health. Zeb.

[June 18, 1853]

My Dear, loved One,

I sit down to day, somewhat in haste, to give you a letter as usual. I have hardly time to write to day, at least anything more than a mere note informing you of my health &c, but you know my dear, that ordinary excuses have never prevented me from doing my duty, and manifesting my devotion to the loved One to whom I have consecrated my whole existence. I have for a long while resolved that nothing over which I can exert any controul shall ever prevent me from giving you my accustomed letter and at the regular time. To day my Sister Sarah[26] is quite sick indeed. She was at-

26. Sarah Priscilla Vance, born January 4, 1838. Dowd, *Life of Vance*, p. 7.

tacked two or thre days since with that terrible disease, the bloody flux (pardon me) and we had almost began to fear a fatal result when this morning she took a slight change for the better. I was up with her nearly all night last night, to releive Mother who was nearly broken down with watching and anxiety. The Dr thinks her still very dangerous, but I hardly fear for her now. I have been compelled to be in town all day on business, and will have to go again directly. Beside this, there are two gentlemen in town who were College friends of mine, the Messrs Wright[27] from Wilmington, who sent for me to see them and I have been with them a good part of my time. So I feared I would not get time to write at all, if I did not seize upon this moment while waiting for my dinner.

I am getting so anxious to hear from you again! I really am getting worse every day about you, Hattie, and find it the more difficult to exercise patience the nearer *the time* approaches. I get especially fretful and *cross*, when I am disappointed in hearing from you. I know indeed that you must be pretty well disgusted and worn out with letter-writing by this time, and if I could *exist* without getting your letters, I would allow you to write less frequently. But really I can not, it seems, live without them, and so I must beg you to hold out only six weeks longer and then I will release you.

Will you be able to let me know shortly, your certain arrangements about how our wedding is to come off? You told me when I left you that you would let me know soon; whether it should be private or other wise. You know my preference in regard to it, but I beg you to beleive me when I tell you, as I have often done, that my preference if I have any, is so slight that I dont wish it, and dont intend it, to have any influence with you whatever in determining your own proper choice in the matter. I beg you therefore to act upon this fact, and be assured I will be not only content, but pleased, delighted—I want only *Harriet*, and am solicitous about nothing else, which I am sure you believe to be true; dont you? Please write me something about it, whether you have made up your mind or not for I take a great pleasure in talking and writing about any thing which concerns or relates to our marriage. I have dreamed of it I reckon a dozen times since I saw you, and dont think it can ever be absent from my mind for a single fleeting

---

27. Probably James Allen Wright and Joseph Hill Wright, who graduated in the Class of 1854 at the University of North Carolina. *Catalogue of U.N.C., 1851-52*, p. 14; D. L. Grant, *Alumni History of the University of North Carolina* (Durham, N.C.: The General Alumni History of U.N.C., 1924), p. 697.

moment. I am reading law now constantly, but you may rest assured I am not thinking much of what I am reading—You may think it scarcely probable, but I am sometimes taken with fits of impatience much, *much* more violent than those I sometimes have with you so much to your amusement. At those times I really get miserable and desperate. But even while I write, time is flying and each successive tick of the C'l'k brings me nearer, nearer, nearer. Well, I will set down now and eat my dinner and be a good boy, and not "take on" any more to day if possible—

I hope My Dear your health is still improving and that when you write you will be able to inform me of your complete restoration—I hope too that Sam McD——s health is still improving, and that he will be able to visit us here in Buncombe soon. You say you think he will be here next month. I have not heard anything from Sister Ann for some months, only word occasionally that she was well. I forgot to ask you when I was with you, whether you had ever written to her.

I must really close and go up to town—some gentlemen are waiting upon me. Do write. My Dearest, beloved Harriet, may Heaven bless you and protect you is the sincere prayer of your ever truly devoted

       Zebulon.

Asheville
June 18, 1853

June 21st 1853—

My beloved Zebulon,

  I was truly sorry to disappoint you last mail, but you were partly the cause of it, as you wrote me you would probably be absent from Asheville ten days—however, this was not the only reason for my not writing, neither was it because I was not well enough, for my health is much improved since I last wrote, but we have had a great deal of company & besides I wrote a note to Dorcus Happoldt the evening before she went over, requesting her to say to you I was pretty well—I hope she did so, & you have not allowed yourself to be uneasy—I intended writing to you by Miss Dorcus & must acknowledge that negligence was the principal cause of my not doing so—I hope tho' you will pardon me this time—you know I do not often fail to write you every week, unless I have the very best of reasons—but enough of this.—

I received your last letter, by Thursdays mail—it gave me as usual, great pleasure—I was pleased to learn you had returned safely & I hope you will not experience any inconvenience from the trip: you write that it is still doubtful whether you can visit me again before August—now dearest you know I would be delighted to have you do so, but not unless you can with safety leave your studies—If you should fail in obtaining Licence, you know I should attribute it to your visiting me, partly at least—tho' your visits have not been very many, indeed I think they have been rather few—but I know you came as often as possible—& you well know my own one I would not have you neglect things of more importance mearly to afford [me] pleasure—you say you sincerely rejoice to know that the time is so near at hand when you can be constantly with me—well dearest I must acknowledge the thought is by no means unpleasant to me—I have always looked forward to that time when we would be constant companions as a period of great happiness & I now feel assured if love can make persons happy—we will be—for I can but think that we are more devotedly attached & have more confidence in each other, than usually falls to the lot of mortals—but let us remember, my love, that there is *One* above who should occupy that place in our hearts, which we too often allow this world & the things pertaining to the world to occupy.— My daily prayer is my Dearest One, that such may not be the case with us, but that we may both remember & perform our duty to our merciful Father—for unless we do, we cannot be truly happy;—I wish I could write longer upon this subject, but I must be brief, as I am visiting —I left home this morning to be absent several days—indeed I am going to spend most of the week with Sallie.—I am truly happy to inform you of the improvement in Brother Samuels health—he was much better this morning than he has been since his return home— we were quite uneasy about him last week—I did not consider him near so well as when he first arrived & he seemed very much discouraged & low spirited himself, but he appears in fine spirits to day, & we all think decidedly better & I am in hopes, in a fair way to to get well—he returns his thanks for your kind rememberance & desires his regards to you—I think he will be able to visit Asheville in about a month or six weeks, perhaps earlyer—I design going over near about that time—what think you of my intention? approve it, of course.—I suppose you have seen a good deal of Miss Dorcus Happoldt since she arrived at your place—is she much admired? I hope she will be pleased with her visit—& as Asheville is, I guess to be my future home, I want as many of the Burke society to go over there, as possible, so I wish very much she could fancy some one of those clever fellows you have over there, & make her home there—she accompanied her father over I believe. I presume he renders himself as disgusting as usual—I guess he either has or will give you an account of a discussion he & I had at his table a few days before he went over—he thuraly disgusted me but this is not very interesting so lets change the subject.— Have you seen my friend Clara since you were over? She came over on Sabbath in the stage & she, Mr Murphy & Col Walton left early monday morning for the North—wont she & Mr Murphy have a nice time? I regretted not seeing Clara. I suppose I will have bidden adieu to single blessedness before her return—Notwithstanding all the pleasures & enjoyments attending this step, it makes me sad—I so much fear I will not be able to come up to my idea of what a wife should be; I know that I will not without divine assistance—I am still in the notion of having a very private marriage—& if Uncle is perfectly willing I'm most certainly to be married in the church—do you know if we marry on the 2nd of August it is only six weeks from today—how near it is at hand—perhaps tho' you are willing to defer it—use your own pleasure, you know I have told you after the 11th of July[28] it would be left entirely with you to appoint the time. But I must close—my much love to your mother, how near & dear she feels already, to me—to your Aunt Mary & Mrs Neilson remember me kindly also to your Sister Ann when you write—And now My Own beloved One, adieu; May the blessing's of God abide with you & may we be happy companions not only for time but through eternity.

I hope to hear again from you by Thursdays mail—I will write soon again.—I am beginning to feel quite encouraged again about my health—I think I will be quite well before long—My love to Annie Lester & Dorcus—I will write to them soon—perhaps this evening;—Say to Dorcus Morganton is more quiet than I ever saw it—quite changed in the last two weeks—I had almost forgotten to tell you of the interesting meeting we had in our church—Miss Tene Avery, & Cousin Kate McDowell connected themselves with the church—how happy it makes me feel to see any one coming out & confessing Christ but especially happy when my companions & those who are dear to me are among the number—Really I must quit writing. I expect my letters to you in future will be quite short as I am so busy. I will write often however—Hoping to hear

28. HNE's twenty-first birthday.

very soon of your continued health & happiness, I am sincerely your own devoted Hattie

---

[1853]

My dear Harriet,

 I sit down this morning quite hurriedly to write a few words to you by Miss Dorcas. I did not know untill last night that she was to leave so soon and was then engaged until quite late, and having been unable to call on Miss Dorcas yesterday I had to do that early this morning before I could write. I can only say a few words as they will probably be in waiting. Sister S. is this morning some better, but her health is still very low, and it is yet somewhat doubtful I think as to her getting up again. I trust for the best however and earnestly hope that God will spare her life. I am anxious, very anxious to get your letter which has been so long defered! Miss Dorcas tells me your health is some better, tho' I at first understood her to say when I first saw her that your health was no better than when I left you. I am delighted to hear from you in health, by any means—but my dear, messages ill supply the place of a letter. But let me say nothing more about my disappointments —your excuse as given by Miss Dorcas is sufficient, and I am confident you never neglect me when you can avoid it.

 Lest they are allready waiting for me I must seal this up and hurry down with it. This is court week and I am somewhat busy trying to make arrangements for getting off my hands the management of my crazy wards estate and hope I shall succeed.

 Excuse errors, as I have not really time [to] read it over and correct.

       Your Own devoted
       Zebulon.

Asheville, June 25. 1853.

My Dear Harriet,

 I find myself seated this morning in the act of again writing to you, and almost without matter enough to make up a letter. We have had quite a poor court indeed—very little business done and I am almost bored to death with the court, myself, and every thing else. I did not have but a few moments conversation with Miss Dorcas while she was here but am glad to learn that she will be back again soon. I hope you received my letter by her hands— it was a short one, but all that I could write in the midst of the week. Sickness still continues in Mothers family—Sister Sarah is slowly improving, but Sisters little boy Archie, is very bad off in the same way. He is quite a delicate child any how and he is attacked so severely that we fear he will not recover. Poor Sister is nearly heartbroken about her little boy, her only child, and his Father and protecter in a distant land! We have indeed been very much afflicted of late and I seriously fear that our troubles are not yet over with. Sister Ann is now at home—She came home on thursday last. I dont know when she will return She does not want to go back atall, but I suppose when the sickness in the family has subsided, she will return and finish her engagement for the present session. She looks quite pale and thin from study & confinement, and I am anxious for her to leave Burnsville entirely. Some of our negroes too are down with sickness, so you may well believe we are in a disturbing situation.

Gov Swain arrived here last evening with his family. I have been spending the morning with him and his family. His daughter Miss Anne, is in feeble health—I did not see her this morning, but hope to this evening. He was a most noble friend to me, and I feel desirous of showing him and his family all the humble attentions within my power—during his stay up here, which will be four or five weeks at least.

My dear Harriet, I thought this morning, I would mention a little matter to you, in order to have your opinion (or rather your wish) upon it. I have made no sort of contract yet for the purchase of a lot, altho' I have had two or three pretty good offers, because I wished you to be pleased in the selection of a residence for us, and because I felt averse to giving all I possess for a house and lot. I know that Asheville is not your choice any how, and since you have so generously sacrifised your own preferences to what you believe is my interest, I intend if possible, at least to have your preference consulted in regard to the selection of our home. With this view, as you have often told me that you wished to go to housekeeping right off which is my desire also, I have been looking about to see if we could rent a comfortable house, where we could live and not be hurried in looking out for a permanent home. Mr J. M. Smith has a little house to rent on the street leading from Mr Woodfins to the Boarding house, that I have been thinking of.

Its not such an one as I could wish, but I think its the best chance I know of at present. Its a small one story house, with two convenient rooms, a good kitchen, smoke house &c. with good water convenient. Mr Smith proposes to build a good dining-room to it, and if he does I think it would do for us a short while. Please write upon this subject in your next, and if you like it, I will engage it from Mr Smith, have him put up the additional room, and bespeak from the Messrs Hildebrand[29] some furniture. You can get some knowledge of the situation from James McDowell if you would ask him. It is the house formerly occupied by Mr Israel. I think with the addition proposed and a little whitewashing &c, it would be pretty neat and comfortable. If you think you would not like it, please dont feel any hesitation in saying so, for I could not be pleased unless you were, so perfectly dependent is my own happiness upon yours—

I am really doing no reading at all now, scarcely—my situation makes it almost impossible—sickness in the family—the courts—visitors &c take up a great part of my time and distract my attention—Besides Hattie, I can think of nothing scarcely but *August*! You cant imagine how much I do think of that time, and what emotions rend my breast when thinking of it! I really feel sometimes that it is almost impossible for me to get license, unless the judges would consider my exciting situation and favour me. Dont you think they will? They are not human beings if they dont.

The bells are ringing for dinner, and I must close this letter and go down home. I hope you will not be so busy my dearest love, but what you can write to me by next mail giving me your opinion on the things above mentioned. Earnestly hoping these lines may find you in still improving health and happy in the hopes of the future I remain your

       truly devoted Zebulon.

       Morganton June 28th 1853

My beloved Zebulon,

You will perceive from the caption of this letter that I am not at Quaker Meadows tonight—I left home this morning—have been visiting all day & although I feel quite tired I can not retire

---

29. J. H. Hildebrand and his son, J. H. Hildebrand, Jr., German-born cabinet makers, operated in Asheville under the firm name "J. and J. Hildebrand." *Census* of Buncombe County, 1850; *Asheville Messenger*, January 8, 1851.

without writing at least a short letter to my own beloved one—the mail has already closed, but I will write at-any-rate, & send it by Mrs Lester who does not leave until day after tomorrow, but I will be engaged all day tomorrow spending the day with her in company with several other friends, so I think I had best write tonight as I might perhaps allow tomorrow pass without writing you as I have to day—I am spending tomorrow at Cousin Robert Pearson's[30] & it is now after ten o'clock so I must be brief.

I received your letter yesterday & regret so much to hear of the affliction of your mother's family; your mother, Dr Lester tells me is also quite unwell, however he says she were improving when he left & I hope he is not mistaken—I would feel truly sorry if your sister's little boy were not to recover—Dr Lester says he is much better & doesent seem to consider him dangerous atall—I sincerely hope to hear by next mail the family are all decidedly better & that all will very soon be well—I had not heard when I wrote you last of the illness of your Sister Sarah, as I did not receive your letter until my return home from Sallies—your letter by Miss Dorcus I received at the same time—Your Sister Ann, you write me is now at home—please remember me particularly to her—I should have written her long before this, but have neglected doing so & I now am so much engaged that I can find time to write to no one but my beloved Zebulon—I will write when I can, but if I should not I hope she will excuse me—

You ask me if I will be pleased with the arrangement about our going to house keeping—certainly, my dear; I will be perfectly willing to go in that house if Mr Smith will have the proposed room put up—As I have told you before, I would greatly prefer going immediately to housekeeping if it is just as convenient to you—& I have no doubt but that place will suit us very well, for the present. —I must tell you also, that Uncle has given his consent for me to use my pleasure in having a private wedding, though he greatly prefered I should have a large party—but he has left it with me & I propose we shall be married at the church about twilight or early in the morning—which time do you prefer? I guess you think it a strange fancy, dont you? I hope though you are quite willing to it— I know you will not object at-any-rate.—

I was in hopes I could write you in this letter that my health was still improving, but I fear this is not the case—Although I have

---

30. "Cousin" to HNE through his marriage to Jane Sophronia Tate. Robert Caldwell Pearson was at this time a prosperous merchant in Morganton. Ashe, *Biographical History*, pp. 362-66.

been out visiting to day—I am not atall well—I find a great deal of exorcise or excitement does not suit me—so I think after this or next week I will spend my time quietly at home & I hope it will prove benificial—I think however I shall be better in the morning—after a good night's rest—but enough about my health.—

I am sorry Annie Lester is making such a short stay with us —I have seen but little of her—Dorcus does not return with her as they expected but will go over next week or the week after—Miss Sallie Grier, a very lovely friend of mine I expect will accompany her—I hope you will call upon her & cultivate her acquatance— she is indeed a charming girl—Have you called upon Maggie McDowell?[31] if not, I hope you will, she is a very particular friend of mine, & quite an agreeable girl.

You say, my love, that you are reading none atall & that you think some times that it is almost impossible for you to obtain license— now if you really have serious fears—I would rather you would not apply—but you know best—I dont want you to be rejected of course. It is quite late & my letter is growing quite long so I must close— but before closing I must tell you some good news—The Rev. Daniel Baker,[32] the great revivalist I suppose you have heard him spoken of—he is a Presbyterian—has been preaching in Charlotte for some time & I am happy in saying has had a revival of religion down there.—Mr & Mrs Barringer have both connected themselves with the church—also June Fox,[33] besides numerous other careless young men as well as ladies—many gentlemen who were really skeptics Maria writes seem deeply concearned about their soul's salvation— & indeed the whole community seem awakened to their guilt & are flying to Christ for pardon—what an interesting time it must be— Mr Sheetz has written soliciting Mr. B—— to come up here &

31. Margaret Erwin McDowell, daughter of Mrs. Charles McDowell's brother James McDowell and Margaret Erwin McDowell. After the death of her mother the infant "Maggie" was reared at Belvidere. *Census* of Burke County, 1850; McDowell, *McDowells, Erwins, Irwins*, pp. 211, 261, 262.

32. In August of this same year the Reverend Daniel Baker, D.D., of Texas held a revival at Providence Church at Fullwood, now Matthews (ten miles south of Charlotte). Of the meeting there Baker wrote, "Immense congregations attend my preaching—every Sabbath perhaps three thousand. People come from a great distance . . . I am told there has not been such a glorious revival in North Carolina for the last fifty years. . . ." "Records of Providence Church, Mecklenburg County, North Carolina," by H.D.H. (2 vols.), State Library, Raleigh, N.C., 1 (October 1, 1951): 6, 16; Powell, *North Carolina Gazetteer*, p. 316.

33. Junius A. Fox, Charlotte lawyer, was a son of Dr. Stephen Fox. His mother was the former Cynthia Erwin of Burke County. *Census* of Mecklenburg County, 1850; McDowell, *McDowells, Erwins, Irwins*, p. 194.

I sincerely hope he will do so—he goes from Charlotte to Davidson College, then to several other places down in that country & then we hope to have him with us—I can but hope he will be the instrument of doing great good in this community—I flatter myself that some one or more of our young men are concearned upon the subject of religion now—Cousin Kame among the number—how happy it would make me to have my own beloved one among the number who are anxiously enquiring the way of salvation—Oh dearest it is a blessing for which I sincerely pray.—I think perhaps if Mr Baker comes up here he will probably go on to Asheville if Mr Allen[34] will write & ask him—I hope he will do so—I hope dearest you dont think it amiss for me to mention to you so often the subject upon which I am most interested—your soul's salvation—When I see and hear of others being concearned you know it is but natural that I should speak to him who is the nearest & dearest friend I have, upon the subject—I wish my sheet was not filled & it was not so late—that I might write more upon the subject—but it is now too late & my heart is too full to write much more—I have been very much excited & quite happy ever since I heard this glorious news—you must know dearest that I could but wish you were among the number—but I do not despair—"All things are possible to them that believe"—The many promises contained in Gods holy word are truly precious to me—"We are told to ask & ye shall receive; seek & ye shall find"—indeed we should come expecting the blessing—believing that God will perform that which He promises—He will hear & answer the prayers offered in faith—& I will & do endeavor to exorcise faith but really I am sitting up too late—I could write all night to you upon this subject, but must now say "Good night" —May heaven protect you my dearest one & fit you for an inheritance incorruptable, undefiled & that fadeth not away is the heartfelt prayer of her who daily impotunes at a throne of grace for you. Brother Sam—I am thankful to a merciful Providence is still improving—My love to your mother, Sisters, & Aunt—I feel quite anxious about those who are ill & I hope you will let me hear from them every mail—I will write by next Tuesday's mail I think—And now again good night—truly I am happy in the hopes of the future —just think, only five weeks from to day—until we shall be united—

Your own Harriett—

34. From early 1852 until 1854 the Reverend M. T. Allen served the First Presbyterian Church in Asheville and the churches in Swannanoa and Reems Creek. George W. McCoy, *The First Presbyterian Church, Asheville, N.C., 1794-1951* (Asheville, N.C.: The First Presbyterian Church, 1951), p. 30.

I hope to hear from you soon again & that you continue in good health & are still quite happy—I am dearest

---

Asheville June 28. '53

My Dear Harriet,

Do you like to get a letter from me every mail? Or are you getting tired of receiving them so often? I hope not, for I am never tired of writing them and I hope you can *read* them without getting wearied. It seems almost singular to me—the disposition I have to be ever with you or writing to you or something of the kind and never feel the least weary, and no matter what I have to do or how busy I am I always find time to write you. When the time rolls around for the mail to leave for Morganton, the writing of you a letter occurs to me as naturally as the call to dinner at the ringing of the bells, and I think sometimes that the only object of the line from Asheville to your village is to carry my letters to you and receive yours in return—my trust is however, that my task will be done in a few weeks, our probation which has been a rather severe one ended, and we shall receive the reward our constancy and devotion deserves, transcendant happiness. How the time has flown! Notwithstanding my eager impatience I must confess the moments fly rapidly and I fear will outstrip my preparations for the great event. One short month only intervenes between us and our happiness! Really, as you say, after all, the near approach to this important change in my condition fills me at times with something of solemnity and awe! I hope to proffit by the reflections that come over me on such occasions, and that I may become the better prepared for the responsibilities about to devolve upon me. But I cant moralize much this evening—its too dreadful warm. I never felt such melting weather in my life scarcely—

I think Harriet, that the time we have appointed, the 3rd of August, will be a little inconvenient for some of my friends on account of the election. Brother Robert who is a candidate for re-election, has pretty strong opposition and says he dislikes for me to be out of the county at the election especially as I will have with me several young men who would all be friends of his. But I cant see how it can be helped, for I cant consent to defer it, and have to go back again after getting my license. So we will have to trust things as they are, and I hope Brother will not be so closely run as to need my help. His friends think he will beat his opponent by an almost overwhelming majority, although he, Mr Moore,[35] is said to be as strong an opponent as he could possibly find in the county. If things could change however, so as to make my presence actually necessary here on election day I will write you again and we will put our wedding forward a day or so instead of backward.

Sickness, sickness, nothing but sickness still in our family. We have five in bed yet—Mother, Sister Sally, and little Archie, and two negroes. They are all improving to day, except a negro woman who will probably scarcely get well. I am fearful, if our family continue sick much longer it will interfere with my preparations for August—but I trust they will soon be all well again.

I have been with Gov Swain and his family all the time I could spare and have been spending the time quite pleasantly. He has been teasing me about you a great part of his time. He says he knows you must be pretty if you resemble in any degree your mother; whom he knew. I told him you *resembled her most perfectly*. I have heard so, at any rate. He left town this morning to go to Col Lowreys[36] from there to Macon &c.

I can not think of anything more to put in this letter, I write so often—I will go up to the office and see if you have written to me.

God bless you my dearest Love and preserve your health is the constant prayer of

Your devoted Zebulon.

Mother, Sister, and Aunt Mary desire to be remembered—affectionately.

35. Exact identification cannot be made, but it is likely that he was a member of the family of Charles Moore, farmer and respected resident of the Hominy Creek section of Buncombe County. *Census* of Buncombe County, 1850; Minutes of the Buncombe County Court of Pleas and Quarter Sessions, Minute Docket, October 8, 1852, Book C, p. 658.

36. Colonel James M. Lowrie, half-brother of David Lowry Swain, was a resident of Madison County. Both Arthur and Connor spell his name "Lowrie" although the accepted spelling of Governor Swain's middle name was "Lowry." Arthur, *Western North Carolina*, p. 196; R. D. W. Connor, comp., *A Manual of North Carolina Issued by the North Carolina Historical Commission for the Use of the Members of the General Assembly Session 1913* (Raleigh, N.C.: E. M. Uzzell and Co., State Printers, 1913), p. 517.

[1853]

My dearest Hattie,

I recd yours yesterday evening per Mrs L—— [Lester] and really considered it a treasure—it has been so long since I rec'd such an one from you. I was much disappointed in not getting one by mail and was really much delighted to get one by our friend, and with it also a large bundle of Burke gossip. I called up this morning and had a long talk with Mrs L—— and the Dr. They tell me that you are in very low spirits about your health, and really I cant help but feel quite melancholly about it myself, when I see you so, who are generally so cheerfully resigned to every dispensation of providence. Dr Lester tho' solemnly assures me, that he does not think you have any reason for believing your health so near gone— he thinks you will recover, and do very well yet. I hope you will cheer up and that I may find you hale and healthy when I go over to seperate you from the friends and haunts of your childhood.
Before going any farther in this letter, let me inform you of a very unexpected event—nothing more nor less than the arrival home of our brother-in-law, Dr Neilson! He got home last night at 2 O'clk on the stage from Charleston, when we were expecting every body else in the world but him, as his last letter some two weeks since recd said nothing atall of returning before next fall or winter. You may be sure his arrival in this manner created quite a sensation in our family. He is looking quite stout and robust and is apparently in excellent health. He has I think, made a big pile of money *over the left*, but we are all satisfied to see him safe and well and able to take care of his family—Our sick folks, by the way, I beleive are all improving, and I am in hopes will soon be quite well. Sister & her little boy are both quite overjoyed, and the latter is nearly well—Sister Ann has left Burnsville for good and will stay at home all the time hereafter. She is obliged to you for your remembrances of her and desires me to return her affectionate regards to her future Sister-in-law.

Well now to business, having discussed other more general topics. So your Uncle has consented for you to do as you like about the wedding—I am really glad to hear it—And you say it shall be quite private, and in the church, to which of course I am perfectly agreed. You ask which I would prefer, getting married at twilight in the evening, or early in the morning? I dont know my dear, that I have any more choice in that matter than in the other, only it seems to me that it would probably be more conventient to have it take place in the evening, since we wish (at least I do) to start quite early next day in order to get into Buncombe for the election, and we could I amagine, be better prepared for such a start, if the wedding were to take place in the evening—But I assure you I will be content either way. Please inform me in your next if you intend to have any attendants, I presume not tho', but if so, how many. Also, if I should bring any one with me or shall I come quite alone? I had invited some young gentlemen to go over with me, but all of them conditionally—in case there should be a wedding—so there will be no inconvenience about that and I am glad there is going to be none—Please explain to me your entire arrangements this time so I may have my mind as much at ease as possible and study as well I can. About my getting license, I dont think there is any danger—I had studied pretty smartly several months since, and am getting under pretty good way again—Dont fear for me. You said when I was last over that I must provide some way for Cousin Mary Jo to come over with us—if she will come certainly, I will take a gentleman with me to bring her—Please let me know if she will certainly come so I may be prepared to take her—

I have seen Mr [Daniel] Baker that you speak of, in Tennessee and heard him preach, and hope he will come to Asheville—Be assured my Dear One, I donot take it amiss for you to speak to me so often on religious subjects; on the contrary I am much obliged to you, and hope I may proffit by it. My sheet is exhausted—please write me on all the topics I have spoken of, and may the God of Mercy bless you and keep you in health & strength—Your devoted Zebulon.

Quaker Meadows July 4th 1853

My beloved Zebulon,

With usual pleasure, I perused your letter this morning & it affords me equal pleasure to spend a short time in replying to it this afternoon. I am truly sorry our friends Dr & Mrs Lester have told you that I seemed low-spirited about my health—they are mistaken in supposing, I am—I thought I appeared quite cheerful while with them, although I was more unwell that day than usual—really I endeavor to be cheerfully resigned to every dispensation of providence & I hope I am to my ill health—however I fear sometimes I donot bear it as cheerfully as I should—I will try to though, hereafter—I know it's right that we should pass through afflictions in this life—it causes us to feel our dependance upon a supreame power—I feel that if it is right He will grant me health & if not I pray for grace to say "thy will O Lord be done."—I think I am better today & have been for a day or two & I certainly hope, with you dearest, that you will find me when you come over, much improved—the time is drawing very near—I can scarcely realize that it is so near—Before going farther, my love, allow me to say, if the appointed time (2nd of August) be atall inconvenient to yourself or friends I hope you will write me—I am perfectly willing either to defer it or have it come off a few days earlyer—just as it suits you—as we are going to have such a private wedding you know it wont make any difference with me.—I will tell you the arrangements I have concluded up if we are married on the evening of the 2nd—I don't wish to have any attendants or at least as I cant well have the number I desire, I would rather have none atall & besides I dont wish a party atall so I think it best that we should not have any attendants—I design being married about twilight in the church of course, from there we go to sister Mag's & will start from there the next morning as early as you wish—If you would rather be in Asheville the morning of the election, I would just as leave be married on the morning of the second & go immediately over that morning—either way suits me—I hope dearest if you find any objections to these arrangements you will let me know immediately—perhaps the time we have appointed doesn't suit your mother; if it doesent I hope you will not hesitate to say so;—Mollie Jo's intentions I can tell you nothing about as I have not seen her for more than three weeks—she went over to Rutherfordton about that time with the Misses Carson[37]—very much against the wishes of all her friends, & has not returned yet—I dont know when she will be at home—but when she does come I will ask her if she still desires you to provide a way for her to go over with us & let you know—I am sorry to say it, but it is so—Mollie has been acting, not atall as she should—her friends (all of us) to tell the truth, are very much put out with her—for reason that I will give you when we meet—I wish she would go over with us. I think perhaps you might influince her to act differently—Dont let her know that I have written in this manner to you—I really feel very anxious about her—I hope she will return home soon—I will then let you know her desire in the matter.—

37. Probably Mary Moffett and Margaret Ann, daughters of Jonathan Logan Carson and Mary Sturdivant Presnell Carson. Moffett Sinclair Henderson, *The Flags of Destiny* (n.p., n.d.), p. 60.

How delighted I was to hear of the arrival of Dr Neilson—your sister must really be over-joyed—we can judge of the excitement his arrival must have produced in your family having so recently welcomed Brother Samuel; Dr Neilson you say is looking so well—this I am also pleased to hear—I wish I could say this of poor brother—he is looking so badly & I think improves very slowly—he spent a very sick day yesterday—I think he is better today though.—I was glad to hear the sick of your mothers family were improving—I hope they will all be restored very soon—Your sister Ann you say is going to remain at home—I am quite pleased to hear it—My much love to her—Remember me also to your mother & Aunt.—My sheet is almost filled so I must prepare for closing & I know no better way than by invoking the Divine protection for you—May God ever be near you & keep you out of all temptations my dearest one—.

Miss Dorcus & Miss Sallie Grier go over tomorrow—this will be quite an agreeable surprise to Annie & the Dr—Kate says she thinks she will accompany you & I over—I hope she will. I hope you will be pleased with Miss Sallie—she is indeed a lovely girl—one I have a very high regard for.—Well, I had almost forgotten I was writing to upon the 4th of July—I suppose it has been a *great* day in your Village—as usual our Villagers spent it in a quiet way.—We are having such a nice shower of rain this evening—it is truly refreshing—everything seems quite revived—I must close as it is so late & I will be out visiting tomorrow with several lady friends & must prepare my letter this evening for the Office—I will write soon again you know—dont allow yourself to be uneasy about me, I assure you I feel better this evening & think I'm going to be well soon—Farewell dearest—I will expect a letter by next mail—I suppose you cant visit me again before the time of our happy union—I am afraid to ask you—in haste—

Your own affectionate
Harriett—

Asheville July 9th [1853]

My dearest Harriet,

I am in the proper trim for writing a love letter this evening according to Voltaire. He says that when one sits down to write a love-letter, he ought to begin without knowing what he is going to

say and quit without knowing what he has said. I am this evening in precisely that condition, at least as to the beginning part and therefore I can but hope that this letter may prove vastly interesting to you on that account. I am writing this evening from a sense of duty, and because my love is so great that I am loath to lose any opportunity of communing with you, and not that I have matter sufficient to write. I write so very often that I exhaust every thing of a general nature most completely, and if I did not draw heavily upon that *one grand inexhaustible* fund, (you know what I mean) I should have sometimes nothing at all to say—.
Well, the preface being read, let us enter upon the main subject, or if you will excuse the pun—the *august* theme. I know you dont like puns, and that is one reason why you have never suffered from my perpetrations like the most of my friends. I rec'd yours and was delighted, as usual, with its contents. I am always so delighted to receive those continued assurances of affection—those silent but eloquent messengers of love and happiness! I was glad to learn also that you were in better spirits concerning your health. I have suffered a great deal of unhappiness when thinking about it, and earnestly hope that a merciful Providence may yet enable you to see many years of health and happiness. I am likewise pleased with your preparations and arrangements for our marriage. I approve of them most cordially in every particular. As to altering the day appointed for the convenience of my friends, I positively can not hear of it. I have been waiting so long already that I cant consent to its being defered for a single moment, and as to having it come off sooner, inasmuch as I would be obliged to be in Morganton on the 2d to get my license, that wont do either. Nothing but continued and dangerous illness of our family can induce me to defer it. I am sorry to state in this connection, that Sister Laura is still very ill and has been ever since monday morning. She is getting some better now however and I have no doubt will be well in a week or so. I wrote you I believe, that I was threatened with sickness myself, and that I was quite uneasy. I am happy to say, that I think I am going to escape entirely—at least I feel to day extremely well. I beg you to feel no uneasiness about me whatever.

I have been studying very hard for some time past as I wrote you before & regret exceedingly, that I shall have to lose next week. But as I have a pretty large State docket and will make some money, I am somewhat reconciled to it—I have to attend Madison court also, as I have some business there that can not be neglected. I will only be there two days tho', and then I will read dilligently untill I have to start to You. It will not be in my power to write to you again next week so you must not be looking for a letter untill the close of the week. I intend getting to Morganton on Saturday evening the 30th. Could you permit me to spend the Sabbath with you? I do hope you will, at least a part of it—Has Cousin Mollie got home yet? I know your reasons for censuring her—I got them from Mrs Lester who told me you were very much disturbed at her wild manners. I think you are right—most assuredly.

Miss Dorcus & Miss Grier did not come as you wrote me. I could not have much time to visit them if they were here. I believe this evening I will ride out to Dr Hardy and see Cousin Cecelia Erwin[38] and Miss Mag McD——as I am really tired of my room. I am sorry to hear that Mr Sam McD's health improves so tardily—His friends here wish very much to see him. Perhaps he will come over about the time *we* do. I hope he will. Where is Jim now? My love to him, and tell him to come over, and return to Burke as I go over— I shall be entirely alone I suppose—Mother, Sister and Aunt all desire to be mentioned—.

  And now my Dear, I am again at the end of my letter, and thinking of nothing else to write it only remains for me to invoke the blessing of Heaven on you, and to assure you that I am still, as I hope ever to be, your Sincere and truly devoted

         Zebulon.

Please recollect Hattie, that tho' I shall be too busy next week to write you a letter, yet I will have ample time to *read* one if I could get it by Wednesday's mail—Zeb.

         Asheville July 16. [1853]

My Dear Harriet,

  Tho' scarcely able to sit up I can not suffer the mail to leave this evening without a letter for my Own beloved Harriet who has now been a week without hearing from me—I would not tell you of my illness, if it were not that I have determined never to conceal anything from you whatever, and because I trust too

  38. Cecilia Erwin of Belvidere was a sister of Mrs. J. F. E. Hardy. McDowell, *McDowells, Erwins, Irwins*, pp. 261, 262.

much to your good sense to beleive that you will disturb yourself with needless alarms when I assure you of the full extent of my illness—When I wrote you last Saturday I told you I was getting well, and really thought I was going to escape altogether—But the disease began to return upon me, and I feared I should not be able to attend to my business during court week, as I got a little worse each day—But by taking strong medicines and stimulants I kept up untill yesterday, when I was compelled to come home and go to bed from which I have scarcely been up a moment since—Brother Noel[39] was taken down at the same time and he and I are about equally bad off with the same painful disease—Sister Laura continues quite low and improves so slowly as to scarcely be perceptible—We have all been very much afflicted indeed, as two or three only of the whole family have escaped this disease which seems to be if not contagious, at least epidemical—It is obtaining some hold in the village also, as I hear of several families afflicted with it, tho' none have suffered like ours—Under such circumstances my dearest one, I know you will excuse the want of that due preparation for your reception which continued sickness is likely to prevent. Mother is much disturbed in being compelled to forego her preparations for a party by these misfortunes—you may perhaps wonder at my not requesting the postponement of our marriage, but I really can not consent to that untill the last moment. As this disease has been fatal to none of us, and does not keep any of us down for more than a week or so at a time, I am still in hopes that we will all be in health by the 2d. Sister hopes to get well enough to return to housekeeping next week, and Brother and I are almost the last ones to take it—If however we do not get better by that time, the wedding will have to be postponed of course, tho' I will not think of this untill it cant possibly be avoided—I am so selfish, that, if I am well enough myself, I had rather bring you home without the least preparation, than to defer my happiness a single day—The merry-makings, parties &c. usual on such occasions can come off afterwards, when health and other circumstances are more propitious—I care nothing for them at all, and neither I am confident do you, but I am anxious nevertheless, for my friends to show you that respect which in the present instance is peculiarly your due from every one who is a friend to me. I beg therefore Harriet, that you will not ask for our marriage to be put off from any notion of

39. James Noel Vance, an "invalid," probably an epileptic. He died in 1854 of apoplexy. *Census* of Buncombe County, 1850; Dowd, *Life of Vance*, p. 7.

the time being inconvenient to my friends, for I assure you if it should become necessary or proper, the request shall come from me—

I beg also My dear, you will not suffer any undue uneasiness about my health, for tho' I will not deny suffering a great deal and being pretty bad off, yet I am taking all proper steps for checking my illness, and think quiet and medicine will restore me in a few days—The Dr says if I had kept my room instead of undergoing the labour and excitement of the court house, I would not have been down at all—I am of course compelled to lose Madison court, where I had a few cases and some important business that I would have been glad to attend to. But it cant be helped—

Miss Dorcas and her little Sister [Laura] are here but I have been unable to see them—My great distress is about losing my time for studying—for tho' I have been trying to read here all day, I can do no good at it as you may well imagine—I could tell you of a great many things of a general nature, but I am really getting quite weak & giddy, and so must get back to bed—Mother and all send their love—Please let me hear from you soon—as to your own health, which I hope is improving, and other things—

Truly your own devoted and affectionate

Zebulon—

July 19th 53

My beloved Zebulon,

I have just received your letter, that I should have gotten yesterday morning, & how unhappy I am to hear of your illness, but dearest I will endeavor to look on the bright side & do sincerely trust the next mail will bring me more consoling intelligence—Do take care of yourself—& I beg your good mother not to be disturbed with regard to my reception—I was much in hopes she would not put herself to any trouble atall—I was not thinking of her giving a party, particularly as her family have been so much afflicted & continue to be—Under the circumstances I dont think she ought to give herself the least uneasiness—please say to her for me, I hope she will lay aside all her fears & receive me with as little trouble as possible—Do Dearest let me hear from you at every opportunity. I will be so anxious about you—If you find it necessary to postpone our wedding, I hope you will not hesitate—I do sincerely trust you will soon be well—I am writing in great haste—I had written you and was just about closing the letter, when I recd yours. I will not send it now—I also wrote you by last Wednesday's mail, but did not get it to the Village in time to be mailed—I feel thankful to tell you of the improvement in my health—I am vastly better than I have been—Your severe illness dearest is the only thing now to mar my happiness & I trust in an all wise power that you will soon be restored to your usual good health, for which you should be so thankful—I regret so much to hear your Sister improves so slowly—indeed you all have been afflicted—this dreadful disease seems to be prevailing every where—Bro. J. is waiting to go to the village so I must close my note—I will wait impatiently for the next mail—Will write again Monday—wish I had time to write more but have not—How much I wish I could be with you in illness—I think I could nurse you so well—no doubt though you have the greatest attentions—Brother hurries me & I must say farewell, however against my will—God bless you my own one—

Your own Harriett—

Morganton July 23rd 1853

My beloved Zebulon,

I can't express to you my very great disappointment at not receiving some tidings concearning you by last mail—I suffered great anxiety before it came, but since it came in without a letter from you dearest, I have really been quite unhappy, & you can judge of my uneasiness when you remember my having told you, that I would never again write you by the Sabbath mail.—I fear you were too ill to write—Do dearest, if you are not able to write to me yourself, get some of your friends to write at least a line, that I may know your real situation,—you know there is nothing worse than a state of suspense—so will you not let me be informed, precisely, with regard to your situation? I do endeavor to bear this (affliction I may call it) submisively; but I cant refrain from giving way to my feelings at times; I hope though, I do not do so, murmeringly—I earnestly pray for grace to bear patiently the dispensations of an all wise Providence; Though His hand may appear to bear heavy upon us for a season, we should remember it will all work togather for our good, if we love God—Does not your affliction, my own one bring you to feel your dependence upon a merciful Father, who does not chastise in wrath, but mercy? I sincerely beseach a throne of Grace that this affliction may be sanctified to your soul & my dearest I have faith, I trust, to believe, that my prayers, will be answered but they must be accompanied by yours—God's Holy Spirit has no doubt often striven with you & is now waiting to bless you—but we should remember that it will not always strive with us; if we continue to resist, it may take its flight; —but I must cut my letter short, as Sis has called to me to go to walk—I have been spending to day with my dear friend Maria Barringer—She desires her regards to you, so does Sis—Do dearest relieve my anxiety by next mail,—you cant know how anxious I feel—I have shead many tears, will you believe.

How sorry I was to hear of the very sad illness of Dr Lester. Do you find it necessary to postpone our marriage?—Do let me know as soon as possible.—I must not close without apologizing for my last hasty note as well as this one—I am too uneasy to collect ideas enough to fill a sheet.—My much love to your Mother & other friends—If you should not be able to write me yourself, I hope some of them will grant me the pleasure of hearing from you—God bless you my dear one—I can but hope to see you soon in health—I leave all things in the hands of God—I know He will do all things well—Do excuse haste.—Your own Hattie

P.S.
I must tell you how very slowly poor Brother Samuel improves—He was very sick yesterday—but is better to day.—I will write again by Wednesday's mail   Hattie

---

Asheville July 23. 53

My Dear Harriet,

I am very much disappointed in not getting a letter to you by last mail—Indeed I expect I was fully as much disappointed as you were in not getting one, for I wished greatly to allay your uneasiness about my health, which I knew must be very great after getting my last letter. The reason why you did not get a letter was because the one I wrote for the mail, I gave to Miss Dorcas who intended going by that Stage, but on account of Dr Lester being taken sick she gave it out, and did not think to send my letter to the office. This is I trust a sufficient excuse, and yet I regret the uneasiness you may have felt. I stated in that letter that I was getting better, and now I am happy to state that I am almost entirely well. I have nothing to fear from a relapse if I stick to the *regimen* prescribed for me by the Drs and you know I'll do that. I have been taking medicine like a good boy (as I am you know) in my great anxiety to get well. I have been up in town attending to business &c, as usual—I met Miss Grier at Dr Lesters yesterday and was much pleased with her. I hope to see more of her—Bro Noel is improving slightly to day, and Sister continues to improve also—so that I hope yet you may find us all in health when you come among us. The Circus has been here two days and has had a great crowd at each performance—This Company goes through your village I believe—

You must excuse me for not writing a long letter this evening as there is a friend in my room now waiting for me to get done so he can talk to me—I will write you next week again and, as it will be the *last* one I may ever write to you as Miss Espy, it shall be a long one. You have not yet answered my enquiries about my visiting you on the Sunday after I get to Morganton—I wish you would in your next, as I will certainly expect *one more* letter from you by next mail—As to news I can not think it important enough to interest you, since judging by myself I feel no interest in anything now scarcely but the one grand event—So I will conclude. I hope your health is still improving—God bless you my dearest One—Adieu, Adieu—

Zebulon—

Quaker Meadows July 26th 1853

My beloved Zebulon,

Your letter of last mail I can assure you, relieved my mind greatly—I remained in the Village Sabbath night, in order that I might hear from you as soon as possible. I was so uneasy, but I am thankful, I trust, to a merciful Providence that my dearest love is again restored to usual health & is still so happy in the contemplation of that future, which appears so bright.—I was also pleased to learn that the family were improving—I should be pleased to see some of them on the evening of the 2nd of August at the Presbyterian church—by the way, have you written to Mr Sheetz? I presume you design having him marry us, do you not? You say I may look for you on Saturday evening—I am delighted you are coming then; I hope you will come over to the Quaker Meadows that evening & I will also be pleased to have you with me during the Sabbath—we must go to church though—you can remain over here that night & go in to church & we can then return.

I suppose you rec'd my letter by last mail; I was so uneasy, I could not refrain from writing. I hope it did not prevent you from attending church—Bro. J. is waiting to mail my letter so, as usual, I must close in great haste—I hope to see you certainly Saturday evening & I will then talk over all—I hope to receive, by next mail, the promised long letter. My love to all your friends I hope to see them soon in good health—How is Dr Lester? In great haste—

       Your own Hattie

P. S. If you dislike to come alone why not bring one of your young friends with you—Do excuse the greatest haste—

Appendixes and Index

Appendix A

FAMILY RECORD.

MARRIAGES.	MARRIAGES.
[handwritten entry: Z. B. Vance and Harriett N. Espy, were married, by Rev. Wm. C. Sheetz, August 2d 1853, in the Presbyterian Church, Morganton, N.C.] *[handwritten entry: Chas. M. Busbee and Kate V. Tate were married by Rev. A. A. Harding, Nov. 5th 1879 at the residence of M. P. Pegram Esq. Charlotte N.C.]*	

Z. B. Vance and Harriett N. Espy, were married, by Rev. Wm. C. Sheetz, August 2nd 1853 in the Presbyterian Church Morganton N. C. [*Notation in the Bible inscribed: "Harriett N. E. Vance From Her Husband 1857"*].[1]

1. This Bible is in the possession of the editor.

Appendix B

My dear Sir

Some time Sins I Receivered a letter from you asking from me a precious favor in the person of my niecs. I have Raised her and a think a greate dale of her Had your Character not been Represented to me in the light it has I might have held my Consent you say your patrimony is all gon to Secure you an education poverty under Sutch Circumstances is I think a blessing it shows that you are determined to Relye on your Resorses for a living may you be successfull is my Cincear wish you have been represented to me as an ennerJetick Sober young man I have a high Regard for your family there four I give my Consent and trust you and my Nice may live hapily and long in the enjoyment of all nesary Earthly Blessings.

Charles McDowell

April the 25th 1852

Source: Frontis W. Johnston, ed., *The Papers of Zebulon Baird Vance, 1843-62*, 1: 16-17.

Index

A

Adams, Lawrence Augustus: married Mary Joe Tate, 227n
Adams, the Reverend Stephen B.: identified, 215
Alexander, Jane: identified, 115
Allen, the Reverend M. T.: identified, 248
Asheville, N.C.: prosperity of, xv; description of, xvii, xxii; social life of, xviii, 100, 108, 110, 112, 113, 115, 126, 128, 163, 166, 184, 190, 204, 212
Aston, Edward J.: identified, 154
"Aunt" (of HNE). *See* McDowell, Anne McDowell (Mrs. Charles)
"Aunt" (of ZBV). *See* Baird, Mary Adelaide
Avery, General Clark Moulton, 207; identified, 184
Avery, Harriet Eloise Erwin (Mrs. Isaac Thomas), 30n, 44n
Avery, Harriet Justina (Tene), 207; identified, 44; joins church, 242
Avery, Isaac Erwin: identified, 44
Avery, Colonel Isaac Thomas, 30n, 44n, 77n, 155n, 184n; identified, 199
Avery, Mary Corinna Morehead (Mrs. William Waightstill): identified, 101
Avery, Mary Martha, 207; identified, 77
Avery, Thomas Lenoir, 156; identified, 155
Avery, William Waightstill, 33, 156, 199n; identified, 30n-31n; murder of Fleming by, 30-31; defeated by ZBV for Congress, 213n
Avirett, James Battle, 123; identified, 127
Azalea (summer home of William Patton in Buncombe County, N.C.), 112n

B

Baird, Bedent, 73n
Baird, Christiana Weaver (Mrs. William R.), 127n
Baird, Hannah Erwin (Mrs. Zebulon; ZBV's grandmother), xiii, 16n, 17n, 51n
Baird, Israel, 73n
Baird, Margaret Jane (Mag), 83; identified, 73n; and Augustus Summerfield Merrimon, 73, 76, 115. *See also* Merrimon, Margaret Jane Baird (Mrs. Augustus Summerfield)
Baird, Mary Adelaide (ZBV's "Aunt"), 122, 132, 133, 138, 144, 156, 160, 168, 172, 176, 180, 188, 195, 218, 220, 222, 224, 228, 235, 242, 254, 256; identified, 127; wants to meet HNE, 169
Baird, Mary Tate (Mrs. Israel), 73n
Baird, William R., 127n
Baird, Zebulon (ZBV's grandfather), xiii, 15n
Baker, the Reverend Daniel, 252; identified, 247
Barringer, Daniel M., 51n
Barringer, Maria Massey (Mrs. Victor

C.), 98, 260; identified, 51n; wedding of, 94, 95; joins church, 247. See also Massey, Maria
Barringer, Victor C., 115, 163; identified, 51n; engagement of, 51; marriage of, 94, 95; joins church, 247
Battle, Kemp Plummer, xvii, xviii, 13n
Battle, Lucy Plummer (Mrs. William Horn), 13n
Battle, Richard Henry, 13n
Battle, Susan Catherine, xxiii, 17; identified, 13
Battle, Judge William Horn, xii, 13n, 31n, 42n
Bellevue (James Erwin plantation in Burke County, N.C.), 187n, 190n
Belvidere (plantation in Burke County, N.C., owned by descendants of William Willoughby Erwin), 58; sketch of, 51n; HNE visits at, 51, 227; some people reared at, 71n, 123n, 209n, 256n
Bingham, Anna J., 226n
Bingham, Eliza, 226n
Bingham, Eliza Alves Norwood (Mrs. William J.), 226n
Bingham, Robena: identified, 226
Bingham, William J., 226n
Blackstock, Emily: identified, 137
Blackstock, Nehemiah, 137n, 204n
Bleak House, 91
Bowman, Grace Greenlee (Mrs. John; HNE's great-grandmother), xix. See also McDowell, Grace Greenlee (Mrs. Charles)
Bowman, John (HNE's great-grandfather), xix
Bowman, Mary (HNE's grandmother), xix. See also Tate, Mary Bowman (Mrs. William)
Boyd, Dr. J. D., 190, 208, 214; identified, 143
Boyd, Mary: identified, 113
Brank, Rebecca, xiv
Brank, Robert (great-grandfather of ZBV), xix, 96n
"Brother James." See McDowell, James C. S.
"Brother Samuel." See McDowell, Samuel Moffett
"Brother William." See McKesson, William F.
Brown, Ann Evans (Mrs. John), 165n
Brown, John, 165n
Brown, John Evans, 168n

Brown, William Caleb: identified, 165; and Clara Patton, 165, 172; and California gold rush, 169, 191, 228; and Mary Joe Tate, 194
Buck Hotel, Asheville, N.C., xviii, 100n
Buncombe Turnpike, xiv, xv
Burgin, General, 119, 199; identified, 116
Burke County: social life of, xx, 46, 148, 206, 207, 216, 217, 234, 235. See also Reading Society
Burnsville Academy, Burnsville (Yancey County), N.C., 215n
Butler, Margaret Tate (Mrs. William Claiborne), 9n
Butler, Sarah Louisa (Sallie): reared in home of Captain Charles McDowell, xx; identified, 9; engagement and marriage of, 36, 37, 39, 44. See also Greenlee, Sarah Butler (Mrs. Ephraim E.)
Butler, William Claiborne, 9n
Bynum, General John Gray (HNE's "Cousin Gray"), 14n, 147; in W. W. Avery trial, 31n; identified, 51n; illness of, 148, 149
Bynum, Mary McDowell (Mrs. John Gray; HNE's "Cousin Mary"), 14n, 95, 148, 149; education of, 30n; identified, 51n; ZBV's opinion of, 144; approves HNE-ZBV marriage, 145
Byrd, Cornelius, 112

C

Caldwell, Jane Eliza, 79, 84; identified, 77
Caldwell, John, 77n
Caldwell, Tod R., 77n
Calhoun, John C., xv
California gold rush, xxii, 37n, 39, 45n, 48, 55; ZBV on, 60, 109, 112. See also Avery, Thomas Lenoir; Brown, John Evans; Brown, William Caleb, and California gold rush; McDowell, Samuel Moffett, and California gold rush; Neilson, Dr. Morgan Lines, and California gold rush; Tate, Junius Constantine, and California gold rush
Campbell, Thomas, 4n, 174
Capers, Bishop William, 132, 135; identified, 128n
Carlisle, the Reverend John M.: identified, 226
Carson, John, 50n

Carson, Jonathan Logan, 253n; identified, 50
Carson, Margaret Ann: identified, 253
Carson, Mary Moffett: identified, 253
Carson, Mary Sturdivant Presnell (Mrs. Jonathan Logan), 179, 253n
Carson, Samuel, xiv
Carson's (stage stop in McDowell County, N.C.), 103, 175, 176, 179; description of, 50n
Chapel Hill, N.C., xxii, 47; social life at, 13, 20, 35; ZBV's attachment to, 41
Chapel of the Cross, 40n
Chapman, the Reverend Robert Hett, 130
Cherokee County, N.C.: court in, 93, 151, 156, 157, 158
Chunn, Alfred B., 220, 224n; identified, 152n
Chunn, Julia: identified, 224
Chunn, Sarah M. (Mrs. Alfred B.), 156, 224; identified, 152
Clingman, Thomas L.: identified, 213
Coleman, Cynthia Swain (Mrs. William), 112n
Coleman, David: identified, 112
Coleman, William, 112n
Corpening, Mr., 226
Corpening, Salena M., 44n
"Cousin Eliza." *See* Woodfin, Eliza Grace McDowell (Mrs. Nicholas W.)
"Cousin Gray." *See* Bynum, General John Gray
"Cousin John." *See* Woodfin, John W.
"Cousin Mary." *See* Bynum, Mary McDowell (Mrs. John Gray)
"Cousin Mira." *See* Woodfin, Mira McDowell (Mrs. John W.)
"Cousin Woodfin." *See* Woodfin, Nicholas W.
Crockett, Davy, xiv
Czar, His Court and People, Including a Tour in Norway and Sweden, The, 103

D

Davidson College, 11, 94n
Deaver, R. Pinckney (Pink), 23, 171; identified, 169
Deaver, Reuben, 169n
Deaver's Springs (summer resort in Buncombe County, N.C., no longer in existence), 169n
Dickens, Charles, 91
Dickinson, William T., 137

Dickson, Henry Robertson: identified, 116
Dickson, the Reverend John, 116n
Dream Life: A Fable of the Seasons, 80, 91

E

Eagle Hotel, Asheville, N.C., xviii, 100, 108, 109, 115, 143n, 190
Edney, General Bayles M., 112
Edney, James M., 80, 121, 143, 237; identified, 79n; attacks ZBV, 79, 82
Ellet, Elizabeth Fries (Lummis), 46
Erwin, Adolphus Lorenzo, 211; identified, 209
Erwin, Alexander (ZBV's great-grandfather), xiii
Erwin, Arthur Leander, 53n
Erwin, Cecilia Matilda, 256
Erwin, Clara, 167; identified, 162
Erwin, George Washington Phifer: identified, 187; loses child, 190, 194
Erwin, Harriet Esther, 211, 220; identified, 209; ZBV's opinion of, 213, 216, 231
Erwin, James, 187n, 190n
Erwin, Marcus, 92, 95, 188; identified, 51n; praises ZBV, 51; ZBV's opinion of, 58; runs for North Carolina Senate, 62, 66, 87, 111
Erwin, Margaret Phifer (Mrs. James), 187n, 190n
Erwin, Mary Gertrude Simianer (Mrs. Adolphus Lorenzo), 209n
Erwin, Matilda Walton (Mrs. William Crawford), 162n, 234n
Erwin, William Crawford, 162n, 203, 234n; identified, 190; marriage of, 217, 223, 227, 233, 234
Erwin, William Willoughby, 51n
Espy, Harriett Newell: description of, xi, xx, 74; youth of, xiii; birth of, xviii; death of parents of, xviii; taken into Captain Charles McDowell's home, xviii, xix; meets ZBV, xviii, xxi; relationship of, to Captain Charles McDowell, xix, 45n; family life of, xix, xx; joins church, xx, 131n; inheritance of, xx; characteristics of, xxiii, 16; death of, xxiv; ZBV receives ring from, 20; "addressed" by Augustus Summerfield Merrimon, 24n; education of, 155n; on living in Marion, 179, 180, 186, 208, 209, 211; opinion of, of ZBV's ability, 210; attitude of, toward ZBV

and politics, 217. *See also* Marriage of HNE and ZBV
Espy, Mary Louisa Tate (Mrs. Thomas; mother of HNE), xv, 75
Espy, Thomas, the Reverend (father of HNE), xviii, 75, 76

F

Fagg, Colonel John A., 111
Fleming, Samuel, 30n
Fox, Cynthia Erwin (Mrs. Stephen), 247n
Fox, Junius A.: identified, 247
Fox, Dr. Stephen, 247n
French Broad River, xiv, 21n, 85, 137n, 184n

G

Gaither, Alfred, 175n
Gaither, Alfred Haywood: identified, 174
Gaither, Burgess Sidney, 123n, 159n, 174n; runs for Congress, 213
Gaither, Catherine Reese Erwin (Mrs. Alfred), 175n
Gaither, Elizabeth Sharpe Erwin (Mrs. Burgess Sidney), 123n, 159n, 174n
Gaither, Julia Matilda, 186; identified, 175
Gaither, William E., 159; identified, 123; courtship and marriage of, 202, 217, 223
Garrett, James R., 21n
Garrett, Jane Neilson (Mrs. James R.), 21n
Garrett, Sara L.: identified, 21n; rumor concerning, threatens HNE-ZBV romance, 21-24 *passim*; HNE accepts ZBV's explanation concerning, 25-26 *passim*; attitude of, toward ZBV, 84; HNE's opinion of, 86; rumor concerning, recurs, 92, 95; illness of, 120, 123, 132; marriage of, 135
Garrett, Stephen, 21n
Gaston, Lauretta Murphy (Mrs. Alexander Francis), 233; identified, 217n
Gilliland, Cordelia: identified, 154n; marriage of, 154, 157
Gilliland, Lewellyn, 154n
Gilliland, Mary; identified, 170n-71n; going to Happoldt-Lester wedding, 170
Goldsmith, Oliver, 6n
Gould, Miss R., 155n
Graham, Alexander, 113n
Graham, Harriet, 115; identified, 113

Graves, Magie (M. F.): identified, 154. *See also* Smith, Magie Graves (Mrs. Jesse Siler)
Graves, William B.: identified, 154
Greenlee, Ephraim E., 48, 80, 82, 123, 127, 207; identified, 36n; engagement and marriage of, 36, 39, 42, 44, 45; trip to Tennessee of, 50, 54, 77, 78; housekeeping in Morganton, 86
Greenlee, Ephraim M.: and W. W. Avery case, 30n; identified, 186n; HNE once lived with, 186; offers land in McDowell County to HNE, 211
Greenlee, Sarah Butler (Sallie; Mrs. Ephraim E.), 42, 48, 82, 101, 127; trip to Tennessee of, 50, 54, 55, 77, 78; HNE's affection for, 62; housekeeping in Morganton, 86; HNE visits, 203, 241, 246. *See also* Butler, Sarah Louisa
Greenlee, Sarah Hollingsworth Brown (Mrs. Ephraim M.), 186n
Grier, Sallie (schoolmate of HNE): spends summer in Burke County, 217, 218; visits in Asheville, 247, 254, 256, 261

H

Happoldt, Ann Judson: identified, 55n; courtship of, 55, 67, 77, 79, 102, 106, 110, 115; confirmed, 107; wedding of, 138, 156, 158, 167, 171, 174-75 *passim*. *See also* Lester, Ann Happoldt (Mrs. Thomas C.)
Happoldt, Dorcas, 175, 202, 207, 247, 254, 256, 260; identified, 44; confirmed, 107; visits in Asheville, 240, 241, 242, 243, 244, 246, 258
Happoldt, Dr. John Michael, 44n, 55n, 66, 156, 175; identified, 50; party of, 171; HNE's opinion of, 242
Happoldt, Laura, 258
Hardy, Cordelia Erwin (Mrs. James F. E.), 71n, 209n, 256n
Hardy, Dr. James F. E., 171n, 199, 204, 256; identified, 71n-72n
Hardy, Washington Morrison (Wash): identified, 171
Harper's Magazine, xxii, 39, 46, 51, 67, 89, 91, 100, 132, 187, 218; ZBV's opinion of, 40
Haywood County, N.C.: court in, 11, 164
Hemans, Felicia D., 206n
Henson, Freeland, 115n

272

Henson, John McKamie Wilson (Kame), 33, 73, 76, 213, 218, 220, 229; identified, 17n; death of mother of, 17, 20; returns to Morganton, 202; courts Mollie Jo, 203, 207; engagement of, broken, 226, 227, 230; concerned about religion, 248

Henson, Mary, 224, 231; identified, 115

Henson, Sarah Myra Erwin (Mrs. Freeland), 115n; identified, 17n; death of, 17, 20

Hickory Grove (plantation in Burke County, N.C., where HNE's mother was born), xviii, 33n

Hildebrand, J. and J.: identified, 245

Hilliard, Dr. William Lewis, 204; identified, 169

Holston Annual Conference of the Methodist Episcopal Church, South, 110, 128, 129, 132, 135

Holston Conference Female College, 82n-83n, 143n, 152n, 226

Hutchison, James Marion: identified, 94

I

Israel, Claudia Blackstock (Mrs. Jeptha M.): identified, 204n; death of, 204, 206, 214

Israel, Jeptha M., 245; identified, 204n

Ives, Bishop Levi Silliman: identified, 107

J

Johnson, Robert Bruce, 43, 231; identified, 32n

Johnson, William, 32n

Jones, George, 135n

Jones, James: marries Sara Garrett, 135n

Jones, Kesiah Sevier (Mrs. George), 135n

K

Kerr, John, 143; identified, 112

L

Lapland (site of Marshall, N.C.), 184n; ZBV's family lived at, xiv, xvii, 71n, 137n

La Rochefoucauld, 3, 32

Lester, Ann Happoldt (Mrs. Thomas C.), 193, 207, 211, 213, 216, 228, 230, 235, 242, 246, 247, 254, 256; visits in Charleston, 175, 187; Asheville parties for, 177, 184, 189, 190; HNE's opinion of, 194, 202, 224; Asheville home of, 221-22; ZBV's opinion of, 231. See also Happoldt, Ann Judson

Lester, Dr. Thomas C., 192, 199, 202, 204, 207, 213, 252; identified, 55n; courtship of, 55, 67, 77, 79, 100, 102, 106, 107, 115, 147, 148, 151; wedding plans of, 138, 152, 158, 167, 170, 171, 172, 173; wedding of, 174-75 passim; Asheville parties for, 177, 184, 189, 190; visits in Charleston, 181, 187; home of, 221-22; attends Vance family, 246, 251; illness of, 260, 262

Love, Colonel James Robert, 226n

Love, Margaret, 230; identified, 226

Love, Robert G. A., 111

Lowrie, Colonel James M., 111; identified, 250

M

McDowell, Anne McDowell (Mrs. Charles; HNE's "Aunt"), 62, 78, 102, 104, 159, 207; relatives of, 9n, 50n, 55n, 190n, 209n, 247n; identified, 45; visits in Rutherfordton, 51, 55, 58, 61, 63, 121, 122, 125, 224, 227; visits in Asheville, 127, 130, 133; favors delay in HNE-ZBV wedding, 201; goes to ailing son, 232, 233

McDowell, Captain Charles (HNE's "Uncle"), 62, 63, 66, 73, 78, 80, 81, 122, 159, 165, 179, 211, 213, 217, 227, 233, 242, 251; sketch of, xix, 45; household of, xix, xx; indulged HNE, xx; relatives of, 9n, 14n, 15n, 24n, 25n, 30n, 32n, 67n; relationship of, to HNE, 45n; writes ZBV, 267

McDowell, General Charles, xix, 45n

McDowell, Grace Greenlee (Mrs. Charles), 45n. See also Bowman, Grace Greenlee (Mrs. John)

McDowell, James, 93n, 209n, 247n

McDowell, James C. S. (HNE's "Brother James"), 17, 32, 37, 48, 80, 86, 89, 91, 93, 95, 99, 101, 107, 113, 115, 123, 127, 159, 176, 178, 180, 184, 193, 220, 226, 245, 256; sketch of, 9; and Mary Wheat, 13, 28, 53, 60, 63, 83; in Butler-Greenlee wedding, 44; goes to Charlotte with Massey-Barringer party, 90, 95; and Martha McEntire, 109; resumes law study in Asheville, 175, 181, 201, 203, 211; in McEntire-Gaither wedding, 223; goes to ailing brother, 232

273

McDowell, John (brother of Mrs. Charles McDowell), 55n
McDowell, Dr. John Calhoun: identified, 190
McDowell, Joseph (grandfather of Captain Charles), 15n
McDowell, Colonel Joseph, of Pleasant Gardens, xixn, 45n
McDowell, Colonel Joseph, of Quaker Meadows (uncle of Captain Charles), xixn
McDowell, Dr. Joseph Alburton: identified, 93
McDowell, Katherine Ann (Kate), 51n, 220, 242; identified, 209
McDowell, Margaret Erwin (Mrs. James), 209n, 247n
McDowell, Margaret Erwin (Maggie), 51n, 207, 256; identified, 247
McDowell, Mary Moffett (Mrs. Joseph, of Pleasant Gardens), 45n
McDowell, Samuel Moffett (HNE's "Brother Samuel"), 39; identified, 32n-33n; to take law examination, 32, 34, 35, 36; and the California gold rush, 37, 45, 48, 55, 64, 73, 93, 97, 99, 102, 107, 156, 159, 228, 232; obtains superior court license, 38; in Butler-Greenlee wedding, 44; education of, 94n; illness of, 232, 233, 235, 236, 238, 254, 256, 260
McDowell, Sarah, 234; identified, 55
McDowell, Sarah Erwin (Mrs. John Calhoun), 190n
McEntire, John, 109n
McEntire, Martha (Muff), 113, 145, 148, 149; identified, 109n; and James McDowell, 109; ZBV's opinion of, 115, 147; and William Gaither, 159; engagement of, to William Gaither, 217n
McEntire, Thomas: identified, 113
McKee, James, 100n
McKee, James L.: identified, 100n; married, 100, 102
McKesson, Anna Maria: identified, 25
McKesson, James (contemporary of HNE's), 207, 217; identified, 61
McKesson, James (father of William F.), 61, 78, 170; identified, 14n; Miss R. Gould's school in home of, 155n; praises ZBV, 172
McKesson, Margaret McDowell (Mrs. William F.; HNE's "Sister"), 51, 58, 101, 110, 172, 183, 194, 211, 213, 217, 224, 232, 260; identified, 14n, 25n; new home of, 78; ZBV asks consent of, to his marriage, 62, 66, 80; approves marriage, 76, 81; relationship of, with ZBV, 127, 132, 193; favors ZBV's moving to Marion, 180; ZBV and HNE to spend wedding night in home of, 253
McKesson Maria (Mrs. James), 14n
McKesson, Sarah (Mrs. Thomas), 61n
McKesson, Thomas, 61n
McKesson, William F. (HNE's "Brother William"), 25n, 44, 76, 121, 127, 131, 136, 137; sketch of, 14
Macon County, N.C.: court in, 96, 112, 157, 161
McRee, Dr. William Lucius: identified, 217
Madison County, N.C.: court in, 88, 127, 128, 129, 133, 135, 157, 168, 181, 214, 219, 255
Maltby, Miss, 179, 185, 186, 218; in Morganton for Happoldt-Lester wedding, 172, 175, 177
Marion (town in McDowell County, N.C.). See Espy, Harriett Newell, on living in Marion
Marriage of HNE and ZBV, xxiv, 20; regarding date of, 31, 182, 184, 200, 201, 202, 242; jeopardized by rumors concerning ZBV, 117-18 passim; not cancelled, 119-20 passim; plans for, 159, 246, 249, 251, 253, 255, 256, 257, 261, 262; record of, 265
Marshall, N.C., xiv; located on Vance property, 183-84
Marvel, I. K. (pseudonym of Donald Grant Mitchell), 80n, 82n, 89
Mason, David: hanging of, 88
Massey, George, 51n
Massey, Maria: identified, 51n; coming wedding of, 51, 76, 79, 80, 86, 87, 88; Charles McDowells to entertain for, 90. See also Barringer, Maria Massey (Mrs. Victor C.)
Massey, Maria McKesson (Mrs. George,) 51n
Maxwell, John S., 103
Merrimon, Augustus Summerfield, 39; ZBV reads law with, xviii, 51n; sketch of 24n-25n; and Sara Garrett rumor, 24, 26, 27, 30; law licenses of, 36, 38, 170; ZBV's opinion of, 38; interest of, in HNE-ZBV engagement, 51, 53, 82; defeated by ZBV for solicitorship, 72-74 passim, 76; and Margaret Jane Baird, 115n-

116n; wedding of, 127, 132; Nicholas Woodfin's party for, 132, 136
Merrimon, the Reverend Branch Hamlin (father of Augustus Summerfield), 24n, 73, 76
Merrimon, Branch Hamlin, Jr., 115n-16n
Merrimon, Margaret Jane Baird (Mrs. Augustus Summerfield), 124. *See also* Baird, Margaret Jane
Mitchell, Dr. Elisha, xii, 52
Moore, Mr. (opposed Robert B. Vance for clerkship), 250
Moore, Charles, 250n
More, Hannah: identified, 132
Morehead, Emma Victoria: identified, 101
Morehead, John Lindsay: identified, 101
Morehead, Governor John Motley, 101n
Morehead, Maria Louise: identified, 101
Morrison, Julia Adelaide (Ada), 181, 184, 187, 230; identified, 170
Morrison, Washington, 170n
Morrow, Mary Jane, 85, 162, 231
Mountain House Hotel, Morganton, N.C., 50n
Munday, Stephen, 112
Murdoch, Robert J.: identified,150
Murphy, John, 158n, 217n
Murphy, John Hugh: identified, 158n; and Ann Happoldt, 158; and Clara Patton, 194, 202, 221, 234, 242; ZBV's opinion of, 230
Murphy, Margaret Stringer Avery (Mrs. John), 158n, 217n

N

Nash, Judge Frederick, 42n
Neilson, Archibald (Archie; son of Dr. Morgan Lines), 48n, 83, 244, 246, 250
Neilson, Archibald D. (father of Dr. Morgan Lines), 48n
Neilson, Elizabeth Lines (Mrs. Archibald D.), 48n
Neilson, Laura Henrietta Vance (Mrs. Morgan Lines; ZBV's "Sister Laura"), 16n, 55, 77, 83, 127, 138, 177, 180, 188, 215, 220, 222, 224, 228, 233, 235, 242; identified, 48; illness of, 85, 87, 89, 93, 95, 100, 102, 104, 106, 110, 255, 256, 259, 261; husband of, returns from California, 251; to return to housekeeping, 257
Neilson, Dr. Morgan Lines, 21n; identified, 48; and California gold rush, 55, 77, 83, 89, 93, 95, 104, 109, 150, 157, 159, 195, 215, 251, 254
Neilson, William, 21n

O

Osborne, Harriet, 173, 187, 212; identified, 170; HNE's jealousy of, 175, 176, 178, 186; ZBV calls upon, 181, 184, 230
Osborne, Joseph R., 170n

P

Patton, Clara I., 87, 108, 109, 115, 125, 127, 138, 157, 158, 175, 179, 187, 211, 213, 226; identified, 77; relationship of, with HNE, 79, 132; visits in Rutherfordton, 145, 148, 149; ZBV's opinion of, 146; courted by John Hugh Murphy, 159, 194, 221, 234, 242; ZBV at party of, 162, 163; and William Caleb Brown, 165, 191; coolness of, toward ZBV, 215, 224, 230
Patton, Henrietta Kerr (Mrs. James W.), 184
Patton, James Alfred, 200, 202; identified, 132
Patton, James W., 108n
Patton, John E., 21n, 199-200
Patton, Louisa (Lou), 162, 167, 179, 181, 187, 191, 226; identified, 77n, 146
Patton, Louisa Walton (Mrs. Thomas Taylor), 77n
Patton, Montreville: identified, 100
Patton, Thomas Taylor, 77n, 119, 123, 167, 184
Patton, William: identified, 112
Pearson, Jane Sophronia Tate (Mrs. Robert Caldwell), 246n
Pearson, Judge Richmond M., 42n
Pearson, Robert Caldwell, 77n, 246
Pearson, William: identified, 77; death of, 79, 84
Phillips, Cornelia, xxiii. *See also* Spencer, Cornelia Phillips (Mrs. James M.)
Phillips, Samuel F., xii, 42n
Piedmont Springs (summer resort in Burke County, N.C., no longer in existence), 223, 228, 230
Pierce, Franklin, 121n, 143

Pleasant Gardens (home of Jonathan Logan Carson in McDowell County, N.C.), 50n, 71. *See also* Carson's
Pleasant Gardens (Joseph McDowell plantation in McDowell County, N.C.), xix, 45n, 209n
Pleasant Retreat (home of Thomas Taylor Patton in Buncombe County, N.C.), 77n, 163, 195, 202, 215, 226
Presbyterian Church, Morganton, N.C., 91n, 242; HNE joins, xx, 131n; HNE-ZBV marriage in, xxiv, 261, 265

Q

Quaker Meadows: description of, xix; life at, xxii; origin of name, 15n; HNE's feeling for, 36, 62; Captain Charles McDowell's inheritance of, 45n; farm of Robert Brank near, 96n
Queechy, 218, 220

R

Railroad Convention at Cumberland Gap, 235-37 *passim*
Rankin, David: identified, 169
Rankin, William, 169n
Reading Society, xx, 74; HNE president of, 33; gives party, 46; importance of, to HNE, 132
Reems Creek, xv, 137n; ZBV born in house on, xiii; David Vance II inherits farm on, xiv
Reid, Governor David Settle, 112n, 143
Remine, Miss L. L., 83, 214
Reveries of a Bachelor: Or a Book of the Heart, 82, 90, 91
"River, the," 84, 144, 184. *See also* French Broad River
Roberson, Miss (summer visitor in Asheville), 115
Roberts, Jane, 123n
Roberts, Joshua, 44n, 123n
Roberts, Philetus W., 48, 164; identified, 44
Rose Hill (Asheville home of the Albert T. Summeys), 181
Rowley, the Reverend Erastus, 212; identified, 45
Ruffin, Judge Thomas, 42n

S

St. Mary's School, 13n, 67
Salem Female Academy, 30n
Sawyer, Isaac B.: identified, 72n; opposes ZBV as solicitor, 72; visits at Quaker Meadows, 159; ZBV's opinion of, 190
Scott, General Winfield: runs for president of the United States, 121, 126, 143, 145, 147
Sheetz, the Reverend William C., 247; identified, 91n; comes to Morganton, 91; marries HNE and ZBV, 261, 265
Shuford, Mary E., 154
"Sister" or "Sister Maggie." *See* McKesson, Margaret McDowell (Mrs. William F.)
Smith, James McConnell, 184, 189, 200, 244-45; identified, 100
Smith, Jesse Siler, 171; identified, 154n; marriage of, 154, 193, 194, 200, 203; party for, 208, 211, 214
Smith, Magie Graves (Mrs. Jesse Siler), 216. *See also* Graves, Magie
Spencer, Cornelia Phillips (Mrs. James M.), xxiv. *See also* Phillips, Cornelia
"Springs, the," 84, 85. *See also* Warm Springs
Stock stand, xiv, xv
Summey, Albert T., 170n
Summey, S. Rose (Mrs. Albert T.), 170n
Supreme Court of North Carolina, 222; summer sessions of, in Morganton, xx, 105n; law examinations by, 14n; justices of, 42
Swain, Ann: identified, 244
Swain, David Lowry: lifelong friendship of, with ZBV, xii; recommended ZBV for loan, xviii; sketch of, 7; introduces ZBV in Chapel Hill, 35, 41; ZBV calls upon, 38; uncle of David Coleman, 112n; visits in Asheville, 244, 250
Swan Ponds (plantation of Colonel Isaac Thomas Avery in Burke County, N.C.), 44n, 77n, 155n, 184n

T

Tate, Elizabeth Ann Tate (Mrs. Samuel C.), 44n
Tate, Elizabeth Tate (Mrs. Samuel), 147n
Tate, Julia: identified, 147
Tate, Junius Constantine (June): identified, 33; and California gold rush, 37, 45, 48, 64, 228; in Butler-Greenlee wedding, 44
Tate, Mary Bowman (Mrs. William; HNE's grandmother), 186n. *See also* Bowman, Mary

Tate, Mary Joe (Mollie Jo), 99, 102, 110, 127, 135, 167, 179, 183, 185, 188, 213, 218; and brother June, 33n, 45; identified, 44n; in Butler-Greenlee wedding, 44; friendship of, with HNE, 61-62, 96, 121, 122, 175; ZBV's opinion of, 66; "Tatey" at St. Mary's, 67; going to Charlotte, 95; fondness of, for ZBV, 133; to go to Asheville, 171, 174, 177; and William Caleb Brown, 194; courted by Kame Henson, 203, 206, 207; engagement of, broken, 224, 226, 227, 229, 230; wants to accompany HNE and ZBV to Asheville, 252; friends worried about, 253, 256
Tate, Dr. Robert N. C., 131n
Tate, Dr. Samuel, 131n, 147n, 221n
Tate, Samuel C., 33n, 44n
Tate, Samuel Caspar Wistar (Wistar), 167; identified, 147
Tate, Dr. William C., 33n, 44n, 96
Tate, William Lucius (Lucius), 224; identified, 221
Thompson, Joseph, 162n
Towns, Miss (music teacher in Asheville), 108
Turkey Tail (now Glen Alpine, N.C.), 199
Twitty, Penelope: identified, 143

U

"Uncle" (of HNE). See McDowell, Captain Charles
University of North Carolina, xiv, 17n, 127n, 132n, 239n; influence of, on ZBV, xi-xii; teachers of ZBV at, xii, 42n; ZBV granted loan at, xviii; roughness of students at, xxii-xxiii; ZBV's first day at, 7; ZBV's favorable situation at, 8, 13; vacation between sessions at, 14, 32; ZBV's standing with faculty and students at, 19, 28; ZBV takes "first honor" at, 27; ZBV's courses at, 27; examination week at, 29; ZBV's roommate at, 32; second session begins at, 41; senior vacation at, 43; ZBV plans to leave in May, 49
University of North Carolina Magazine, 60, 63, 132, 136, 218; first number of, 42, 43, 51, 62; ZBV elected an editor of, 53; ZBV gives HNE subscription to, 58; ZBV's "Theorizing" in February, 1852, issue of, 66; ZBV's "Americanisms" and "Indian Legend" in March, 1852, issue of, 66; Editorial Table by ZBV in April, 1852, issue of, 66; ZBV's poetry, "For What I Ask," signed "Halcro'" in May, 1852, issue of, 66, 89, 91; criticism of ZBV's "For What I Ask" in August, 1852, issue of, 113; ZBV's "Calico, Its Wonders and Mysteries" in February, 1853, issue of, 181, 187

V

Vance, Ann Edgeworth (ZBV's "Sister" or "Sister Ann"), 16n; identified, 152n; teaching in Yancey County, 152; comes home, 205, 206; to teach again in Burnsville, 208, 211, 215; in Burnsville, 218, 240, 242; comes home, 244, 246, 251, 254
Vance, David I (ZBV's grandfather): established Reems Creek homestead, xiii; achievements of, xiv
Vance, David II (ZBV's father), xiii; inherited Reems Creek farm, xiv; description of, xvi; family of, 16n
Vance, David Leonidas (ZBV's brother), 16n
Vance, Hannah Moore (ZBV's sister), 16n
Vance, James Noel (ZBV's "Brother Noel"), 16n, 261; identified, 257
Vance, Mira Margaret Baird (Mrs. David II, ZBV's mother), xiii, 71, 73, 80, 87, 89, 104, 107, 119, 122, 124, 127, 133, 138, 144, 152, 156, 160, 168, 169, 172, 176, 177, 180, 185, 188, 192, 218, 222, 224, 226, 228, 230, 233, 235, 254, 256, 260; death of, xxiv; library of, xvi-xvii; description of, xvi-xvii; influence of, upon ZBV, xvi, 28; sketch of, 15n-16n; approves engagement of ZBV, 72, 75-76; headaches of, 83; town of Marshall on land of, 184; falls, 190, 193, 195, 201, 206, 213, 215, 220; HNE's feeling for, 242; illness of, 246, 248, 250; party of, for HNE postponed, 257, 258
Vance, Priscilla Brank (Mrs. David I; ZBV's grandmother), xiii
Vance, Robert Brank (ZBV's "Brother" or "Brother Robert"), xv, 16n, 249; identified, 119
Vance, Robert Brank (ZBV's uncle), xiv
Vance, Sarah Priscilla (ZBV's "Sister" or "Sister Sarah"), 16n; illness

of, 238-39, 243, 244, 246, 250
Vance, Zebulon Baird: and politics, xi-xii, xvii, xxii, 25n, 31n, 111-12, 143, 147, 213n, 220, 252; ancestry and birth of, xiii; moves to Lapland, xiv; education of, xv, xvi, xvii (see also University of North Carolina); and religion, xvi, xxii, xxiv, 18, 19, 146, 147, 252; moves to Asheville, xvii; reads law, xviii, 24n; meets HNE, xviii, xxi; law practice of xxii, 97, 110, 129, 135, 137, 149, 151, 157, 161, 164, 168, 181, 183, 214, 219, 234, 255; visits of, to HNE, 7, 71, 103, 118, 143, 168, 174, 199, 233; on marriage, 10, 11, 46, 47; on ambition, 11; on his future, 13, 60, 161; law licenses of, 14, 38, 255; sends ring to HNE, 15, 17; former sweethearts of, 21, 67, 154, 158, 159, 203 (see also Garrett, Sara L.); loyalty of, to mother, 30, 194; sends picture to HNE, 58, 61, 63, 65, 73, 74; returns to Asheville, 71; solicitorship of, 71-73 passim, 74, 79n, 89; accident of, 116-17 passim; estrangement of, from Woodfins, 119, 121, 123, 126, 127, 130, 131, 136, 221, 225; speech of, in Yancey County, 200, 206, 208, 210; finds house to rent, 244-45; illness in family of, 250, 251, 254, 255, 257; illness of, 256-58 passim, 260-61. See also Marriage of HNE and ZBV

W

Walton, Eliza Murphy (Mrs. Thomas George), 234n
Walton, Colonel Thomas George, 242; identified, 234
Warm Springs (summer resort in Madison County, N.C.; now Hot Springs), xv, 21, 22, 115; fire at, 199
Washington College, Jonesboro, Tennessee, xvi
Watauga County, N.C.: court in, 170
Western Carolina Female College, 83, 85
Wheat, John Thomas, 13n, 27n
Wheat, Mary, xxiii; identified, 13; reputation of, 17, 63; and James McDowell, 28, 53, 60, 83; and Mary Joe Tate, 67
Whitsun, Dr. George W.: wedding of, 123, 124, 126, 127
Wide, Wide World, The, xxi, 218, 220, 221

Wightman, Dr. William M., 135
Williams, H. B., 110n
Williams, Mary Ann, xxiii, 127, 138; identified, 110; ZBV's opinion of, 112-13, 115
Williams, William, 164
Wilson, the Reverend John McKamie, Jr., 131n
Wilson, Mary Lizzie, 135, 228, 231; identified, 131
Women of the American Revolution, The, 46
Woodfin, Anna, 223; identified, 78n
Woodfin, Eliza Grace McDowell (Mrs. Nicholas W.; HNE's "Cousin Eliza"), 104, 108; education of, 30n; identified, 67n; visits at Quaker Meadows, 77, 78, 79, 82, 223; and Sam McDowell, 73, 99; gives party, 132; snubs ZBV, 136; goes to Raleigh, 158, 159; invites HNE for visit, 172
Woodfin, John W. (HNE's "Cousin John"), xxi, 9n, 33n; ZBV reads law under, xviii, 24n-25n, 51n; identified, 26n; ZBV displeases, 26-27; in W. W. Avery trial, 31n; to visit at Quaker Meadows, 86; publicly condemns ZBV, 126; ZBV's relationship with, 138, 160, 223; "kind" to HNE, 233
Woodfin, Mary: identified, 78n
Woodfin, Mira (daughter of the N. W. Woodfins), 78n
Woodfin, Mira McDowell (Mrs. John W.; HNE's "Cousin Mira"), 73, 76-77, 104, 108; identified, 30n; ZBV's opinion of, 30; visits at Quaker Meadows, 85, 86, 179; and Sam McDowell, 99, 232; relationship with HNE, 223, 233
Woodfin, Nicholas W. (HNE's "Cousin Woodfin"), xxi, 104, 168, 172; in W. W. Avery trial, 31n; and Sam McDowell, 33n; identified 66n-67n; and North Carolina Senate, 66, 87, 111, 148n; snubs ZBV, 136
Wright, James Allen: identified, 239
Wright, Joseph Hill: identified, 239

Y

Yancey County, N.C.: court in, 99, 102, 112, 127, 129, 135, 136, 137, 167, 168, 169, 172, 174, 214, 219; Ann Vance in, 152, 205, 206; ZBV's speech in, 200, 206, 208, 210

www.ingramcontent.com/pod-product-compliance
Lightning Source LLC
Chambersburg PA
CBHW021355290426
44108CB00010B/258